Walking to the Edge

Essays of Resistance

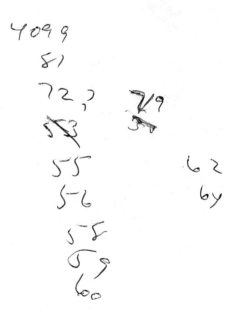

Walking
to the Edge

Essays of Resistance

Margaret Randall

South End Press
Boston, Massachusetts

Cover art by Barbara Byers
Photographs by Margaret Randall

Edited, designed, and produced by Sheila Walsh and the
South End Press collective

Manufactured in the USA

Library of Congress Cataloging-in-Publication Data
Randall, Margaret, 1936-
Walking to the edge: essays of resistance/Margaret Randall.
p. cm.
1. Social history—20th century. 2. Feminism. 3. Power
(Social sciences) 4. Randall, Margaret, 1936- . I. Title.
HN18.R34 1991
305.42—dc20   90-48221
                                                        CIP
ISBN 0 89608-398-5 (cloth)
ISBN 0-89608-397-7 (paper)

South End Press, 116 Saint Botolph Street,
Boston, MA 02115

99 98 97 96 95 94 93 92 91 1 2 3 4 5 6 7 8 9

This book is for Mercy Díaz and Jane Norling

Acknowledgements

"Coming Home" first appeared in my book by the same name (Albuquerque, NM: West End Press, 1990). The book also includes poems written in the context of my immigration case, photographs, and a chronology.

An earlier version of "Notes on the New Female Voice" was included in *Conversant Essays: Contemporary Poets on Poetry*, ed. James McCorkle (Detroit, MI: Wayne State Univ. Press, 1990). "The Woman Hanging from the Thirteenth Floor Window" is from *She Had Some Horses* by Joy Harjo, copyright © 1983 by Thunder's Mouth Press. Used by permission of the publisher.

"Remapping Our Homeland" is based on a talk which I gave at the Alliance for Cultural Democracy's national conference, "Remapping Our Homeland," at Powderhorn Park, Minneapolis, on May 6, 1989. It appeared in *Cultural Democracy* #37, Fall 1989, and was published in Spanish and English in *The Underground Forest/La selva subterránea*, Number 7, 1989.

A version of "Reclaiming Voices" first appeared in issues 8 and 9 of the Association for the Study of Peoples Culture newsletter, 1989. Another will be published in *Latin American Perspectives* in 1991. Excerpts under the title "Power Politics and Gender Awareness: Some Notes on Oral History with Women in Latin America" were included in *Women & Language*, Volume XI, Number 2, Winter 1988.

An earlier version of "How We Clothe and Wear Our Bodies" appeared in *Hurricane Alice*, Vol. 6. No. 2, Minneapolis, Minnesota, Spring 1989.

"Living About Life" first appeared in *Open Magazine*, Westfield, New Jersey, 1989.

An earlier version of "The Human Face of Revolution" was published in *The American Book Review*, September-October 1987. The book reviewed is *Miguel Mármol* by Roque Dalton, trans. Kathleen Ross and Richard Schaaf (Willimantic, CT: Curbstone Press, 1987).

A slightly different version of "Invasion as Metaphor in America" was first published in *The Women's Review of Books*, May 1988. The book reviewed is *The Bean Trees* by Barbara Kingsolver (New York: Harper & Row, 1988).

An earlier version of Part One of "Down Dangerous Roads" was published in *The Women's Review of Books*, October 1987, as a review of *Sanctuary, A Journey*, Judith McDaniel (Ithaca, NY: Firebrand Books, 1987). Part Two was written specifically for this collection.

"Exiled in the Promised Land," a review of *Exile in the Promised Land* by Marcia Freedman (Ithaca, NY: Firebrand Books, 1990) was originally written for *Bridges: A Journal For Jewish Feminists and Our Friends*.

An earlier version of "Art as Information" was written as an introduction to *IKON* Magazine, No. 11, 1990.

An earlier version of "Something About My Pictures" was included in the catalog *Photographs by Margaret Randall, Image and Content in Differing Cultural Contexts*, which accompanied a retrospective exhibition at the Everhart Museum, Scranton, Pennsylvania, from May 15 through July 17, 1988. Robert Schweitzer curated the exhibition.

Different versions of "Woman to Woman, Our Art in Our Lives" appeared in *The Taos Review*, Vol.1, No.2, Spring 1990, and in *The Minnesota Review*, 1990.

A slightly different version of "Alice and Carlos" appeared in *IKON*, Second Series #10, Summer 1989.

Contents

Photographs *by Margaret Randall*

Introduction

Walking to the edge is what I've done most of my life. Walking to the edge: taking conscious risk. Calling up, even in the most difficult of circumstances, this courage of vulnerability. Honoring process, a profoundly female business.

So engaged, I have often felt painfully alone. Then, in instant recognition and warmed by its consequent explosion of tenderness and life, there is the presence of that millennia of sisters. Sisters, as well, in the here and now. And yes, also brothers.

If I have learned little else, I have learned that I have no choice but to walk again and again to the edge. Because there is no choice, and because there are so many of us walking out here, I am not alone. There is challenge and also a steadiness in our discovery.

This is writing of resistance. I want to say right off that this collection speaks from and addresses an abusive economic and socio-political system. These essays describe a world that is classist, racist, sexist, heterosexist, ageist, and able-bodyist. They are also written in the heat of the struggle for social change. And I will identify myself: as an aging, white, middle-class lesbian of Jewish heritage, a socialist and a feminist, a mother, grandmother, artist, and teacher, I am speaking to you and also reminding myself that here on the edge we can be unashamedly creative. We must reclaim our voices in order to create the women (indeed, the people) we must be: no more conditioned dichotomy between emotions, mind, and body; no further need for the fragmented or reactive response.

I deeply believe in the importance of language, that we must retrieve ways to say what we mean, assign responsibility, give the perpetrators as well as the victims and survivors first and last names. We must teach ourselves how to use language powerfully; only then will its reclaimed and highly charged memory enable us to create ourselves into the world of equality and justice we so urgently need. I'm not talking about vision without work. Bumper stickers like "VISUALIZE WORLD PEACE" annoy me. It's not enough to see with the eye—even the mind's eye.

We must work on every front to undo the damage that's been done. Analysis; scholarship; standing up for what we believe; changing society; writing poetry; painting pictures; parenting; healing humans, animals, and earth; farming; producing heavy machinery; learning and teaching; scrubbing floors; safely recycling or disposing of waste; making music; restoring to language the meaning that will help us live: all are necessary tasks. For all we must hone our tools, and—until we are certain of victory—our weapons.

After twenty-three years in Latin America, these are essays and other non-fiction pieces written since my return to the United States. Essays of the eighties. They are varied in subject matter, ranging from an attempt to describe what it feels like to live under the constant threat of deportation, to a fresh-eyed commentary on different aspects of U.S. popular culture; from literary criticism to an essay on the changing dress codes for women in Cuba and the United States, and my personal experience of teaching.

Here is memoir: something of my personal history, in order to provide a context for much of what this book is about. What it's like to come out as a lesbian in mid-life. The difficulties and complexities (as well as the rewards) of writing and publishing about incest. What photography means in my experience. The book ends with a piece that comes as close to being a short story as anything I've written. In fact, I would like to think that one of the threads that unites this collection is the breakdown of arbitrary divisions between non-fiction and fiction, commentary and formal essay, poetry and chronicle. Our rebel vision defies these patriarchally imposed labels.

I was moved to write (or speak) the original pieces upon which these (usually reworked) versions are based in a number of different circumstances. Sometimes the circumstances changed, and the rewrites followed that process. I have mostly resisted the temptation to bring some of these pieces "up to date" for this collection, by adding more recent examples of U.S. government abuses or people's mobilization in protest. The lists on both sides would be endless; and so I have preferred to trust the reader to fill in the blanks. Take these ideas, often inspired by those of others: add to them, stir, and make them work for you.

The opening essay, "Coming Home: Peace Without Compla cency," emerges as the piece I've wanted to write since winning my case against deportation. The U.S. Immigration and Naturalization Service (INS), invoking the ideological exclusion clause of the 1952 McCarran-Walter Act, for more than four years sought to deport me because of the content of my books (several contain strong criticism of U.S. government policy during the Vietnam war years and towards Cuba and Central America, and commentary on racism and sexism here at home).

The deportation order was issued in October 1985. For the forty-eighth International PEN[1] Congress in January 1986, I followed its theme and prepared a paper called "When the Imagination of the Writer is Confronted by the Imagination of the State." Later I wanted to go more deeply into the phenomenon of deportation itself. All through the immigration battle, the case motivated poetry and other short pieces. Several weeks after it finally ended, with a July 1989 Board of Immigration Appeals (BIA) ruling that I had never, in fact, lost my U.S. citizenship, I was able to finish the essay you have here.

Having lived for substantial periods of time in countries like Cuba and Nicaragua, where people are attempting to build a producer rather than a consumer society, my return to the United States naturally found me with new eyes. My roots were here, particularly in the land and light of New Mexico, so there is always a solid sense of recognition. But I have come home with a different way of seeing much of this country's plastic culture: money machines, credit cards, our particular U.S.-style racism and sexism, the establishment's vision not only of the home terrain but of the world at large.

A feminist publication in the Midwest planned an issue on women's adornment. Its call for submissions prompted my writing "How We Clothe and Wear Our Bodies: Cuban and U.S. Women's Adornment in the Seventies." Often a magazine's plan to publish around a particular theme, or an anthologist's call for work on a particular subject, has reminded me that I have cross-cultural observations that may be worth sharing. Similar announcements or requests were what prompted me to write on oral history, to ponder parallels between sixties and eighties art, or to write the several book reviews which, out of the forty or so produced during this time, I've chosen to include.

Most of the other pieces in this collection fall into the more conventional categories of literary criticism or cultural analysis. There is an essay on what I perceive as a new female voice in North American literature, another comparing mass cultural and artistic responses to two conservative periods in U.S. history, one on the making and uses of women's art. A brief commentary takes as its starting point the viewing of two independent films—part of the 1988 Public Television series called Point of View. The essay on my experience with teaching was written especially for this collection.

Surely one of my most important—and painful—experiences since returning to the United States, was the process of re-membering an incest experience previously deeply hidden in my childhood. Feminist therapy was the vehicle through which I began that unfolding, and my exploration is the subject of a book: *This Is About Incest*,[2] which was published several years back. Naturally, neither the writing nor the publication was free of personal trauma, and "Some of you are saying we are both wrong ..." is based on the letter I wrote to members of my immediate family in the context of trying to work through residual feelings about my having gone public with that experience.

Feminist theory and therapy have helped me make the connections that powerfully inform my developing analysis of history and society. More than a decade ago, in the introduction to another book, I said that socialism and feminism need one another.[3] Now I would add that we must work hard, individually and collectively, to reunite body and mind—and learn about the ways in which they work together—for the health of our planet, our society, ourselves. Through these years which have proven so difficult and discouraging for the socialist dream I continue to nurture, this seems more than ever important.

There are family, friends, and colleagues with whom an ongoing discussion of these issues has been essential to my ideas and energy. I especially want to thank my life partner Barbara Byers. Her love and support always include the courage to criticize. My gratitude also to my son Gregory Randall, my therapist and friend Becky Bosch, dear friends Ruth Hubbard, Susan Sherman, Liz Kennedy, and Jack Levine. My appreciation to South End Press editor Karin Aguilar-San Juan who gave me valuable feedback and creatively challenged every essay during the final preparation of this manuscript.

A word about the dedication: Mercy Díaz was a Cuban friend from my years in that country. A brilliant political analyst and teacher, a wonderful loving woman, she committed suicide in 1988. News of her tragic decision reached me as I was beginning to work on this manuscript. Many of the questions examined in these pages were ones we probed together. Jane Norling is an old friend, a powerful artist and muralist whose work continues to inspire me. Her successful battle with breast cancer, also during the making of this book, reminds me of the epidemics —named and unnamed—against which we must continue to fight.

So, these are the pieces that fit nowhere else. But they are not gathered here without reason. Together, I hope they form a chorus of voices walking to the edge. Linked by a feminist perspective; class, race, and gender analysis; the conviction that the invasion of a body and the invasion of a nation are sad reflections of one another; a fascination with language and with people's culture; and a delight in the breakdown of conventional genre; they are a part of my homecoming response to this land in which I was born, grew up, and to which I return—not without struggle, and powerfully cognizant of its multi-cultural terrain.

—Hartford, Connecticut
April 1990

Notes

1. PEN is an international association of poets, playwrights, essayists, and novelists.
2. *This Is About Incest*, Margaret Randall (Ithaca, NY: Firebrand Books, 1987).
3. *Cuban Women Twenty Years Later*, Margaret Randall (New York: Smyrna Press, 1980).

Coming Home
Peace Without Complacency

A room is not a world. A city is not a continent. These streets do not border the edges of a universe. But the people who move in them, the people who live in them are a world, a continent, a universe.
—Susan Sherman, from "Ten Years After"

I think I was a teenager but I may have been older during a passionate discussion between my father, mother, and myself. In any case, it's one of the few family events about which all three of us retain similar memory. We were driving somewhere, and I think it was my mother who mentioned a current news item: the ACLU's defense of some Neo-Nazi organization's right to hold a public rally. My father regularly contributed to the ACLU, my mother was of liberal persuasion as well, and I had been brought up in this middle-class, white, second generation North American family to believe that defense of difference was an important part of the national conscience.

But there was no agreement in this particular discussion. My mother thought defense of *any* rights for fascists was unthinkable. "If a group advocates hate and killing," as far as she was concerned, "they can have *no* rights!" With all my youthful passion, I agreed. My father, against both of us—both of us could usually talk faster and turn a more intricate phrase than he could—was adamant in his defense. He hated anything fascist as much as we did. But this would cease to be a democracy, he kept saying, unless we make sure we defend *everyone's* freedom of expression.

A week or so after the victory in my struggle against the U.S. Immigration and Naturalization Service (INS), the memory of this old argument surfaced. The experience of hard years of fighting deportation has taught me a great deal. If it wasn't absolutely clear to me before, censorship, as a vehicle for so-called protection, has become increasingly repugnant. The government attempted to exclude me because of my ideas. I continue to believe that human beings must be allowed, in fact

1

encouraged, to express our ideas and feelings—in all their plenitude and difference.

Today I can better understand my father's plea. But something of my mother's point of view continues to speak insistently in my gut. If freedom is important to us we must fight against the spread of a fascist ideology in every way open to us, so it's hard for me to defend *everyone's* rights. It's hard for me to defend the rights of racist and other hate groups to promote their corrupt and corrupting world views.

Certainly, given a Constitution like ours, we must struggle so that its protection extends to the commonly disenfranchised, not just to those in power. But that's the key question: who holds the power? If the power is held, as it is in this country, by a bourgeois minority within a context of class exploitation, then the powerless shouldn't have to worry about protecting the interests of those who already have all the power. The powerful are quite capable of protecting themselves.

"And what about the fascists?" some would say. The American Nazi Party and the Ku Klux Klan don't govern this country (though the latter certainly holds a dangerous measure of power). I guess there my bottom-line response is that in a life and death struggle—which I have no doubt we are waging, on all sorts of fronts—we must consistently choose life if we hope to survive.

I'm troubled by instances of censorship within certain socialist societies. If they are truly workers' states, how can the accessibility of a range of ideas be closed to working people? Denied the opportunity to discuss opposing views, how can we learn to think for ourselves, to develop our own convictions? Perhaps this is not really a censorship issue, but one of how functional (in this arena, at least) the workers' society in question really is.

Frequently, in countries whose territorial integrity is being threatened, there are also extenuating circumstances: in wartime, certain types of censorship may be necessary, even when they are not desirable, and this necessity may be heightened as well by the fact that a small country is struggling against the multiple pressures of a much larger power. Socialism, even in peacetime, defines itself as a transitional society. Capitalism proudly asserts it is "the best there is."

So, I would argue, censorship is to be avoided wherever possible, but it's never exercised in a vacuum. Censorship by and for (or against) whom? In each case, context and interests served must inform the answer.

Working within a bourgeois democracy, we are too easily trapped by the myth that all views are honored. The myth encourages ordinary men and women to respect this principle, while those who govern continue to abuse our rights. Today, faced with the reality of a Neo-Nazi rally, I don't think I would actively support the ACLU in its defense of the "rights" of hate-mongers, although I certainly support that organization's defense of issues and people I respect. Faced with a Neo-Nazi rally today, I wouldn't actively promote its freedom of expression, but neither would I propose that it be suppressed. Instead, I would attempt to mobilize everyone I could to the understanding that such anti-human views mean death to us all.

What I know without a doubt is that there are other ways in which we can, and must, struggle against fascism in the United States. We must retrieve our common histories, educate, alert, and mobilize: against fascism and racism, nuclear irresponsibility, the so-called right-to-life ideology, destruction of our earth and atmosphere, privilege for the rich, blind protection for the powerful, sexism, homophobia, homelessness, ignorance, exploitation and oppression of all kinds.

A great deal of what I know about the importance of freedom of expression and freedom of dissent I have learned from personal day-in and day-out experience over the past five years: since the U.S. Immigration and Naturalization Service issued a deportation order against me because of my ideas—the nature of some of my books, and my refusal to retreat from my position, that of my constitutionally protected right to think, write, speak, and teach what I believe.

I am one of millions. Millions of women and men who espouse hundreds of differing ideas about the nature of society, history, and the changes we believe would improve the life of our planet. I am not a member of the ruling elite. I didn't write the laws—protecting many of us on paper, but in truth only the governing few. I learned that I must fight for my right to be heard, included, respected; and I must fight for the rights of others.

I. Some History

In 1961, at the age of twenty-four, I left New York City and went to Mexico. I already considered myself a writer (I wrote a lot of romantic poetry, and had completed a first very bad novel) and expressed incipient left political views—more radical than those of my family and, I should add, of most of my artist friends. I was also a single mother; my son Gregory was born in October 1960.

The sixties in Mexico had something in common with the sixties elsewhere. Poets and writers in general began talking to one another through a laborious network of independent readings, broadsides, little magazines, presses, and forums. Student-led protest movements erupted in the wake of the Cuban Revolution; 1968 would produce Mexico City's own version of New York's Columbia University, or May in Paris. Mexico had invested heavily in hosting the 1968 Olympic Games, though, and a repressive government couldn't afford to see that investment lost; at the Plaza of Three Cultures, more than 1,000 unarmed demonstrators were massacred on October 2nd, an event that would change that country's history—and mine.

In early 1962, Mexican poet Sergio Mondragón and I began editing a bilingual literary magazine which was to provide a coming together for the most exciting new voices of North and Latin America. The journal, which was called *El corno emplumado (The Plumed Horn)*, proposed a bridge—between the plumes of Quetzalcoatl and the jazz horn of the United States. And it echoed our own development through those years: starting as an eclectic showcase for young writers and artists and eventually becoming a more cohesive mirror of work by intellectuals on both continents; in most cases we were creative thinkers and activists who were deeply concerned with injustice and who directed our creativity towards change.

There was intense correspondence, now spanning five continents. There was an increasing interest and energy in translation: we wanted to make our work available to one another, in all its formal subtleties as well as in its content. We sponsored and attended gatherings of young nonconformist artists and writers. With our energy and exuberance, we believed we could change the world.

Cuba was essential; today it is chic to espouse long-distance views on that country's successes and failures, but it would be impossible here to overemphasize the impact made by the Cuban Revolution on the lives of generations of Latin Americans. Quite simply, David reenacted his struggle with Goliath. A tiny island nation had showed the world that it was possible to stand up to the United States and reclaim its identity and dignity. My first trip there to a gathering of poets in 1967, and another in 1968 for a meeting of more than 600 Third-World intellectuals, had a lasting effect on my outlook. In a complex and profound sense, my own life and work were becoming a bridge.

During the Mexican years Sergio Mondragón and I were married. We had two daughters: Sarah and Ximena. There was a great cultural richness in the early life of this new family of five; Sergio brought to our relationship the Quetzalcoatl myth, the bird rising above its conquerors. I brought the quick though perhaps somewhat innocent energy of New York streets, the new Beat consciousness of North America. But the construction began to come apart over time as my husband moved in the direction of certain eastern philosophies and a more ascetic lifestyle, and our daily sustenance depended increasingly upon my efforts.

As a woman in a particularly misogynist society, as a foreigner in Mexico, it was never easy for me to obtain adequate or adequately paid work. In 1966, on the misadvice of a lawyer, I took out Mexican citizenship. It was an economic move, an effort to support my three children (then all under the age of six). I was motivated by the emotional pressure of a marriage and the urgent and practical needs of my family.

In the acquisition of Mexican citizenship, which was completed in 1967, I was under the impression that I had to relinquish my U.S. nationality. Dutifully, I turned my passport over to the American consular authorities. Less than two years later, beginning to understand that Mexican naturalization would make it problematic for me freely to visit my parents and country of origin, I tried to undo what I unwittingly had done; I attempted through what's known as an administrative recourse to retrieve my U.S. citizenship. Although I had been very clear that economic duress was the reason for the unfortunate switch, the State Department turned down my request. They never explained their refusal.

Meanwhile, I continued to grow—as a woman, a writer, an editor, and a politically aware person. Sergio's and my differences became insoluble, and we separated in 1967. I established a relationship with a U.S. poet, Robert Cohen. Our daughter, Ana, was born in 1969. By this time Sergio had also left the magazine, which I continued editing—first alone, and later with Cohen. Feminism hit me; initially as one more of a series of issues I wanted to embrace, then as a necessary way of connecting the pieces of my own life which had previously seemed so at odds with one another. In the summer of 1968, the Mexican student movement exploded, held forth for several extraordinary months, then was decimated by repression. Throughout the following year, those of us who publicly protested the death sentence imposed upon that movement began to experience repression of different kinds. The government tried to shut down our magazine, but impressive reader support, from many parts of the world, enabled us to survive. To the regime, our survival must have stung like an open sore. In July 1969, my youngest daughter barely three months old, *El corno* could finally resist no longer.

I was forced from any possibility of a normal life in Mexico. Paramilitary forces came to our home, stole my Mexican passport, forced me into hiding. The experience of several months of underground life, in which Mexican officialdom always insisted they knew nothing of what was happening, nor had they anything against me, made it clear I was no longer welcome in that country. My four children traveled to Cuba, where they were lovingly cared for as the Cuban Revolution cared for thousands of children of those engaged in struggle. In September, sick and without papers, I left Mexico. My circumstances made it necessary for me to travel halfway around the world to join my children in Cuba. Robert had arrived there the week before.

I was now in my early thirties rather than twenties. The impact of feminist thought, as well as the experience of national liberation struggles on several fronts and in several stages, turned me towards oral history as a viable means of bridge-building. I wanted to know about women's lives in Cuba, and in other parts of the so-called Third World. I wanted to listen to women speak about their lives, about the problems and changes wrought by struggle and sometimes by victory; and I wanted to write books that would offer a context for those women's voices, so they might speak to the people of my own country, the United States.

For I never stopped thinking of the United States as my home. In forums and at conferences around the globe, I represented my country of origin. Interviewing women in Vietnam, Nicaraguan women, Chilean women, or women from Peru's jungles and mountains, I was the *gringa* who asked them to talk about what concerned us both—from the unique vision of their lives. Years later I was able to regain my Mexican passport, but I was still a *norteamericana*—a woman of white, middle-class, U.S. roots, from the cultural mix of New Mexico, whose Marxism and even feminism were most often spoken in Spanish, for whose children that language was their mother tongue. A transplant, a hybrid of sorts, who remembers a momentary feeling of confusion when a Puerto Rican TV show host in Boston, 1978, asked me to tell him how I approached a particular problem "as a North American living in Latin America." Was I really a North American in Latin America, or a Latin American in this country? Or neither? Or both?

After ten years in Cuba, I moved on to Nicaragua. By that time Robert's and my relationship had disintegrated and I had lived my last five years in Cuba with a Colombian poet and musician by the name of Antonio Castro. My children were older; one had finished college and the second was about to get her degree. The Sandinistas had won in that

Central American country, and once again I was curious—particularly about Nicaraguan women, who had made such a startling contribution to their people's struggle. My old friend Ernesto Cardenal—poet and Catholic priest when I knew him in Mexico—was now also Nicaragua's Minister of Culture. "Come and talk to our women," was how his invitation read. And I did.

Throughout the years in Cuba, I continued to be a bridge; not only through my own writing—dozens of poems and articles, short stories, books of oral history, and essays on women and culture—but through my translations of important Latin American poets' work. And also by my presence: as a woman, a mother of four, a North American living and working within the revolutionary process. I believed that passion and reason, socialism and feminism, art and responsibility all needed one another; and I wanted to bring them together in my life and work. Members of the Venceremos Brigades, from the first contingent on, and many other travelers as well, would come to visit; and I felt I was able to help translate the Cuban experience in words that respected cultural difference. With the Cubans I was also able to discuss the various idiosyncrasies and differing political perspectives of my U.S. sisters and brothers.

This continued in Nicaragua. I was there for three months in late 1979 and early 1980, then returned to live, with my youngest daughter, in December of that year. Soon my second youngest daughter graduated from high school in Cuba, and chose to join us. I was interested in women's lives, in the experience of writers and other cultural workers, and my books from this period reflect that. I was fortunate to have arrived at a time when writers, photographers, and other creative artists were beginning to come together, devising organizational forms which provided infinite new possibilities for our work within a rapidly changing society.

Having lived in a country like Cuba, where the history of Church and State had been such an antagonistic one, I also became absorbed in the role of Christians in the Nicaraguan revolution. This was another bridge, and it drew me—fascinated and energized—to the connections it made. Although they longed for the same peace and justice on earth, believers and non-believers had traditionally been pitted against one another by the forces intent on maintaining the status quo, especially in the poorer countries. In Nicaragua, recent history had exploded that myth of "irreconcilable differences."

Again, my family and I were not tourists in the superficial sense.

I worked at the Ministry of Culture, for the women's organization, and with media; my children went to local schools; my vantage point was one of engaged participation rather than what the guardians of the "free" press would call impartial observation. By this time I was doing photography too. My late entrance into that medium was a way of seeking another bridge: I was frustrated by the language barrier between my poetry (the best of which is in English) and my Spanish-speaking colleagues and friends. The photographic image transcended that barrier. Photography has its own language, though, and I soon began to search for my voice. Most of my books, from the end of the Cuban period on, include my own images as well as my words. More recently, photography has moved beyond illustration in my life; a variety of exhibitions and reproductions in magazines and books attest to that process.

II. Coming Home

I lived in Nicaragua for almost four years before returning to the United States in January 1984. I've gone into some detail about my life, because I want to share something of where I came from and who I've been, in my early years in this country and during my almost quarter century in Latin America. Now I want to speak at greater length about the woman who came home, and what happened when she did.

The last couple of years in Managua had been intense. The *contra* presence was already escalating as a vehicle of U.S.-backed opposition to the Sandinistas, and as a part of its ongoing program of low intensity warfare against that nation's sovereignty. Many of the innovative and courageous new programs aimed at improving the quality of life for Nicaraguans were suffering as a result. Military attacks in the north and along the southern border were beginning to hit the capital city.

In a nation of young soldiers, I was a woman in my mid-forties—exhausted by years of long hours, with questions about the contribution I was making, needing to come home. Essentially a writer, I knew I had to slow down, to tackle larger and more complex writing projects than those I had been able to complete during my years in Latin America. I believed I no longer had U.S. citizenship, but I had never ceased to think of New Mexico as my special place.

And so I applied for a tourist visa, and boarded a plane one morning in Managua's 114-degree heat. That night I stepped down from another, into the cold of a January evening in Albuquerque. On a reading and lecture tour the year before, I had fallen in love with an old friend, American poet Floyce Alexander. We were writing to one another; and making a life with him as well as moving closer to my parents, brother, and sister, were all aspects of the human ties that brought me back. My essential reason, however, was much deeper.

I'm not sure I could have articulated that reason, at least not at first, or not completely. I intuited it, and that was enough. There were those in Nicaragua—among them a psychologist, an exceptional woman named Tony—who helped me nurture the courage to make the move. They made me see that following a clear destiny does not by necessity imply denial of the people or places I'd leave behind. Cutting out on a war-torn nation wasn't easy. I didn't want to rationalize, but I did need to understand. The transition, for me, was one of addition, not one of subtraction or denial.

In recent years, when I've been asked, I've tried to be honest about the several parts of that process. Talking about coming home—and being home—have allowed me to understand it more fully. In the first place, it has always, powerfully, been a *coming home*: through the confusing days of reentry, bombarded by the dozens of ways in which I had to adjust to a society I knew intimately and yet hardly knew at all; even, or perhaps especially, during the times in which I felt most tangibly the threat of deportation.

I came home because this is my land: this New Mexican space of light and openness. For while I was born in New York City, and returned there for four years as a young adult in the late fifties, I was raised in Albuquerque from the age of ten. My parents' choice of this city proved prophetic to my own later needs and choices. These mountains and this desert are my place of physical and emotional regeneration.

I came home because the creative work I feel called upon to do must be done here. I needed to retrieve and feel surrounded by my own language, my culture; and to understand how the places I've lived and the experiences I've had engage that language and culture in my life. In my late forties and early fifties, bridge-builder still, I wanted to put the pieces of myself together. Conscious of the importance of New York, Spain, Mexico, Cuba, Vietnam, Peru, Chile, and Nicaragua, I had to return in order to make sense of the powerful mix that informs my life.

Certain yet uncertain, overwhelmed by change, continually thrown off balance by seemingly insignificant details: I remember those first weeks and months. Floyce offered a loving home, and tried hard to cushion the blows. But I couldn't stay inside his apartment forever. I had to emerge, out into a world I claimed. Nevertheless, I had little practical idea of how that world really worked.

The therapist I'd seen in Managua had advised me not to take a job for a while. In fact, she said, two years might be needed—for rest and adjustment. But that kind of time is rarely available to those of us who must support ourselves. After a couple of months, I was wondering how I could earn a living—what I might contribute to society, from my long experience in Latin America. And also where I might reasonably expect to be hired with my particular qualifications—or lack of qualifications.

I thought about teaching. I knew I had a lot to share, and I believed college-level students in this country might find my experiences useful. I also sensed that I could learn a lot about my nation's current heartbeat from them: the problems, ideas, and aspirations of a new generation. But would college administrators or department chairs find me hirable? I vividly remember the gestures of friends who put themselves on the line for me, showing me how to write a curriculum vitae, what a syllabus was, what teaching at a university entailed (when I had never graduated from one); I didn't have a formal degree, but I had published more than fifty books. Somewhere, I reasoned, equivalency must be possible.

To make a long story short, I was able to get a job as Adjunct Assistant Professor at the University of New Mexico, beginning that first September. Women's Studies was a natural home for a woman like myself, who had written more than twenty books of women's oral history. American Studies was also receptive to what I had to offer. Three years later Trinity College in Hartford, Connecticut invited me to be a Visiting Professor in its English department. Since then I have taught at Oberlin and Macalester, and have plans to return to Trinity, and to teach at the University of Delaware. Teaching has become important to me: another kind of bridge-building. But I'm getting ahead of my story.

III. The Case

Floyce Alexander and I were married in February 1984, and—as we believed I was a citizen of Mexico—he petitioned for my permanent residency status in March of the same year. I remember the day we went to the Immigration and Naturalization Office in Albuquerque; it's in the old downtown center of the city where I used to walk, filled with a sense of adventure, with my high school girl friends in the early fifties. We filed the appropriate papers, and one of the officers (Douglas Brown, now CEO of the Albuquerque office) interviewed me briefly. He was casual, interested in "what it was like to live in Cuba and Nicaragua." I understood that those were countries upon which the Reagan administration did not look favorably. And when Brown mentioned that "the FBI would probably be around to ask some questions," I wondered why he couldn't have asked them himself. But there was nothing in the man's initial manner to warn of what would come.

Sixty to ninety days, the INS in Albuquerque informed us, was the usual time-frame for obtaining a green card, the lay person's description of residency. We were happy to wait. I was beginning to become accustomed to life in a consumer society, as opposed to a society of scarcity. I felt slightly more able to shop at the large department stores, and wasn't as surprised as I'd once been by people's inability to understand where I was coming from much of the time (or my difficulty in transmitting ideas and events outside their immediate life experience). A new love as well as reunification with my parents took the sharp edges from this time. An uncle died, and my father generously decided to use the inheritance to build me a house in the foothills next door to his. That was an exciting project, and a stabilizing aspect of the physical process of homecoming.

Sixty days passed, though. Then ninety. Then more than a year. I didn't get my green card. It became clear that mine would not be looked upon as the usual case of a "foreigner" marrying a U.S. citizen and applying for residency. In fact, it was not only my husband whose application for my change in status was approved; the INS also approved applications from my son (who, along with one of my daughters, is a U.S. citizen), and from my mother. But nothing seemed to be happening.

The FBI didn't come to our home, but one day in June I was summoned to a taped interview with another INS official. This was our first indication that residency, for me, would not be about family ties or any of the usual questions an applicant is asked. When I entered the room where that interview would take place, I immediately saw a number of my books spread across a large table. They were opened to specific pages, and passages were highlighted in yellow magic marker. I knew then, instantly and powerfully, that my welcome would be pitted against my ideas.

In a friendly, always courteous manner, this new inspector collected further information about my life in Latin America. He seemed most interested in the opinions—my own and those of others—taken from my books, and frequently asked me to elaborate upon one or another of the passages he'd marked. They seemed quite straightforward to me, but I was glad to explain them further. I wasn't given a sense of how much longer this might take, but I understood that I had been naive in presuming I might be granted residency without a struggle. Suddenly, the terms changed; this was battle, and I knew I needed a lawyer familiar with the politics of what was happening. (At first, believing I was dealing with the simple administrative aspects of immigration, we had hired a lawyer who was, in fact, present at that interview about my writing. But he knew, as well as we did, that mine was becoming a different kind of case.)

That was when I called my old friend Michael Ratner at the Center for Constitutional Rights in New York City, and asked him if he thought the Center would be willing to represent me. He immediately said yes, and from then on I was fortunate to have his counsel as well as that of Michael Maggio and David Cole, the wonderful attorneys who saw us through to victory.

Seventeen months elapsed between our March application and the October 1985 deportation order issued by A. L. Guigni, Immigration and Naturalization's District Director in El Paso, Texas. I was beginning to be able to feel the nature of the government's anger towards a woman, a writer, who holds, expresses, and defends her opinions—even when they dissent from U.S. foreign policy positions—concerning the Vietnam war, Central America, and other questions.

I've been asked why I point to my womanhood as a target. I know that a man writing what I've written could just as easily have been subject to the persecution I endured. Many have been, and they need our support. In a patriarchal society, however, a woman standing her ground seems to provoke a greater degree of official rage. Women are supposed to cede, acquiesce, say we're sorry. If we don't, we must be punished—at least according to certain fundamentalist principles which are more and more in vogue. Later I'll talk about the particularly gender-offensive line of questioning used by the government attorneys at the hearing in El Paso. Throughout these years of struggle, in press interviews and on radio and TV talk shows, I have frequently been the target of specific assumptions or attitudes directed at me as a woman.

In spite of the fact that during that first year my contact with the INS was scant and our efforts at getting them to make a decision futile, my feelings about being made a scapegoat were grounded in reality. Once, two of my lawyers came to Albuquerque and we went down to the local INS office to inquire about my case. Douglas Brown refused to shake hands with any of us. He was visibly angered by our presence, and attended to us outside his office, in the common area where people wait endlessly for all sorts of information or responses to their questions.

When the deportation order finally arrived, it was an eleven-page document, ending with the words: "... her writings go far beyond mere dissent, disagreement with, or criticism of the United States or its policies.... Your pending application for adjustment of status is hereby DENIED." The word denied was written in capitals, as if to avoid confusion. I was given until the 30th of October—twenty-eight days—to pack up and leave my husband, my parents, the land where I grew up and to which I had come home. And I was being refused residency explicitly because of what I had written and published. The First Amendment of the Constitution, which I had been raised to believe was an inalienable right, clearly did not protect me from the INS.

I remember taking that letter from the rural mail box by the road in front of my home. There was a blaze of yellow topping the chamisa, and the air was alive with light: October in these foothills. The Justice Department return address prompted me to open the envelope and read its contents standing out in the midst of all that beauty. As I pondered the deportation order, I was determined to fight, for myself and for others, and to win if I possibly could.

Had I been one of the thousands of ordinary people from other countries, applying for U.S. residency without the benefit of my professional position or legal help, I would have had no alternative but to brutally disrupt my life and the lives of those closest to me; I would have had to pack up and leave. But I was lucky. Michael and David assured me those twenty-eight days limited only those who had not taken the decision to struggle. I had the right to appeal and could remain here while I did so. I knew I had support, and was ready to do battle.

IV. The Feelings

I don't want to give the impression that I never suffered down times. There were plenty of tears—of sorrow as well as of rage. There was the anxiety of not being able to plan a future, secure steady employment, concentrate on my writing. I couldn't visit my children who live outside the country because I would have forfeited my appeal by crossing the border, nor could I greet my three grandchildren as they came into the world. How do I measure the weight-gain of compulsive eating, or a variety of physical ills—suddenly poor eyesight, nervous tension, hypothyroidism, among others—that may or may not have been intensified by the harassment? And I didn't *ask* to have to struggle with the INS and menopause at the same time.

The news media began their complex dance around my case, retreating during the long waiting periods but moving to center stage every time a motion was made or denied, or some phase of the process began or ended. This made me a public person in a way no one would wish for. Vicious hate mail, threats upon my life (often accompanied by a detailed description of how the writer intended to kill me), sudden encounters with strangers who were encouraged by the atmosphere—which eight years of Reaganism had consolidated—to take my person as a target for their anticommunism or fundamentalist righteousness: incidents of these kinds became part of the fabric of my life.

I remember almost being pushed off the freeway one afternoon by the occupants of another car who glared and pointed as they maneuvered towards me. Once I was threatened in my University of New Mexico office, and the campus police had to attend to my situation as an ongoing task. Sometimes as I entered a movie theater or restaurant, a stranger would scream obscenities, and others would turn and stare. Radio or TV talk shows were the worst; I tried to prepare myself for their high percentage of callers who assuaged personal frustrations by demanding I "go back where I came from(!)" or, more simply, "die."

It's important to make clear that for every one of these attacks, there were at least forty or fifty supportive encounters. Now that the struggle's over, I would like to be able to speak to every person who went out of his or her way to wish me well, offer a few words of encouragement, or—without knowing me personally—involve themselves in the hard work of this case. If I try to list them all, I know I'll leave out many; but I must at least mention Jane Creighton, Ruth Hubbard, Marty Fleisher, Jane Norling, Trisha Franzen, Liz Kennedy, and Bobbi Prebis. They dedicated large and ongoing parts of their lives to working for my freedom.

In 1987, a man on the street in Berkeley pushed a twenty dollar bill into my hand, urging me to "spend it on yourself.... We need roses as well as bread," he said. A few months later, an American Indian shaman, standing in front of me in an airport counter line, recognized me from my picture in the papers. He said he was on his way to a pow-wow in Oklahoma, and would pray for me there.

A woman in Arizona wrote a moving letter, folded around a five dollar check from her social security income. A classroom of fifth-graders at the Albuquerque school I had attended as a child made my case their year-long project. From them I received letters, drawings, songs, and a great deal of love. Some of the most gratifying demonstrations of support came from people who made sure I knew they didn't agree with my politics, but strongly supported my right to express my ideas. There was infinitely more support than harassment, but the constant tension that comes from having to be prepared for harassment palpably changes the daily texture of one's life.

Once the official deportation order was served, my status also became a matter for interpretation. Legally, according to the U.S. system of justice, I had a number of appeals open to me. And while the case was on appeal, obviously I had to continue to support myself. The U.S. Immigration and Naturalization Service disagreed. At different times throughout these past three and a half years, it wielded its own interpretation in whatever way it could in order to cause me more distress. Douglas Brown, from the Albuquerque INS office, appeared on television and publicly threatened more than one institution that offered me employment. Eventually, it was due to the courage of places like Trinity College in Hartford that I could work at all. They defied the threats, standing by their commitment to the First Amendment.

The INS also offered some interesting interpretations of my person. On a 1988 Albuquerque Public Television special, the same Mr. Brown got red in the face as he called me "an alien anarchist"! Only the seriousness of the situation kept me from laughing at his ET-vocabulary.

At first I applied for extended permits to work, which were issued without a problem by the Albuquerque INS office. As a person on appeal, with what they call first category family ties, my requests were more a matter of courtesy than anything else, and they knew that as well as we did. In 1986, though, the immigration law changed, and as soon as it did the INS regional director in El Paso revoked my work permit. Agency lawyers at my subsequent hearing before an Immigration judge were quick to point out that I continued to teach without permission. The judge gave this charge only "one scintilla of importance." I now want to talk about that immigration hearing in some detail, because it was there, I believe, that we all came to understand the government's hard-line position in my case.

V. The Hearing

The law under which aliens may be excluded or deported from the United States is the McCarran-Walter Immigration and Nationality Act of 1952. President Truman vetoed the Act, but a McCarthyite

Congress overrode his objections. With some modifications, McCarran-Walter continues to govern immigration today. One of its thirty-three parts, known by lay persons as "the ideological exclusion clause," makes it possible to deny entry to those whose writing or speaking "advocates the international, economic, or governmental doctrines of world communism."

That's the way the statute reads, and it is obvious there may be as many interpretations of what those words actually mean as there are officials with the power to interpret them. In fact, this is very much a matter of interpretation: what does advocating the doctrines of world communism really mean, where does freedom of expression come in, and *who* has the ability or right to do the interpreting? Can we expect intelligent literary criticism from a middle-level INS official? Or even a rational interpretation of political and historical texts?

And that's what those four days in an El Paso courtroom were all about. Judge Martin Spiegel heard "evidence" from both sides. We brought witnesses who attested to my family ties and contributions to the community. We brought witnesses who were granted expert status by the court, who spoke of my literary work, my photography, my teaching; who addressed the political and literary language used in the sixties and seventies, as well as realities of life in Cuba and Nicaragua. My daughter Ana testified, as did my parents and my husband. The courtroom was packed with friends and colleagues from the University of New Mexico, students of mine, women from the feminist communities of Albuquerque and Las Cruces, old union organizers from the Salt of the Earth miners strike in Silver City, and farm workers from the border area.

The prosecution produced no human witnesses at all. What chief lawyer for INS Guadalupe Gonzalez presented to the court was my work and my work alone—2,270-plus pages of it! Some of the poems or articles, originally written by me in English, had been translated by hurried or quasi-literate INS translators from published Spanish into a crude English I could neither recognize nor acknowledge. At one point the INS prepared to show what they termed "anti-American cartoons" published in the magazine I edited in Mexico. The judge said he didn't think that was necessary.

Those four days of testimony are available in a court transcript numbering close to 1,000 pages. It's difficult to choose examples, from the many I might quote. But I want to continue to talk about freedom of expression and dissent, and what that freedom really means; how it is frequently betrayed, and how it may translate—subtly or blatantly—into censorship or self-censorship, deeply affecting a person's capacity for thought and action. So I'll stick to the line of questioning that most clearly addressed those issues.

After doing her best to define me as a wanton degenerate (some of her questions included asking me if it were true that I had posed nude for art classes in the fifties in New York, waitressed in a gay bar there in the same decade, and why several of my children had different fathers), Guadalupe Gonzalez asked me what it had been like to "publish in a magazine that also published communists?" She pointed out that one issue of *El corno emplumado* had been dedicated to Black Panther leader Huey Newton, that a poem of mine had been titled "Che," and that Marxist material had been advertised in a bookstore ad in our magazine.

Judge Spiegel wouldn't let me respond when Gonzalez asked if I "would take up arms to defend the United States against Castro communist Cuba," reminding her that conscientious objection exists here for citizens and therefore certainly for aliens. But he did let her ask if I had ever written a poem in praise of free enterprise. When she questioned my 1960s spelling of America with a K, sometimes even with three Ks, and I replied that it was a metaphor, she did not understand what that meant.

If it hadn't been clear from the beginning, the hearing in El Paso solidly established mine as a First Amendment case. It was all about what I had written, my opinions which differed from those of a series of U.S. administrations over issues ranging from racism and sexism at home to foreign policy in Southeast Asia, Cuba, and Central America. Sometimes there didn't seem to be enough in my own writings to damn me as conclusively as the INS lawyers would have wished. So they introduced as evidence things written about me by others.

Of course, many of my opinions, particularly those about U.S. policy in Vietnam, were shared by hundreds of thousands of others in this country. But they were citizens, the government said; they were free to think or say whatever they wished. I had *renounced* my citizenship (this was the word they used, echoed over and over in the press); they claimed it had been a political rather than an economic act, and as a consequence I should be denied freedom of expression or the right to reside in the land of my birth.

The line of questioning during those four days also made clear just how dangerously close to McCarthy-era assumptions the Reagan administration brought this country. Anti-communism was the underlying tenet of the INS position as expressed by its spokespeople, its lawyers, its officials, and even its judges. Judge Spiegel did not challenge INS language with regard to the characterization of places and people; he reflected similar biases in the opinion he eventually rendered. During the hearing it was always "Castro's communist Cuba" or "the totalitarian government of Nicaragua," rather than simply Cuba or Nicaragua.

The government lawyers literally went so far as to equate U.S. presidential utterance with papal infallibility; David Cole describes this as the "novel doctrine of conclusive and binding 'Presidential Facts.'" In an article in *The National Law Journal*,[1] Cole wrote that the INS attorneys acted as though administration political claims cannot be questioned in a court of law: "It is a 'Presidential fact,' for example, that the Sandinista Front is an evil force of communism, because the president says it is. It therefore follows that Randall, who has dared to write positively of the Sandinistas, should be excluded from this country for 'advocating the doctrines of world communism,'" According to the INS brief, Cole explained, "'the American nation, [presumably through the voice of Ronald Reagan], has decided communism is 'bad' and capitalism is 'good,' and anyone who fails to toe that line should not be permitted to live among us."

We made a brilliant showing in El Paso. Some of my witnesses, like Adrienne Rich, Nelson Valdes, my mother, my daughter, and others were eloquent. The government's testimony was based on a flimsy portrayal of guilt by association, and its 1950s tone and implications alternated between the frightening and the absurd. But we were yet to discover just how close to fifties thought and action the eighties had become.

VI. Immigration Law

Before the year was out, Judge Spiegel upheld the District Director's deportation order. His thirty-two page decision was most interesting, though, in how it differed from Guigni's. While Guigni hadn't actually found me ineligible under McCarran-Walter *but had based the order upon his discretionary powers to exclude me*, Spiegel said that in his *discretion* he would have granted me the right to stay, because of family ties and service to the community. He, however, did find me ineligible under McCarran-Walter.

Both men claimed to have read my work, but they came to opposite conclusions about its bearing on my eligibility for U.S. residency. Freedom of expression, protected by the First Amendment, should render the ideological exclusion clause of McCarran-Walter unconstitutional. However, it was becoming more and more clear that immigration law in this country is used as a political weapon in the hands of people unfamiliar with the literary nature of language and incompetent to agree about the definition of the relevant statute.

Had I been less naive about INS and its self-conceived independent status vis-à-vis U.S. constitutional guarantees, I might not have been so surprised. In the same *National Law Journal* article, David Cole points out that "in more than 200 years, the U.S. Supreme Court has never held an immigration law unconstitutional." And "at least since the turn of this century, U.S. immigration law has authorized the deportation and exclusion of aliens for their political beliefs and associations. Aliens can be deported or excluded for uttering statements, admitting beliefs, or joining organizations that would be constitutionally protected if uttered, admitted, or joined by a U.S. citizen." Xenophobia, racism, and in my case sexism, are tools with which popular support has been garnered for this type of truly un-American activity.

El Paso is history, and I won't go into detail about the way this case began wending its way through the system. We (Norman Mailer, Arthur Miller, Toni Morrison, Anne Noggle, Grace Paley, PEN American Center, Rose Styron, William Styron, Helene Vann, Kurt Vonnegut, Alice Walker, Dr. Mary Martha Weigle, and myself) launched a countersuit, which didn't fare well in Washington District Court. Later, the Supreme Court refused to hear it.

Meanwhile, the deportation case proceeded to the next level: the Board of Immigration Appeals (BIA), in Washington, D.C. In October 1987 it was heard before that five-member board, with fifteen minutes allotted to the attorneys for each side. Guadalupe Gonzalez, who traveled from El Paso to argue for the Service, continued her virulent attempt at character assassination and guilt through association. But here she went further than she had in Judge Spiegel's courtroom. Rather than cite from cases or points of law relevant to the government's position, she simply quoted from Allan Bloom's *The Closing of the American Mind*:

> [T]he danger is that we will dilute the battle between freedom and communism to the level of no fault auto insurance. The danger is that we will view this case in a context where there is no right or wrong. But there is a right and a wrong. The American Congress has stated that

our system of government is right, and it is good, and the communist system is bad. We are an intolerant government. We are intolerant of world communism, and we are intolerant of those individuals like Randall, who attempt to increase its hold on the world.[2]

There's really no clearer example than this of the government's point of view on this issue. At least the point of view of those within our government—the zealots—who would reduce complex social and political thought to the simplicity of fundamentalist gibberish. The Board of Immigration Appeals heard the oral arguments and then sat on my case for more than a year and a half—through the passage of a 1988 Senate Foreign Relations Authorization Act that did away with some of Mc-Carran-Walter's worst features, as well as a reversal, one year later, of the part of that act which favored my situation. When the BIA finally ruled, it was a surprise to us all. But more about that later.

A number of congresspeople, over the past several years and during the time in which the BIA was deliberating my case, have attempted to pass legislation designed to modernize important aspects of McCarran-Walter. Barney Frank (D-MA) has been one of the most ardent proponents of more rational immigration law, and Alan Simpson (R-WY) has proposed modifications that also address some of that law's most antiquated clauses. It is clear that we need to keep fighting for the repeal of McCarran-Walter. There is no reason that a country that holds itself up as a model of democratic principles should deny entry to people like Pablo Neruda, Gabriel García Márquez, Carlos Fuentes, Farley Mowat, Hortensia Allende—and deny the people of the United States access to their presence.

Back, though, to the particulars of my case. As the summer of 1989 began, almost four years had passed since the District Director's deportation order (more than five years since I returned to the United States), and the case still hadn't made its way into the federal court system. Now that it's over I think it's important to explore the issues of free expression, dissent, censorship, self-censorship, harassment, and innuendo as they played themselves out in my life. So what I want to talk about here is what it felt like to take this kind of battle on. How it changed the nature of my thought, work, interaction with others, relationships, energy, confrontation, sense of self. How it affected my body, my mind, my individual and collective memory, my consciousness.

VII. The Hidden Threats

Before exploring what it has meant in my life to have my freedom of expression threatened, it might be useful to define the basic concept of expression. Expression is the externalization of thought and feeling. It is the exposure to others of that thought and feeling, and, in the process, ours and theirs interact to form the bridge across which the human condition itself must pass if it is to live and grow in all its disparate complexity. Forcible opposition to expression, or its denial, constitutes repression. We have come to identify repression with acts of foreign totalitarian dictatorships, or with police brutality against the unarmed communities of our own inner-city neighborhoods. Repression is most often directed against a particular group—the poor or homeless, people of color, gays and lesbians, people with AIDS—by a state that fears their struggle for justice, or by the authoritarian head of a family (usually male) against the women and children he batters in an attempt to alleviate what he may perceive as the system's battering of him.

But the repressive act always begins with the repression of an idea, be that idea one of freedom, justice, or simply the recognition of difference. With particular attention to expression and its repression as concerns the writer of books, Kurt Vonnegut offered some insightful testimony before the International Economic Policy Subcommittee of the Senate Foreign Relations Committee in August 1986. Speaking for the 2,000 members of PEN, Vonnegut said:

> [P]recisely because we are writers, we know that reading one another's books does not replicate face-to-face confrontation. That is, as readers of foreign literature, we respond with particular commitment to the truth of expression inherent to all literatures; as writers, we are acutely aware of the social and cultural contexts that are lost in translation. But when we meet, the insistent articulation of these dialogues fuses those perceptions and experiences we have in common, and this fusion in turn yields a common perspective from which we begin to comprehend the other's differences and singularities. Such exchanges might have once been deemed the luxuries of the intellect. Today, in a world overwhelmed by internationalism, they are morally imperative.

Vonnegut told the committee that "International PEN—the only worldwide association of literary writers—has survived, and thrived, throughout its sixty-five years of existence for one reason: its members, who together represent the sweep of cultural histories and political systems that define the world today, have met and continue to meet, annually at conferences and congresses held in different countries." He went on to reproach Congress with the irony implicit in the fact that "when America's turn came to host a PEN Congress in January 1986, there was doubt and consternation as to whether such a meeting of PEN could take place in the United States, in one of the leading democracies in the world and the only one with a First Amendment. PEN members from everywhere in the world," he said, "had been welcomed to meet in far less free countries, such as Yugoslavia."

The INS's deportation order against me threatened my sense of identity every day from October 2, 1985 to our victory in August 1989. The message was clear: if I did not relinquish my ideas, and my right to express them, I risked losing my home—in the profound definition of that word: history, memory, place, family, cultural context, personal process, and ability to function.

But if I gave up, if I said I was sorry and wouldn't write those things again—something they seem intent upon forcing women, particularly, to do—if I accepted their patriarchal punishment, lowered my voice and turned against the truth of my struggle, I would lose much more. I would lose the very meaning of that truth, for myself and for all those who believe my freedom of expression is linked to theirs.

These are big words and concepts. They tend to become rhetorical or even meaningless if divorced from the daily examples of what this can mean. Throughout these four and a half years, every time I stood before a lectern I wondered who the INS agents in the audience were. (On several occasions they themselves announced their presence: in Buffalo the local INS director attended one of my lectures; in Minneapolis two men who showed up at a fund-raiser identified themselves as working for the Service).

Teaching, I was always conscious of the possibility that Accuracy in Academia, the ultra-conservative bulldog group dedicated to attacking dissent on campuses, might have student-spies in my classes. It was important to me not to allow the shadow of these presences to change what I wanted to say. I literally and consciously recommitted myself daily to that determination.

I often wondered who I was in the eyes of my students. The vast majority of them were born when the McCarthy era was history. We know how quickly history itself becomes distorted or even erased completely in today's educational system. What was happening to me—someone who had been served a deportation order because of what she wrote—was almost impossible for many of my students to comprehend. Besides, they had come to know me; I didn't *seem* like a threat to national security. Over and over again, they told me they couldn't understand it.

It was a delicate balance, in this respect, between keeping news reporters and television camera crews out of my classrooms while at the same time being willing to talk about the case and use it as an educational tool through which my students might understand what's possible, even in a democracy, when constitutional principles are undermined or ignored. I want to say that throughout my three years of teaching while under order of deportation, my students were wonderfully and movingly supportive. Some of them came to El Paso. They worked on my defense committees, launched educational or fund-raising events, passed unanimous motions through student governing bodies; and, with the victory, congratulations have come from supporters whose names I barely remember.

One of the most satisfying incidents with a student goes back to my days at the University of New Mexico. She remained silent in class through the first month at least. When I questioned her lack of participation, she said she was nervous about giving her opinions because she didn't agree with my politics, or with those expressed by most of her classmates. "I'm a Republican," she told me, "I voted for Ronald Reagan. And I don't think that would go over very well in here."

I used that student's concerns to reiterate my belief that all opinions are important, and in my courses all opinions are respected. Months later, just before the El Paso hearing, this young woman was willing to testify to the court that studying with me she had never felt disrespected in her beliefs or coerced into changing them. She, like all my students, I hope, found my classroom a place in which the most important process was that of learning to think, not learning to mimic the professor's ideas, or anyone else's.

VIII. To Keep Doing the Work

I wrote and published six books between the date of the deportation order and the end of the case. I also completed one novel and part of another, which are still unpublished. Every written word carried with it the double-edged question: if I say this, will it make things worse? But how can I not?

One book became a battlefield upon which these questions played themselves out in a particularly painful way. It's called *This Is About Incest*[3] and is a collection of poetry, prose, and photographs detailing my personal struggle to come to terms with the reclaimed memory of my grandfather's sexual abuse.

The struggle itself was interesting, in the context of the case. I didn't *ask* for abuse memories to surface; no one does. But when they did—in the office of a wonderful therapist who made a great difference in my life throughout these difficult years—I took them on as I've accepted other challenges: with the full power of my creative capabilities.

An eating disorder and a phobia marked the way back to the memories I needed to reclaim. I remember experiencing my first body memory signaling the incest itself, just days before we had to pack up our lives and go to the immigration hearing in El Paso. My therapist packed up her practice as well, being one of a large group of supporters and friends who accompanied me on that part of the journey. The case was the priority then; other work would just have to wait.

A month or so after the hearing, I was able to resume the incest work. As an artist, as someone whose natural tendency is to resolve problems through the creativity of writing and photography, I found myself searching for images, hunting down old family portraits and letters, looking at eyes and hands in new ways. I found myself writing out the discovery and the anguish, turning the reclaimed memory into something I believed would be useful in my own healing and as an offering to others going through the same unraveling of secrets that the patriarchy protects.

And so that little book was born. But if writing it was the logical product of my process of abuse discovery, it wasn't an easy book to publish. There were other people's feelings to consider; several in my immediate family asked why I had to put it all out there for everyone to see. In time, most of those close to me have come around; different levels of struggle, and in some cases memories of their own, have made it possible for them to understand and even support my decision.

In a more public sense, *This Is About Incest* found a place for itself that continues to tell me it was an important risk to take, an important statement to make. Letters have come to me from all over the country, from readers who have been helped in their own struggles by my revelation of process. When I read the poems to small groups of women or before larger mixed audiences, there are always dozens of survivors who tell me they're glad the poems are part of our collective history.

Taking the risk implicit in making public my experience with incest taught me a great deal. On a personal level, it enabled me to think about and recognize abuse in the lives of my own children; and it opened the possibility of their dealing with these issues in whatever ways their particular processes demand. In a larger sense, and because I don't separate what some people refer to as personal from political issues, my struggle with incest has provided some insights for my struggle with the freedom to dissent. In both cases I had to protect and nurture my integrity against covert or overt pressures from an authority that preferred my silence, promising rewards if I would only be good, punishment if I wouldn't. In both cases I learned that my integrity was the only thing they absolutely could not take from me.

But there's another area in which I wasn't able to externalize the full dimension of my beliefs, in which I couldn't risk speaking out. About a year into the fight, my personal evolution was taking me to a recognition of my identity as a lesbian. The public assumption of sexual or affectional preference is difficult for many in this country, who simply choose not to take that battle on in our heterosexist and homophobic society. Increasingly, many gays and lesbians *are* taking it on because they believe that coming out ultimately makes it easier for our children as well as for ourselves. Given the consistency with which I've spoken out in my life, my emotional tendency was towards the latter option. My immigration case, however, restricted that choice.

Among McCarran-Walter's thirty-three clauses, there is one that makes "sexual deviancy" grounds for excludability or deportation. That is this particular law's euphemism for homosexuality. Privately, I opened my arms to my lesbian identity and to the extraordinary relief and community it brought with it. Close to three years ago now, I began living with the woman who is my life partner. Together we were forced to deal with the public limitations of our life in the context of my case.

It was clear to us that homosexuality is as unconstitutional a ground for deportation as the expression of so-called subversive ideas or the association with a variety of progressive organizations (most of them legal within this country). It will be important to fight the battle for freedom of sexual preference. But that wasn't a fight to which I could commit myself in the context of this case, and introducing this new element would undoubtedly have complicated the process enormously. My lawyers wanted me, if possible, not to be explicit about my lesbian identity. If it came out, so to speak, we would deal with it; and I want to acknowledge their willingness to take it on if it came to that. Our feeling was that raising this issue would have detracted from the important First Amendment question, however, and so I agreed to try to keep it under wraps.

What did this mean, though, in terms of daily life? At what personal cost was I forced to keep this "secret"? Obviously, my partner and I suffer the oppression of all lesbians and gay men in a heterosexist society. But in our case there was always that extra burden, pressured as we were by the rigors of the case, unable to publicly express our caring, as release or panacea. Hundreds of thousands of lesbians and gay men in this country cannot come out for fear of losing jobs, children, support of family or friends. For us, there was the additional threat of instantly losing my case—which meant struggle, choice, place. My parents as well as my children were solidly and lovingly with us from the beginning. And the lesbian community proved sensitive to our need for discretion.

For my partner, this situation brought a particular brand of invisibility which was often painful to endure. Her courage and commitment contributed enormously to keeping us both on track. For me, perhaps the most difficult aspect of my inability to be fully who I am was the fact that I could not write out of my lesbian sensibility. Not just the obvious restriction on a love poem or in a review of another's work, but the barrier to deep, engaged, honesty that is possible only when one is able to write from every part of one's identity.

This was particularly difficult in the process of Ruth Hubbard's and my book, *The Shape of Red: Insider/Outsider Reflections*.[4] It's a volume of letters, in which the two of us, as women and friends, discuss everything from politics and work to sexuality and motherhood. I agonized over the final publishable form of one of my letters, and almost decided to give up on discussing my sexuality at all. Ruth was thoughtful and patient; she urged me to walk right up to the edge, exposing what I could and leaving the rest to the reader's imagination. As always, when faced with choices about how much to risk, I'm grateful for the vision and support of someone like Ruth, who believes, as I do, that risk itself most often points towards freedom.

Just as the repression of ideas evokes resistance, this limitation on my writing, because I couldn't express my whole identity, also resulted in some not altogether negative byproducts. One day, when I complained bitterly that I wasn't doing the writing I needed to be doing, one of my lawyers said "Why don't you write a novel?" My son also encouraged me in that, and the almost finished two novels I've been able to produce since then might not have happened were it not for my need to express ideas and feelings I couldn't deal with in the first person.

As with other areas of this struggle, though, there are things the government took from me that are lost forever. One is the experience of joining 600,000 lesbians, gay men, and others for the great march on Washington in October 1988. We could have gone, of course; in retrospect I'm sure it wouldn't have meant anything in terms of the case. But several years of media coverage had accustomed me to being picked out in a crowd. I played it "safe." It was one of a number of times in which censorship became self-censorship: the worst kind.

In close emotional association with issues like incest, and even with a particular sexual identification—especially if the society in which you function constantly holds them up to negative scrutiny—is the problem of *shame*. Women, especially, are conditioned to feel shame almost as a matter of course and in a wide range of situations. I wasn't vulnerable to shame as a lesbian (perhaps I was too old for that). Neither was it a significant part of dealing with the incest (enough others had spoken out before me, to create a community in which I could feel supported). But shame did have its place in the feelings generated by this case.

When the anxiety over the possibility of losing their daughter was stark on my parents' face, I told them: "I'm sorry." When I had to ask for help from friends who were already overburdened with multiple issues in their own lives, I'd hear myself prefacing a request with the words: "I'm really sorry but ..." It was hard to sustain the knowledge that this wasn't my fault. The government had launched this battle, not I. Yet how quickly and easily I assumed the blame!

Early on, a wonderful muralist, single mother and close friend, Jane Norling, organized the Northern California Friends of Margaret Randall. It remained one of the most active of more than twenty defense committees across the country; at one time even assuming tasks of nationwide coordination. I remember Jane, overburdened and harried, telling me a couple of years into the struggle, "If it hadn't been you, I never would have taken this on!"

And after it was all over and I was talking about how badly I felt about the time and energy so many had expended on my behalf, Jane again was the one who cut me short: "We didn't do this just because a woman somewhere was being deported. We did it because of what you've given us, your books ... they're important to so many people."

When sticking to one's principles seems to produce nothing more than rage, exhaustion, and ongoing depression, when it would seem so much easier to cede just a bit, to imply a change of voice or heart, it's important to remember what's at stake. Integrity and dignity are qualities that can be taken from a person only in extreme situations of isolation and torture, and sometimes not even then. In my situation they would have to have been willingly forfeited. And integrity and dignity become enormously important in a struggle of an individual against a system. You come to realize that, yes, they can indeed separate you from family, from place, from many of the choices you have made. But they cannot strip you of your core identity; they *cannot* diminish your dignity. In fact, they strengthen both and make them easier and easier to hold onto.

IX. The Support

When I say an individual against a system, I'm not saying I was alone in my struggle. Far from it. Thousands—family and friends but also people I've never met—came with me every bit of the way. And many of the ideas and activities that informed my fight against deportation are themselves extraordinary examples of creative expression and activism.

The Center for Constitutional Rights (CCR) estimates that it cost us a quarter of a million dollars to fight this case. And that doesn't include what we've been charged as taxpayers so the government could wage its side of the battle. The money came from direct mailings, button and poster campaigns, house parties, raffles, auctions, media coverage, and many uniquely original efforts on the part of hundreds of people who gave up pieces of their lives to work on committees or involve themselves in other ways.

Audre Lorde, Adrienne Rich, Sonia Sanchez, Robert Creeley, Diane diPrima, Floyce Alexander, Luci Tapahonso, Joy Harjo, Gene Frumkin, Larry Goodell, Dennis Brutus, John Nichols, Ron Kovic, Alice Walker, Omar Cabezas, Manlio Argueta, Denise Levertov, Susan Sherman, Howard Zinn, Merle Woo, Harold Jaffee, and many others read or spoke for the case. Holly Near, John Bucchino, Casselberry and Dupree, Marta Hogan, Linda Collier, and others played and sang for it. Crowsfeet, The Dance Brigade, and Streetwise danced for it.

The great (and, sadly, recently deceased) painter Elaine de Kooning made an old portrait she'd done of me into a beautiful full-color poster, which was then sold to benefit the cause. It was Helene Vann who made the first "Keep Randall—Deport McCarran-Walter" button; later

Jane Norling added a beautiful design to a reissued version. In Seattle the Red and Black Book Collective organized a Bowl-a-Thon for Free Speech, complete with special T-shirts. David Wilk, of Long River Books in Connecticut, printed a pamphlet of my coming home poems; the proceeds from sales, including his percentage, were donated to my defense fund. Master printer Kathy Kuehn produced an elegant broadside from a short poem of mine, with specially stamped envelopes, a thousand of which were sold to raise money. Peter Stambler, in Wisconsin, organized a marathon fund-raising reading of my work. The Syracuse Cultural Workers Collective dedicated the page for May in their 1989 Peace Calendar to a collage representation of my fight. These are only a few of the great number of offerings, activities, and events that kept the issues alive and some money coming in.

At Trinity College in Hartford, 165 faculty, administrators, and staff members signed a petition urging immediate granting of my residency. Berkeley, California proclaimed February 2, 1986 Margaret Randall Day in their city, and Cambridge, Massachusetts distinguished me with a certificate—not because either had any previous knowledge of me, but because they deem freedom of expression essential to this country's way of life. Unions, religious orders and councils, professional organizations, and conferences unanimously raised their voices against the affront to freedom of expression and dissent symbolized by the deportation order against me. All these, and many more, are examples of communities of people confronting official censorship with creative struggle.

X. Family

I hope this conveys something of the texture of these years. As the case moved from defeat to defeat, I continued to write, make pictures, teach, love, mother, bake bread, and breathe in the rocky juniper-dotted foothill country surrounding me in the home I hoped I would not have to leave. My partner hoped this too, as she adjusted the daily contours of her life to the demands of the struggle. My parents—now eighty and eighty-four—also hoped. Their little adobe house sits between ours and the mountain face. It had taken me almost three decades to come home; my mother and father did everything in their power to help make sure I could stay.

Everything in their power ... thinking back, from this place of having won, I imagine it may have been my parents who felt most powerless through these years of struggle. My mother worried each time a news report reprinted a lie about her daughter. I'm still not sure if this experience managed to teach her—against a life-long barrage of media conditioning—not to believe it " 'cause it says so in the paper." She spent hundreds of hours, over these years, urging people to write letters on my behalf. She was the one who carefully kept the scrapbooks: a record of every brief, opinion, affidavit, affirmation, article, poster, flyer.

Early on, she also had an experience that probably helped to keep her going, in the context of such continuous pressure: sitting in the car one day, waiting for my father to return from an errand, she told herself that if he was the twentieth person to emerge from the door he'd entered, we would be victorious. And she started counting. As time went by, when we were most depressed she often reminded us that he had, indeed, been the twentieth person. When we won, she reminded us again.

One of only two times I cried during the hearing in El Paso, was when my mother was on the stand. She is a small woman, almost so thin as to appear frail. But she rose to enormous heights of energy and righteous indignation when one of my attorneys asked if she had anything further she wished to address to the court. It was 1986, and she spoke about the nation's anniversary, about the Statue of Liberty and what it could mean if freedom of expression was not only honored but guaranteed. It was an extraordinary moment, one that I don't believe many in that room will forget.

My father was a rock of support, in his constant, quiet way. I know that he sent every spare penny to CCR; again and again, when xeroxed sheets of donation checks would come for me to respond to with the letters I always wrote to everyone who gave, I would see a copy of a check from him. But the greatest strength I got from my father was the fact that he never wavered in his pride. I felt that he was proud of the stand I took, and wouldn't have wanted me to back down—even if it eventually meant another (and certainly final) painful separation.

When I think about where my stubborn attachment to honesty comes from, I know I owe that to my father. "It's just not right," he would say. I remember his tone of voice throughout my childhood and growing up years. He'd be talking about some injustice, someone who had been wronged, however small the offense. Throughout my struggle with immigration, my father held to his belief that justice would prevail. A great example of that belief is the house he built for me, while I was still under order of deportation, next door to his own.

My children were always with me, each in his or her own way and from the several countries where they make their homes. They rallied support and tried to keep up with each new turn of events. It must have been hard for them, as their mother went through this, to be so far away. They were raised on struggle, and in places where it has been particularly raw at times. So they understood the forces at play. But that probably didn't make it any easier for them when I sometimes expressed my anxiety in letters or on the phone.

My son and his wife live in Paris, with their two small children. My oldest daughter lived in Cuba for most of these years; communication with her was difficult because of the fragmented relations between the two countries. Now she's in Mexico and we can reach one another more easily by phone; while my next daughter—also in Mexico—has recently moved to an apartment without a phone. There have been a number of times during these years in which I could not travel, that I felt an intense need to be with my children: after the terrible 1987 earthquake in Mexico City, or when they've suffered more personal problems of their own. We've managed one large reunion here in Albuquerque as well as other more partial get-togethers, but I've yet to see any of those who live outside this country in their own space.

My youngest daughter, Ana, has been in the United States since my struggle with the INS began. We are on opposite sides of the country now, but visit frequently; the problems of contact haven't been the same as with the others. Three years back she was living with me, and I remember her coming home from a waitressing job one day and talking about a co-worker who'd asked: "Aren't you the one whose mother is a commie?" So that kind of harassment hasn't been totally absent from my children's lives either. Ana was also on the stand at the El Paso hearing; hers was the second testimony that brought tears to my eyes. It was simply about seeing her there, seventeen years old and participating with such dignity.

If I had to isolate the single most difficult thing about this case in terms of family, I'd say it was not being able to be with my children when they had their own. As a former midwife, as well as a mother, that was a dream I had nurtured. It became one of the irretrievable things the INS took from my life. In October 1987, my first grandchild, Lia Margarita, was born in Paris. Luis Rodrigo followed in Mexico City in February 1988. And Martine came along in August 1989, again in Paris, just weeks before our victory.

XI. Victory

And what about the victory? It came, sudden and unexpected—at least in its origin and form—in the last days of July 1989. I was working on my new novel, sitting before the word processor by my studio window with its dramatic view of the Sandia Mountains. The telephone rang; it was my lawyer, Michael Maggio's, office. "Is this Margaret Randall?" a secretary's voice asked. "Michael wants to speak to you; it's important."

Needless to say, my heart tried to push its way up into the back of my throat. An urgent message: in my mind, battered by a long series of defeats, it could only be a threatening one. At the same time, I knew the case was long overdue for a ruling by the Board of Immigration Appeals. If this was news of that Board's negative decision, well, that was what we had expected.

Then I heard Michael telling me we'd won!

The BIA was the last decision-making body within the administrative INS courts. Its chairman, David L. Milhollan, wrote the favorable decision to which two of the other members subscribed. They found that I had become a Mexican motivated by economic duress, and therefore had not lost my U.S. citizenship. All other issues then became irrelevant. It was a 3-2 ruling, with board member Fred W. Vacca writing a scathing dissenting opinion. His was more or less a rehash of the Guadalupe Gonzalez brand of hysteria, based on lies, innuendo, and half-truths taken out of any recognizable context.

The decision could not be appealed to the courts, and the media immediately wrote the victory as final. I was numb. While the phone rang incessantly, the house filled with flowers, telegrams, and friends with champagne and balloons, I tried to imagine what life would be like, now that I could get on with it. Now that I could hold my grandchildren, tell my partner I loved her—even on our telephone which I must presume is tapped—maybe even get a real job.

But my mind kept telling my body: don't let go, not yet. And my mind was right. Before twenty-four hours had passed, news came that the INS lawyers had requested a thirty-day stay, in order to ask the Attorney General to reverse the decision. We spent close to another month, like human yo-yos, trying once again to bury the emotion and wait. This was a particularly difficult period. Most of the media ran only the initial story; details of complications aren't the kind of things that make the news. So strangers would come up to me in the street and tell me how glad they were that things had "worked out." I never knew whether to launch into an explanation of what was actually happening, or just say, "Thank you very much."

Finally, towards the end of August, the Service "determined that it [would] not file a motion for reconsideration of the Board's decision...." Apparently, they felt it was time to give up. Victory, filtered as it had been through stops and starts, was ours. Eventually, the flowers that arrived in the wake of the absolute win were indistinguishable from those that had brightened our home after the first news. As I write this, several weeks later, the house remains filled with all their joyous colors.

In recognizing my U.S. citizenship, the BIA gave me a full personal victory. Politically, the outcome may seem less clear. The citizenship decision mutes the First Amendment considerations, and that's good for an administration in which many conservatives are fighting against immigration reform; especially as legislation modifying McCarran-Walter once again comes before Congress. But I believe the central issues of freedom of expression and freedom of dissent have not been lost.

Long-time New Mexican political activist Dorothy Cline, among many from whom I've had messages, wrote, "The system worked but the wheels were rusty, out of date and had to be repaired. But *not* replaced— McCarran-Walter is still with us. Certainly the case ... must have helped to influence opinion. When it is repealed, you can take a good share of the credit."

I would argue that we fought an important struggle, one that many within the administration were glad to silence. We educated tens of thousands of people in this country about the nature of U.S. immigration law and about threats to our freedoms which affect us all. We need to keep on fighting, until the laws that govern who may or may not come into our country are brought into line with constitutional principles.

The pragmatists within the administration wanted to see an end to this case. It's interesting that the three Board members who subscribed to the favorable ruling were Nixon and Ford appointees; the two who signed the dissenting opinion were appointed by Ronald Reagan. They, and many others, are the zealots of these years: the Eliot Abramses, Ollie Norths, Jerry Falwells, the names and faces we will continue to see on the other side of the barricades in our battles for human dignity, for just immigration laws, against racism and intervention, for reproductive choice.

The zealots may call themselves "pro-life," but in most of today's battles they come up on the side of death. The pragmatists in many instances may also hold conservative points of view, but they understand that keeping faith with democratic principles can often be important to the maintenance of capitalism. Some also hold constitutional values they don't want to see destroyed.

These are times when victories are scarce. As the reality of this one sinks in, I begin to feel a lightening, a renewal of energy I know I'll need for the other battles we face. Coming home must bring peace, but never complacency. I don't want to forget a single instance of pain or frustration, and I want to be able to place my anger where it belongs: squarely in the laps of those who, from positions of abusive power, would punish, stigmatize, harass, and persecute. But I want also to remember the lessons: how people come together, what creativity is born in struggle, what faith is held in it. As I continue to build my bridges and walk across them, I am filled with the vision of the hands waving behind me and those reaching out to welcome me to the other side.

—Albuquerque, New Mexico
Summer 1989

Notes

1. "The 1952 McCarran-Walter Act: Is It Irrelevant in Today's World?" David Cole, *The National Law Journal*, May 29, 1989.
2. *The Closing of the American Mind,* Allan Bloom (New York: Simon and Schuster, 1987).
3. *This Is About Incest,* Margaret Randall (Ithaca, NY: Firebrand Books, 1987).
4. *The Shape of Red: Insider/Outsider Reflections*, Ruth Hubbard and Margaret Randall (Pittsburgh, PA: Cleis Press, 1989).

Some of You Are Saying
We Are Both Wrong

Throughout several years of feminist therapy (1985-88) I began to retrieve a memory of incest perpetrated by my maternal grandfather, now many years dead. In the process of working through re-memory, I am beginning to take control of a life acutely damaged by an abuse I had blocked out in order to survive. Needing to share this experience with others, I wrote *This Is About Incest*, and included a few of the incest poems in a broader collection, *Memory Says Yes*. A male relative not only took it upon himself to unilaterally decide I was lying about my grandfather, but was unable to respect the boundaries of our separate lives and he attacked me in a particularly sadistic way. His actions threatened to polarize the family, and I began to receive differing and mixed messages from my parents, brother, sister, and others. The following is based on a collective letter of response which I sent to family members (though not to the relative in question) in an attempt to further explain my feelings about going public with this kind of information.

Dearest family:

Some of you are saying we are both wrong.

Me, because I decided to name the man who invaded my trust, who used me for his perverted pleasure and my pain. Me, because I couldn't just "keep it to myself" but told what I have discovered, so many years after the fact. And ——, because he sent me hate mail, pouting in rage because the family name was "dirtied." We are both wrong, you say, you who would rather it all be kept acceptably quiet, not talked about, left unexposed to scrutiny or shame. Both wrong. As if two silences might somehow give birth to erasure, and to ease.

It all begins so many years after the fact. And the fact, some of you say, cannot really be proven. It lives only in my reclaimed body memory. How can I prove it to your satisfaction? It lives only in the

35

hidden center of my fear, my phobia, in the shortness of my breath, in his hideous tongue, safely dead these many years. The fact cannot be proven, except in reclaimed memory. And that, after all, is mine alone. My secret. My responsibility.

And so here we are a half century later. With a woman who has dared to tell what she knows. And a relative who curdles his shame in the clenched fists of denial. As well as some who support me but wish I had considered the consequences before going public, some who feel one way one day and another the next, and some who just don't tell me how they really feel because "why hurt her feelings?"

All of you know I have never kept a covenant with silence. As a child I did not want the brilliant colors to fade. I went after the music and the fire. Even if I sang off-key, I vowed to recover a voice. Through the years, I always went after life, rejected death. When it meant deciding to be a writer. When it meant having my first child on my own. When it meant defending a variety of causes my heart and reason told me were right. There were always obstacles. But, increasingly, there has also been the joy that struggle brings. You, my family, have always been a solid and loving support.

Living in countries where lies explode in harbors or cut the feet off young peasant women, I dragged their stories home with me, pushed them into print, told their truths with my life. Later my country's guardians of law and order said, "If only you hadn't been so strident," and punished me in public ritual. I was strident while they died. And you understood, you supported me then. I don't think you would have been proud of my silence.

Once I read an article about the role of the CIA in the Bay of Pigs. It was 1961, and no one we knew spoke about such things then. I wanted everyone to understand the truth I had uncovered, so I bought dozens of copies of that article, gave them to family and friends. One of you who loves me very much was furious, asked how I could "believe those communist lies!" Years later, coming across the same article in a forgotten closet, you remarked on how visionary its author had been to have understood the connections "way back then." You were surprised when I reminded you of your former stance and agreed that time often helps us catch up with the truth.

The covert actions of a decade ago—then provoking discussion as to whether or not they really could be proven—are overt enough today. Now they bear names like *contra* aid, sending military troops to Honduras, invading Panama and kidnapping and indicting its head of state, justifying shooting down a commercial plane in the Persian Gulf, offering technical know-how on torture, and lying about the human rights violations in El Salvador, Guatemala, South Africa, the occupied territories of the West Bank and Gaza, Chile, and our own inner cities.

Not that long ago, African Americans as five-eighths of human beings, or women as persons or property, were also matters of public disagreement. Slowly (much too slowly for the victims) a struggle was waged so that more than one point of view could be expressed. That which empowered the African-American or the woman was only very gradually the acceptable point of view. And thousands died at the stake or were hanged from trees throughout the long history of struggle to change all that.

The world as flat or round. The earth or sun as center of our cosmic system. Direct communion with God. The very existence of God. Woman as God's representative: all these have been matters slowly, painfully, opened to discussion through lifetimes, generations, centuries. Being ideologically ahead of one's time should not condemn one to silence, but rather commit one to struggle for change.

Silence, secrets: they too often protect the perpetrators.

May we now speak of wife and child abuse? Twenty years ago we couldn't. May we speak of rape? Ten years ago we didn't. May we speak of incest? Five years ago we didn't dare. The hideous reality of satanic ritual abuse is only now beginning to surface—in the reclaimed memories of those courageous enough to speak. Today tens of thousands stand and utter words that make us vulnerable, reveal these painful truths. And the lives of tens of thousands have been changed, empowered, through this new possibility which is our right. And yes, we are beginning to place the nouns and verbs correctly, name the names, show the images, take back that privilege and protection so long reserved for the abuser.

Am I saying that I think I have always held the truth in my hands? That I have always been right—about my personal history or the world out there? No, I am not saying that at all. I don't believe in absolute truth. But I have learned to trust my body when it speaks to me. We need to respect process, rather than only look to product as proof of what we stand by.

What I *am* saying is that authority is not always right, perhaps rarely so, and that powerful interests are well served by our silence. I am saying that superpowers and patriarchs have had authority on their side far too long, and that intimidation is always a part of their game. I am saying undeserved privilege lives because of silence, because who would believe a child (or a nigger, or a fluff-head, or a spick, or a kike, or a queer, or a bum)? You may be seen but certainly not heard. And please don't name any names!

Right now what I am saying is that my grandfather abused me when I was much too small and powerless to fight back, when I was too young to understand what was being done to me, without language to communicate to others the act or the fear it engendered. I am saying his abuse left me with a lifetime of sickness and terror. I am saying that through the difficult (and unfinished) work of feminist therapy I have been able to reclaim that memory, so long ago distorted. And that the discovery has been, for me, the beginning of my road to health.

To those of you who continue to ask me why I didn't think of the effect my words would have on others, I am saying that I *did*. In spite of the discomfort or pain I knew my revelations might provoke, I made a conscious decision to share my discovery—not only the knowledge, but the voice and images which were my particular process of reclaiming. I had to take back my power so I might begin to live in wholeness. And I knew that my process would be useful to others.

The chain must be broken somewhere. When it is, panic often seems the overwhelming emotion. Some may be afraid they will be forced to get in touch with their own story of abuse. Others may fear exposure as abusers. Eventually only healthier relationships and deeper self-awareness result. It is a necessary legacy for our children, so that the cycle is not endlessly repeated, so that new generations may grow free from these fears in an atmosphere that no longer gives tacit permission for violence.

I am saddened that my public revelation, my "washing of dirty laundry in public" (as some have called it), has been uncomfortable for several members of my family. I love you very much. I am angered that naming my experience has enraged ——, and that he has acted in such an irresponsible way, both towards me and towards the events themselves. I am also puzzled that his rage has now assumed a sort of "equal time" with mine. He has chosen to defend the honor of the abuser, protected in death and holding an authority threatened by my memory. He has chosen to attack me, the victim.

And I am angered that I am asked, again and again, to prove my claim. "How do you *know* it really happened?" I am presumed guilty of an over-active imagination, of the need to "draw attention to myself," or of lying—until I can prove myself innocent, on his terms. Why? Why should I, the victim, have to prove myself innocent?

Some of you think us "both wrong." Grandfather wrong in his abuse, perhaps; me wrong in my decision to accuse. Or maybe me wrong in my decision to reveal, —— wrong in his attack upon me.

I want to make it clear that I perceive neither our acts nor the issues they involve as equal in any way. Only in a society that still protects the patriarch (or the imperialist nation, or the capitalist boss, or the machine politician, or the white man, or the foreman, or the wife beater, or the rapist), can it be said that the perpetrator of abuse may be wrong, but so is the victim if s/he makes it public!

When I stand up and read my incest poems, invariably many people in the audience come up to me afterwards to thank me for my courage. They say it makes them feel less alone, or puts them in touch with their own suppressed memories. My book (like others) has brought hundreds of letters from people who no longer feel that theirs is the shame of isolation, the guilt of reverse faulting. I need to say that I feel as good about these letters as I do about those I receive in response to *Cuban Women Now* or *Sandino's Daughters*,[1] letters that tell me how my books open readers to the reality of peoples about whom we are routinely told lies. Even when the people are ourselves.

Would you be proud of me if I had gone along with the mainstream, ingratiated myself with authority, voted only for sure winners, accepted exploitation and greed as "wrongs we simply cannot change?" Would you have wanted me to tell the INS I was sorry I disagreed with U.S. foreign or domestic policy, I'll be a good girl now, I'll never speak my mind again, please just give me my residency?

Much of my courage I have learned from you. In spite of the pain of these struggles, I know you would not have wanted me to bend my principles so my life would be "easier." Anyone with a decent heart and mind knows that ease is often fictitious.

I admit I am sometimes weary of the fight to break with silence, but I suspect I will always be in it. Pointing the finger at my grandfather today is not that different from pointing it at the CIA a quarter of a century ago.

All my love,

Margaret

—Hartford, Connecticut
Spring 1989

Notes

1. *Cuban Women Now,* Margaret Randall (Vancouver, BC: New Star Books, 1981), and *Sandino's Daughters,* Margaret Randall (Toronto: Women's Press, 1974).

Notes on the
New Female Voice

In 1981 June Jordan opened her essay "Many Rivers to Cross" with this sentence: "When my mother killed herself I was looking for a job."[1] Quickly she sets a picture of a young professional African-American mother, jobless, and recently abandoned by a husband she has seen through school. Then she zeroes in on the events surrounding her mother's suicide, and her father's inability even to determine whether or not his wife is dead: his fear, ineptitude, and vindictive rage. This extraordinary piece concludes:

> And really it was to honor my mother that I did fight with
> my father, that man who could not tell the living from the
> dead. And really it is to honor ... all the women I love,
> including myself, that I am working for the courage to
> admit the truth that Bertolt Brecht has written ... "It takes
> courage to say that the good were defeated not because
> they were good, but because they were weak." I cherish
> the mercy and the grace of women's work. But I know
> there is new work that we must undertake as well: that
> new work will make defeat detestable to us. That new
> women's work will mean we will not die trying to stand
> up: we will live that way: standing up.[2]

Central to this new[3] women's work is—I will argue—a new writing, a female voice. A body of U.S. literature which is *qualitatively* different as well as (obviously) written and published in quantitatively greater volume than writing by women has ever been written or published before.

This question of whether or not there is a woman's—or female—voice is not a new one; nonetheless, against growing evidence that there is, it continues to be asked. As with related questions (is there a woman's eye, a woman's musical score or symphony conduction, a woman's art in general?), we have on the one hand an increasing body of first-rate

41

work to which we may go for the answer. On the other hand, mainstream high school and university literature courses, and the traditional anthologies and literary reviews, are as one-sidedly male (and white and heterosexist and elite) as they ever were.[4] One must necessarily conclude that those who continue to turn their backs on this work are doing so, intentionally or not, out of a prejudice which has nothing to do with literature.

The Jordan quote exemplifies something important about the new female voice, about the work of women like June Jordan and Meridel LeSueur, Jane Cooper, Maxine Hong Kingston, Toni Morrison, Adrienne Rich, Audre Lorde, Alice Walker, Marge Piercy, Leslie Marmon Silko, Joy Harjo, Sonia Sanchez, Judy Grahn, Sandra Cisneros, Judith McDaniel. (How absurd to make lists that will forever be partial at best, at worst insulting in their omissions.) What this writing offers is centuries of silent honing powerfully articulated at last, a courageous externalization of the inner map *truly connected to the world out there*. Among its many characteristics are its discussion of body parts and functions far less encoded than in the past, its unselfconscious risk-taking, and a craft by any standard as good as the best. A retrieval of our history has made it possible for us to tap into a great communal re-memory, and there is a dialectical bonding: of women back through time, across the current man-made barriers, and out into a future we envision in our work. Additionally, because of the challenges within the feminist movement, many women writers have been more able than their male counterparts to speak from a history that recognizes difference, that crosses barriers of class, race, ethnicity, age, sexual preference, and physical ability.

For all these reasons, strong women (women who are not victims but who succeed) are finally solidly represented among our literary protagonists. Young women, those just beginning to read, may now select their literary role models from among a much healthier canon. This hasn't always been the case. I think it's important to stop and ask what it meant for women writing (and for people reading) that *The Girl* by Meridel LeSueur remained unpublishable for twenty years because, as one editor after another told its author, "A book about a woman who is not a victim just won't sell."[5]

LeSueur, who was born with the century and is still active—still writing—speaks with authority about a woman's creativity in the context of ageing:

> [N]ow in the experience of ripening and even decaying
> and dropping the seed, it seems to me more inflammatory

to have had communication of a superior intensity and frankness. It would be great if there could be creative hospices, not for the dying but for the ripening. I read somewhere that after seventy you no longer pass through the astrological houses but are freed from them and enter the galactic imagery which is planetary in nature and very strong. Some people die of its intensity, unable to entertain it (possibly alone). We need some kind of monasteries of being together, not to miss this extraordinary crop of the last season or the culminating protein memory.[6]

She has often referred to growing old as a process of decay, in which the cells in decomposition give off a phosphorescence, light.

As a body of work, the new female voice addresses the larger social issues with a power only the most intimate vision can bring (showing how a coherent movement from the general to the particular reflects the fact that, truly, the personal is political and the political personal). Standard textbooks to the contrary, women writers (working women) have rarely lived in ivory towers and so we reject ivory tower notions of art. Our writing involves the breakdown of formal genre divisions through the offering up of the ordinary female voice. We claim this voice as literature by mixing, or choosing to disregard, the traditionally male-imposed categorizations of essay, criticism, novel, and perhaps even poetry (the genres where men are said to excel), and private journals and letters (long thought to be the domain of women). Our voice is a revelation of our female self, calling forth a profound degree of risk (lesbian narrative, work by women with disabilities, incest and abuse stories). This work teaches a willingness, indeed a need, in our commodity-oriented society, to place process up there with product.

This new chorus of female voices has also opened doors for male writers, some of whom, finding their own traditions uncomfortable or alienating, have explored new territories influenced by women's vision. As certain women's work has broken with stereotypical ideas about the "female domain" in literature, a number of men have been freed to write out of the so-called female modes: emotion, sensitivity, re-memory, concern with process.

I prefer female voice to women's writing. On philosophical principle I do not believe these new frontiers can be explored only by women, just as I do not believe only women can be feminists (or that all women are feminists simply by virtue of our gender). Necessarily, however, women are the ground-breakers here; men fear they have too much to lose, and in the short term indeed they do. We of course vastly outnumber men in our explorations of the territory. Many so-called minority writers or writers of color (both labels suffer from the erroneous vision that views only white men as central, everyone else as *other*) express themselves out of an allied if not always identical consciousness. Clearly feminism, as philosophy and experience, has signaled the particular literary renovation which I call the female voice.

As school children most of us—girls and boys—were urged to "write about what you know." But the male province was the standard against which all else was judged. We were already being taught to see ourselves as *other*, long before we were conscious of the imposed condition. As we grew, it was easy to see whose work was noticed, encouraged, published, reviewed. And so (pre-feminist consciousness particularly), we emulated the men, glowed at the "praise" *you write like a man* or *you write as well as a man.*

For the past two decades, with notable forerunners, women writers have come into our own, writing about what we know, and —slowly, painfully—writing ourselves into the center. We have very literally had to make a place for our words on the pages of a literature that judged us trivial, overly emotional, gossipy, infantile, minor.

Rainer had written my requiem—
a long, beautiful poem, and calling me his friend.
I was *your* friend but in the dream you didn't say a word.
In the dream his poem was like a letter
to someone who has no right
to be there but must be treated gently, like a guest
who comes on the wrong day.
      Clara, why don't I dream of you? . . .

This is from Adrienne Rich's compelling "Paula Becker to Clara Westhoff."[7] The passage speaks eloquently about how our history has been distorted. What has come down to us are the words of the great male poet (Rainer Maria Rilke) alone. But Rich, speaking in Becker's voice, tells us where the friendship really was. She mourns her friend's voicelessness even as she reveals the relationships that engendered such silencing. A skewed history erases even dreams.

Many of the most powerful U.S. women writers look to our foremothers for sustenance and voice; poets like Muriel Rukeyser, Jane Cooper, Audre Lorde, Adrienne Rich, Paula Gunn Allen, and others have researched the histories of those women who have gone before us

(Mmanthatisi, Rosa Luxemburg, Molly Brant, Sojourner Truth, Paula Modeson Becker, Willa Cather, Ethel Rosenberg). We have retrieved role models. And we have insisted on speaking in overlay; with their voices stopped in time and with our own: historically erased because they were silenced, sharpened today because they lived. Some of the best among us assume those women's voices, giving them back in rich and varied ways.[8] This actual taking on of another's history/memory, speaking in it, breathing it filtered through a fierce redemption enraged by centuries of denial, is undoubtedly one important component of the new female literature.

Important moments in this ongoing process have been Magda Bogin's discovery that the female troubadours did in fact write differently from their better-known male counterparts,[9] Linda Brent's autobiography,[10] Blanche Cook's gift of Crystal Eastman[11] and her forthcoming biography of Eleanor Roosevelt,[12] Barbara Sicherman's use of Alice Hamilton's letters to weave a plausible and highly readable correspondence-biography of the latter's life,[13] Georgia O'Keeffe's letters,[14] Diane Arbus's personal journals,[15] Evelyn Fox Keller on Barbara McClintock,[16] and teacher/writers like Audre Lorde writing about themselves.[17]

Among the writers inviting us to look into their own lives, a new autobiographical work, *Assata* by Assata Shakur, is not only wrenchingly and beautifully written, but speaks from an experience shared by many but too rarely translated into literature.[18] It is a particular class, race, and gender experience, that of an African-American woman in prison for a crime she has not committed, who preserves herself against terrifying odds, escapes, and makes a gift of the telling. This woman is at once unique and representative of all women of color. This prisoner is at once herself and the inhabitant of a hideously extreme, profoundly compressed version of the prison that our female condition has been for centuries. I want to quote at length from this book. In the opening paragraph:

> There were lights and sirens. Zayd was dead. My mind knew that Zayd was dead. The air was like cold glass. Huge bubbles rose and burst. Each one felt like an explosion in my chest. My mouth tasted like blood and dirt. The car spun around me and then something like sleep overtook me. In the background i could hear what sounded like gunfire. But i was fading and dreaming. Suddenly, the door flew open and i felt myself being dragged out onto the pavement. Pushed and punched, a

foot upside my head, a kick in the stomach. Police were everywhere. One had a gun to my head. "Which way did they go?" he was shouting. "Bitch, you'd better open your goddamn mouth or i'll blow your goddamn head off!"[19]

We are on the scene of a capture, a contemporary version of the capture of Africans for the slave trade almost two centuries ago. As the book unfolds, we understand that the brutality of this initial scene perfectly reflects the fact that these officers of the "law" are guardians of a racist system attacking a vulnerable African-American woman, a woman whose history has taught her there will be neither hope of, nor recourse to, justice. Shakur's consistent naming of the state and its representatives with lower case letters, while reserving upper case for those who struggle (except, interestingly, when she speaks of herself), makes language responsible to ideology. Near the end of the book she chooses to give us this climactic moment, very much a woman's moment, very much a mother's:

> My mother brings my daughter to see me at the clinton correctional facility for Women in new jersey, where i had been sent from alderson. I am delirious. She looks so tall. I run up to kiss her. She barely responds.... I go over and try to hug her. In a hot second she is all over me. All i can feel are these little four-year-old fists banging away at me. Every bit of her force is in those punches, they really hurt. I let her hit me until she is tired. "It's all right," i tell her. "Let it all out." She is standing in front of me, her face contorted with anger, looking spent. She backs away and leans against the wall. "It's okay," i tell her. "Mommy understands." "You're not my mother," she screams, the tears rolling down her face. "You're not my mother and I hate you." I feel like crying too. I know she is confused.... I try to pick her up. She knocks my hand away. "You can get out of here if you want to," she screams. "You just don't want to." "No i can't," i say weakly ... i look helplessly at my mother. Her face is choked with pain. "Tell her to try to open the bars." My daughter goes over to the barred door that leads to the visiting room. She pulls and she punches. She yanks and she hits and she kicks the bars until she falls on the floor, a heap of exhaustion. I go over and pick her up. I hold and rock and kiss her.

There is a look of resignation on her face that i can't stand. We spend the rest of the visit talking and playing quietly on the floor. When the guard says the visit is over, i cling to her for dear life. She holds her head high, and her back straight as she walks out of the prison. She waves goodbye to me, her face clouded and worried, looking like a little adult. I go back to my cage and cry until i vomit. I decide that it's time to leave. [20]

"It's time to leave." Yes it is. Shakur has written as gut-wrenching an exposé of an attack on the mother/daughter relationship as I have read. It is not lost on us that those responsible for this common travesty are the same who loudly proclaim they protect the sacredness of life. Coming down now, this fragment very close to the book's final lines:

Freedom. I couldn't believe that it had really happened, that the nightmare was over, that finally the dream had come true. I was elated. Ecstatic. But i was completely disoriented. Everything was the same, yet everything was different. All of my reactions were super-intense. I submerged myself in patterns and textures, sucking in smells and sounds as if each day was my last. I felt like a voyeur. I forced myself not to stare at the people whose conversations i strained to overhear. Suddenly, i was flooded with the horrors of prison and every disgusting experience that somehow i had been able to minimize while inside. I had developed the ability to be patient, calculating, and completely self-controlled. For the most part, i had been incapable of crying. I felt rigid, as though chunks of steel and concrete had worked themselves into my body. I was cold. I strained to touch my softness. I was afraid that prison had made me ugly.[21]

Although the above is clearly about a particular instance—Shakur's escape from brutal captivity and her arrival in a land of freedom—it is also a powerful metaphor for many women's lives, lives that would seem (from appearances) to be far less dramatic than hers. I would ask, however, that the reader try the above lines out on such common women's experience as incest, rape, battery, or even the less crisis-oriented everyday female oppression. Lines like "Suddenly I was flooded with the horrors of . . . every disgusting experience that somehow i had been able to minimize while inside," "I had developed the ability to be patient, calculating, and completely self-controlled," "i had been incapable of crying," "i felt rigid," "i was cold," "[it] made me [feel] ugly."

Many of our new women writers have looked beyond the limits of the North American and/or western literary scene in our exploration of a whole new genre: testimony. As women listening to women, the pioneering works of Latin Americans and others of the so-called Third World have been important.[22] I'm talking about contemporary classics like *Let Me Speak!* and *I, Rigoberta Menchú*.[23] More recently we have read works by Filipina, African, Middle Eastern, Australian, and New Zealand women. These moving books encourage us in the art of listening. If we can do so, we will hear voices that have always before been ignored, silenced, despised.

Some of us have learned, as well, to listen in a particularly useful way to the multiple parts of our own retrieved identity. Such is the case of Gloria Anzaldúa who explores her many-layered reality as a Mexican/American/female/lesbian in an extraordinary rediscovery of language and meaning called *Borderlands/La frontera*.[24] Straightforward narrative, poetic prose, and poetry combine English, Spanish, Spanglish, and Nahuatl words to reveal a new sense of self, one which because of the existence of this book now belongs to us all.

In this collective retrieval we have also repossessed pages of sheer beauty, forgotten while lesser works by men written in the same period and place continue to receive endless acclaim. I'm thinking particularly of Hemingway's "great white hunter" vision of Africa, as compared with Beryl Markham's *West With the Night*. Both Hemingway and Markham were foreigners on African soil, although she lived and worked there for years while he made occasional visits. His books have become classics; it took the explosion propelled by the women's movement to bring hers to the surface:

"Did you read Beryl Markham's book, *West With the Night?* I knew her fairly well in Africa and never would have suspected that she could and would put pen to paper except to write in her flyer's log book [sic] As it is, she has written so well, and marvelously well, that I was completely ashamed of myself as a writer...." This is Hemingway himself, describing the prose of a woman previously all but lost to literature![25]

I have held hands
with fear;

We have gone steady
together.

Sorrow has been
my mate;
We have been bed-
companions.

The days of my night
have been long.

They have stretched
to eternity.
Yet I have outlived
them. And so shall you.

"I Have Held Hands with Fear" is by Mitzi Kornetz. Out of a
poetry anthology? No. I have taken this poem from the chapter called
"Cancer" in *Ourselves, Growing Older*, the new self-help compendium
from The Boston Women's Healthbook Collective.[26] Women have taken
our literature out of the academic texts and coffee-table artifacts and used
it as well in books on health, exercise, dealing with cancer, addictions,
incest, dying, and other difficult areas of life. And it has not seemed
important to us to limit our field to a chosen few. In our lives and in our
publications we welcome the contributions of women who might not
define themselves primarily as writers, but whose writing speaks to us:

He lets up the pressure for a second. "Mommy!" I scream.
The door opens. She is here. The light from the hallway
is bright; I am safe. In one thousand seven hundred and
fifty seven days I will be sixteen years old. "What did you
do that for?" he shouts. "This has nothing to do with her."
"Mommy," I cry. Her arms are folded across her chest. All
I can ask is that she rescue me. I cannot ask her for comfort.
"Kate," she says. "You shouldn't upset your father ..."

These are a few lines from "Like the Hully-Gully But Not So
Slow" by Anne Finger. It's only one of dozens of nearly uniformly
excellent pieces of poetry and prose in *With the Power of Each Breath:
A Disabled Women's Anthology*.[27] Testimonial writing by women with
disabilities,[28] prostitutes,[29] addicts and codependents,[30] incest and abuse
survivors,[31] lesbians and their mothers[32]—these comprise a body of
literature, not simply a collection of first-person accounts, how-to man-
uals, or scientific theses. When work by prostitutes or writers with
disabilities is legitimized as literature, readers (as well as the authors
themselves) are empowered to push through heavy curtains of fear,

self-doubt, and immobility.

The women's movement taught us how silenced and hidden from us our role models have been. We have founded and sustained women's presses and magazines[33] not simply to publish ourselves (an overriding concern of the largely male-dominated small press renaissance of the fifties and sixties) but to make available this heritage as well. And so we have retrieved our great classics, Zora Neale Hurston's *Their Eyes Were Watching God*[34] and Agnes Smedley's *Daughter of Earth*,[35] to mention only two of the most extraordinary. Classics by any standard, yet in most of our universities still not considered "great books," nor even a part of the standard curriculum, basic reading on a contemporary U.S. literature syllabus.

There is immense variety in this new women's literature. Fantasy is explored in titles like Sally Miller Gearhart's *Wanderground*.[36] Ursula K. LeGuin is only one of a host of women who write science fiction.[37] A feminist interpretation of the natural world can be found in work by writers like Susan Griffin.[38] Anne Cameron's books explore spirituality and traditional women's wisdom.[39] Spiritual and political connections are made in such classics as Marge Piercy's *Woman on the Edge of Time*.[40] Making class/race/gender connections is often, in fact, an essential quality (condition) of this new writing.

> "Why" is not "how"
> is not a recital of physical causes
> physical effects
> it is meaning
>
> The bullet pierced her flesh
> because a finger pressed a trigger
> & she was in the way is "how"
>
> Why that gun was there at all
> why she was in front of it
> why that policeman's finger pressed the trigger
>
> not muscles   but years are behind the answer
> not reflexes
>
> people ...

This is from a poem[41] by Susan Sherman. It's called "Facts," and it deals with the mesmerizing media hype lulling us daily in an attempt to make us think that things are not what they seem, so that *we will not believe we are who we are.* Sherman addresses the way in which *how* is passed off as *why,* even in this country's most interpretive news reportage. As women we must do battle simply to reclaim our history, our memory, ourselves. The classist, racist, sexist, and heterosexist media message, in the United States in the eighties, is technologically advanced to the point where our very identities are jeopardized. Women are creating a literature that attempts to center us in all our multiplicity of mirrors.

> Home once again, I walked out alone
> nearly every day that first week. Or:
> still floating just above my body,
> I watched me walking out alone. The eighth day
> I met my mother, dead eight years.
> As she walked toward me I peered
> into her face. She was crying and smiling
> at the same time. I had questions
> to ask her but we did not speak.
> I wanted to know how I could go on
> living with so much shame:
>
>   I mean
> with the memory of the children sitting
> at their desks in the school that was only
> a roof. Those bright questioning eyes
> welcomed me, tested the cut of my blouse
> and hair, welcomed my foreignness. Last year
> they huddled in ditches as mortars
> shelled their village for twelve days.
> Seven died. I helped buy the bullets ...

Judith McDaniel is dealing here with her own roots and decision to take risks, and with what she perceives as her relationship to events in Central America. McDaniel has been speaking out of the new female voice for as long as she's been writing. Her novel, *Winter Passage,* is about relationships between women. *Metamorphosis* is a collection of poems written out of the experience of alcoholism recovery. The above fragment is from a poem called "Dangerous Memory," in her book, *Sanctuary, A Journey.*[42]

 A finely woven tapestry of essay, interview, poetry, poetic prose, and journal-writing, *Sanctuary* not only crosses the boundaries of literary genre but those of "personal" and "political" concerns as well. A powerful message in this type of work is that the traditional genre divisions are arbitrary at best. The female voice has, I believe, spoken to the problem of form and content in particularly relevant ways. Tracing this to feminist explorations of emotion/reason (and other sexual stereotyping) isn't difficult.

So many of our writers are prolific in the ease with which they inhabit a variety of genres: we have an Alice Walker whose novels, short stories, essays, and poems are equally powerful. We have a Marge Piercy who is as fine a novelist as she is a poet; a June Jordan whose political essays sing right along with her verse. But we do not define the new female voice through "stars" alone. Indeed, our refusal to do so is itself an important part of our commentary upon it.

Our work is peopled by bodies; not the fragmented pieces of ourselves rearranged by those who have crafted a male literature (often resembling the world of advertising). Our bodies age and come in different shapes. They have "unsightly" hair, odors, and sagging flesh. And they are learning, painfully, to feel. The ways in which women write about our bodies, reclaiming our total physical selves, inform a feminist voice more powerfully, perhaps, than any other single feature of our work.

More precise definitions include a repossession of history/memory/self, an attention to and an honoring of process, a gender-, race-, and class-conscious ear. We are concerned with stories, the stories that have been told outside literature for years. We know how important it is to reclaim the ordinary voice. We make connections and search for the multiple faces of a new creative vision: one that insists on a world with everyone in it. Women have begun to produce, as well, knowledgeable compendiums of our own literature. A particularly fine anthology of new women's poetry is *Early Ripening: American Women's Poetry Now*, edited by Marge Piercy.[43] The following is from her introduction:

> Women are writing immensely exciting, approachable, rich, funny and moving poetry that can speak to a wider readership than it usually gets. Women are writing much of the best poetry being written, way more than half of it I believe, but remain poorly represented in anthologies, textbooks, reading series, prize lists, awards and every other institution controlled by white men who like the way things are presently run just fine. Women are still mostly read by women; men remain under the delusion that the poetry women write will not speak to them. I

think that means that many men miss out on poetry that
could get them far more involved than what they're
inclined to read, or more likely, inclined to bow the head
at and pass by: that's high culture, may it rest in peace.[44]

While the proverbial male anthologies have almost always been
homogeneous (read: white, male, middle-class, academic, heterosexist,
safe), this volume of women's work is homogeneous only in its literary
excellence. (Remember the plaintive cry, "We would have published
more women, if we could only have found any good enough...!") There
are many African-American, Latina, Native-American, and Asian-American as well as white women poets represented in Piercy's volume. There
are unpublished as well as well-known names. There are lesbian as well
as heterosexual women; poets who write out of a feminist perspective
and others who simply write as women: poets who are not afraid of anger,
physicality, process. I would like to close by quoting in full one poem
from this anthology. This one, like much of the new female writing
anthologized by Piercy, is strong in the language of our image. It speaks
of a woman in singular, and in so doing speaks about us all. It has memory
and vision, it takes risks. It is Joy Harjo's "The Woman Hanging from the
Thirteenth Floor Window":

She is the woman hanging from the 13th floor
window. Her hands are pressed white against the
concrete molding of the tenement building. She
hangs from the 13th floor window in east Chicago,
with a swirl of birds over her head. They could
be a halo, or a storm of glass waiting to crush her.

She thinks she will be set free.

The woman hanging from the 13th floor window
on the east side of Chicago is not alone.
She is a woman of children, of the baby, Carlos,
and of Margaret, and of Jimmy who is the oldest.
She is her mother's daughter and her father's son.
She is several pieces between the two husbands
she has had. She is all the women of the apartment
building who stand watching her, watching themselves.

When she was young she ate wild rice on scraped down
plates in warm wood rooms. It was in the farther
north and she was the baby then. They rocked her.

She sees Lake Michigan lapping at the shores of
herself. It is a dizzy hole of water and the rich
live in tall glass houses at the edge of it. In some
places Lake Michigan speaks softly, here, it just sputters
and butts itself against the asphalt. She sees
other buildings just like hers. She sees other
women hanging from many-floored windows
counting their lives in the palms of their hands
and in the palms of their children's hands.

She is the woman hanging from the 13th floor window
on the Indian side of town. Her belly is soft from
her children's births, her worn Levis swing down below
her waist, and then her feet, and then her heart.
She is dangling.

The woman hanging from the 13th floor window hears voices.
They come to her in the night when the lights have gone
dim. Sometimes they are little cats mewing and scratching
at the door, sometimes they are her grandmother's voice,
and sometimes they are gigantic men of light whispering
to her to get up, to get up, to get up. That's when she
wants to have another child to hold onto in the night, to
be able to fall back into dreams.

And the woman hanging from the 13th floor window
hears other voices. Some of them scream out from below
for her to jump, they would push her over. Others cry
softly from the sidewalks, pull their children up like
flowers and gather them into their arms. They would help
her, like themselves.

But she is the woman hanging from the 13th floor window,
and she knows she is hanging by her own fingers, her
own skin, her own thread of indecision.

She thinks of Carlos, of Margaret, of Jimmy.
She thinks of her father, and of her mother.
She thinks of all the women she has been, of all
the men. She thinks of the color of her skin, and
of Chicago streets, and of waterfalls and pines.
She thinks of moonlight nights, and of cool spring storms.

Her mind chatters like neon and northside bars.
She thinks of the 4 a.m. lonelinesses that have folded
her up like death, discordant, without logical and
beautiful conclusion. Her teeth break off at the edges.
She would speak.

The woman hangs from the 13th floor window crying for
the lost beauty of her own life. She sees the
sun falling west over the gray plane of Chicago.
She thinks she remembers listening to her own life
break loose, as she falls from the 13th floor
window on the east side of Chicago, or as she
climbs back up to claim herself again.

—Hartford, Connecticut
Winter 1988

Notes

1. "Many Rivers to Cross," in *On Call, Political Essays*, June Jordan (Boston: South End Press, 1985).
2. Ibid., p.26.
3. By new I am referring to women's literature written in the period roughly between 1970 and 1990.
4. A notable exception is *The Heath Anthology of American Literature*, Volumes I and II, edited by a group of scholars headed by Paul Lauter (Lexington, MA: D.C. Heath and Co., 1990). The first volume covers the Colonial period and early nineteenth century; the second, the twentieth century.
5. *The Girl*, Meridel LeSueur, (Albuquerque, NM: West End Press, revised edition 1990). LeSueur's work was in fact silenced almost in its entirety when she was subpoenaed in the early fifties by the House Un-American Activities Committee (HUAC). A byproduct of the McCarthy era, the activities of this congressional committee affected artistic freedom in this country in ways still being felt. Indeed, the censorship and self-censorship generated by that particularly dangerous phenomeon changed the course of U.S. artistic expression. LeSueur's work began to become available again when in the early seventies she was rediscovered by the women's movement. West End Press reissued a number of her books; Feminist Press followed with what remains the most complete collection, *Ripening* (Feminist Press, 1982). LeSueur, born in 1900, is still writing.
6. Meridel LeSueur, letter to author, dated "Last Sunday of March, 1990."

7. "Paula Becker to Clara Westhoff," in *The Fact of A Doorframe, Poems Selected and New, 1950-1984*, Adrienne Rich (New York: W.W. Norton and Co., 1981).

8. This assumption of women's voices from other historic moments has been a poetic practice exercised by North American poets Muriel Rukeyser, Jane Cooper, Adrienne Rich, Paula Gunn Allen, and others. It has also influenced the way women have approached the research and writing of the biographies of our foremothers. See especially *Voices of Women: 3 critics on 3 poets on 3 heroines*, by Martha Kearns, Diane Radycki, May Stevens, Muriel Rukeyser, Adrienne Rich, Jane Cooper, Kathe Kollwitz, Paula Modeson-Becker, and Rosa Luxemburg, with an introductory essay by Lucy R. Lippard (New York: Midmarch Associates, 1980).

9. *The Women Troubadours*, Magda Bogin (New York: W.W. Norton and Co., 1980).

10. *Incidents in the Life of a Slave Girl,* by Linda Brent and edited by Lydia Maria Francis Child was published during the author's life. A contemporary edition was made available by Harcourt Brace Jovanovich in 1973. More recently, a more complete edition, *Incidents in the Life of a Slave Girl Written by Herself,* was attributed to the real author, Harriet A. Jacobs (Cambridge, MA: Harvard University Press, 1987).

11. *Crystal Eastman on Women and Revolution*, ed. Blanche Wiesen Cook (New York: Oxford University Press, 1978).

12. Blanche Cook has been working for a number of years on a biography of Eleanor Roosevelt soon to appear. It promises to combine Cook's meticulous historical research with her profoundly revealing feminist vision.

13. *Alice Hamilton, A Life in Letters*, Barbara Sicherman (Cambridge, MA: Harvard University Press, 1984).

14. Most recently in the catalog book for the traveling show, *Georgia O'Keeffe, Art and Letters* (Washington, DC: National Gallery of Art, 1987).

15. In the 1972 *Aperture* collection of Diane Arbus's photographs, journal entries edited by Diane's daughter Doone. *Aperture* has recently reissued the collection.

16. *A Feeling for the Organism, The Life and Work of Barbara McClintock*, Evelyn Fox Keller (New York: W. H. Freeman, 1983).

17. See Audre Lorde's early biomythography *Zami, A New Spelling of My Name* (Freedom, CA: Crossing Press, 1982). More recent are *The Cancer Journals* and *A Burst of Light*. Among her books of poetry are *The Black Unicorn* and *Chosen Poems, Old and New*. *Sister Outsider* is an important book of essays.

18. *Assata, An Autobiography,* Assata Shakur (Westport, CT: Lawrence Hill & Co., 1987).

19. Ibid., p.3.

20. Ibid., pp.257-8.

21. Ibid., p.266.

22. Although I have sometimes continued to use the term Third World for more immediate reader comprehension, I would like to quote from a note with which June Jordan opens her book *On Call*: "Given that they were first to exist on the planet and currently make up the majority, the author will refer to that part of the population usually termed Third World as First World."

23. *Let Me Speak!* by Domitila Barrios de Chungara as told to Moema Viezzer (New York: Monthly Review Books, 1978); and *I, Rigoberta Menchú, An Indian Woman in Guatemala*, ed. Elisabeth Burgos-Debray (London: Verso Editions, 1983). There have been a number of other such books of oral history with women in recent years, including: *Sandino's Daughters, Testimonies of Nicaraguan Women in Struggle*, Margaret Randall (Toronto; New Star Books, 1981); *Don't Be Afraid, Gringo—A Honduran Woman Speaks from the Heart*, ed. Medea Benjamin (San Francisco: Food First, 1987); and *Enough is Enough, Aboriginal Women Speak Out*, as told to Janet Silman (Toronto: The Women's Press, 1987).

24. *Borderlands/La Frontera*, Gloria Anzaldúa (San Francisco: Spinsters/ Aunt Lute, 1987).

25. *West With the Night*, Beryl Markham (San Francisco: North Point Press, 1983).

26. *Ourselves, Growing Older*, ed. the Boston Women's Health Book Collective (New York: Simon & Schuster, 1987).

27. *With the Power of Each Breath: A Disabled Women's Anthology*, eds. Susan E. Browne, Debra Connors, and Nanci Stern (Pittsburgh, PA: Cleis Press, 1985).

28. I used *disabled* and then *differently abled* until I read E. J. Graff's letter in the January 1988 issue of *Sojourner*. She writes: "I prefer to think of myself as a woman with a disability, not a disabled woman. The former recognizes my handicap. The latter seems to define my entire being ..." See also *With Wings: An Anthology of Literature by and About Women with Disabilities*, eds. Marsha Saxton and Florence Howe (New York: The Feminist Press at the City University of New York, 1986).

29. See *Sex Work, Writings by Women in the Sex Industry*, eds. Frederique Delacoste and Priscilla Alexander (Pittsburgh, PA: Cleis Press, 1987).

30. There are a great number of literary titles in this category, as well as many books by psychologists and others. A visit to a good women's bookstore or library should provide a wealth of material.

31. Among the titles in this category, I would recommend the novel *Searching for Spring*, Patricia Murphy (Tallahassee, FL: Naiad, 1987) and *This Is About Incest*, Margaret Randall (Ithaca, NY: Firebrand Books, 1987).

32. Lesbian literature—novels, short stories, poetry, essays—is much too broad a category to even begin a comprehensive listing here. A look in any good women's bookstore will reveal dozens of excellent titles.

33. Some of the important U.S. publishers of women's writing are Feminist

Press, Firebrand, Naiad, Cleis, Spinsters/Aunt Lute, Seal, and Crossing. Although South End and West End are not women's presses, their feminist titles are worth noting. Among the feminist literary magazines are *Ikon, Sinister Wisdom, Heresies, Calyx, Conditions,* and *Thirteenth Moon.*

34. *Their Eyes Were Watching God,* Zora Neale Hurston (Urbana, IL: University of Illinois Press, 1978).

35. *Daughter of Earth,* Agnes Smedley (New York: The Feminist Press at the City University of New York, 1973).

36. *Wanderground,* Sally Miller Gearhart (Watertown, MA: Persephone Press, 1979).

37. Among Ursula K. LeGuin's many titles, the most important is *The Left Hand of Darkness* (New York: Ace Books, 1983).

38. Susan Griffin's *Woman and Nature: The Roaring Inside Her* (New York: Harper & Row) was ground-breaking. *Made from this Earth, An Anthology of Writings* (New York: Harper & Row, 1982) is a comprehensive introduction to her work; *Like the Iris of an Eye* is poetry.

39. Anne Cameron's books include *The Journey* (San Francisco: Spinsters/Aunt Lute), *Daughters of Copper Woman* (Vancouver, BC: Press Gang), *How Raven Freed the Moon* (Madeira Park, BC: Harbour Publishing), all prose; and *Earth Witch* and *The Annie Poems* (Harbour Publishing), poetry.

40. *Woman on the Edge of Time* as well as most of Marge Piercy's other novels are available from Ballantine/Fawcett (New York). *Circles on the Water* (New York: Knopf, 1982) is an anthology of her poetry books through *The Moon is Always Female.* Also see her new book of poems, *Available Light* (New York: Knopf, 1988).

41. "Facts," Susan Sherman, first published in *Ikon* Second Series 5/6, New York, 1986. It has been reprinted in *We Stand Our Ground,* Kimiko Hahn, Gale Jackson, and Susan Sherman (New York: Ikon Books, 1988). This title is particularly interesting in that it presents the work of three women with a lengthy introductory conversation in which they speak of their origins, politics, feminism, literature, and writing.

42. See these books by Judith McDaniel: *Winter Passage* (San Francisco: Spinsters Ink, 1984), *November Woman* (Glen Falls, NY: Loft Press, 1983), *Metamorphosis: Reflections on Recovery* (Ithaca, NY: Firebrand Books, 1989), and *Sanctuary, A Journey* (Ithaca, NY: Firebrand, 1987; see review in this book).

43. *Early Ripening, American Women's Poetry Now,* ed. Marge Piercy (Methuen, 1988).

44. Ibid., p.2.

Remapping Our Homeland
Some Thoughts on Oral History

Suppose you want to write
of a woman braiding
another woman's hair—
straight down, or with beads and shells
in three-strand plaits or corn-rows—
you had better know the thickness
the length   the pattern
why she decides to braid her hair
how it is done to her
what country it happens in
what else happens in that country

—Adrienne Rich

You must be able to write what you think, and maybe
what you write about your day-to-day, everyday,
ordinary life will be some of the same problems that the
people of the world are fighting out. You must be able
to write what you have to say, and know that that is
what matters. And I hope you can see that you can
begin anywhere and end up as far as anybody else has
reached.

—C.L.R. James

Oral history.

What does the joining together of these two words really mean?

Oral, of course, is from the spoken word, an oral tradition: people, and the stories we tell. Also from a time when peoples' stories were more familiar, valued, honored; not yet pushed aside by the more "educated" written (later, *academic*) telling.

Superseding the oral with the written brought with it an obvious ranking. Those telling the story represent the economic interests of those in power (most often commissioned or paid directly by those interests). White, ruling-class men, and their ideologies. Very occasionally, women trained in the male educational centers, women who could "make it in a man's world" or "write as well as a man."

So we've had the stories, the *his*tories and *her*stories, of those who came before us, all filtered through the myopic lenses of another. More to the point: the *other*, posing as *self*. An ahistoric misarrangement in which we, the people, become *other* to ourselves.

The lives of working women and men, told by those who exploited them. The lives of native peoples offered, presumptuously, by those who came to defile their land, plunder and rape, and finally conquer. The lives of slaves, told by the slave holders. Women's lives, when told at all, distorted through a male lens. Heterosexism making invisible the lives of lesbians and gays.

We read about our forebears. We "learn" our history in books and texts and films and TV specials whose primary reason for being is to falsify our identities: rigged identities which are nothing more than disguises designed to keep us from knowing who we are.

As just one example, think of all the American Indian or Latino children watching grossly distorted images of themselves on mainstream U.S. television or film. There are so many insulting people's images in advertising, school texts, the media. In our multi-cultural society, the current repression of bilingualism is yet another travesty of self.

We learn all this. And then we learn that we must unlearn it. Oral histories have been key in replacing these false identities with bits and pieces of our real selves. We become, once again, the conscious protagonists of our lives.

Even as the system's tools for maintaining this identity-bondage are ever more perverse and refined, we have our own ways of keeping the collective memory alive. We know who we are—in the stories, in the legends, in the voices handed down from generation to generation.

These are the original oral histories, what the grandmothers and grandfathers told the mothers and fathers, what the mothers and fathers tell their children.

And, although the term *oral history* is used to describe stories which are precisely that—a history handed, orally, from person to person—a number of amazing written accounts have also surfaced: narratives such as Linda Brent's extraordinary slave memoir, or Mother Jones's autobiography.

What about the technical components of oral history? How is it made?

First of all, it is not *made*—passive voice—by some invisible power. We ourselves make it.

Originally, and in most cases, we record a voice. We may use a tape recorder or take extensive hand-written notes. Someone, or a group of people, who have lived a particular experience, tell their story to a writer who records, orders, edits. Supplementary supporting data, from the more traditional archives or other sources, may be used as well. But the central narrative comes from the person or persons who have lived the event.

Respect is essential here. I have recorded the stories of people who cannot write their own, and I've worked with those who are able to take an active part in the process. I generally transcribe every word, making two copies of the material; one I file, in order to be able to keep an accurate record of what has been said. Then I am free to apply my creativity to the other. I may feel that a non-linear use of time is more appropriate to telling a particular story. Then I may cut and paste. In recent years I've wanted to photograph the informant and search for other visual images as well. Working in the darkroom, printing these images, has influenced how I might edit a voice; the sound of a voice, in turn, affects how I print an image.

Depending upon the particular project, there are a number of stages and moments when a text may be submitted to the person telling the story. He or she may read it or I may read it to them. Listening to what they've said, they may have valuable input or feedback, enriching even more the final product. In oral history, process is as important as product.

Because working people, inhabitants of rural areas, people of color, and women have for so long been manipulated, used, kept uneducated and without access to the mechanisms of writing and publication, the vast majority of our stories, as uttered by us, have been passed on orally, or told in diaries, private journals, and songs—the so-called lesser literary forms. Only occasionally, and sometimes to be used against us, were out-of-context fragments of these stories passed on by those who had access to the pens and presses.

In some parts of the colonized or neocolonized world, notably in Latin America, people's revolutionary struggles first used the words *testimonio, historia oral,* or oral history, to describe a new genre, one which linked history with literary narrative, a life or lives often told to someone else. Within the cultural context of political change, the ordinary woman and man became the recognized protagonists. We discovered we could tell our own stories, and began to do so.

Often we did this through a listener, someone with the awareness and skills necessary to see a work through to publication. People began to speak of this new category of writing. And discussions about its contours, limitations, and possibilities became more and more widespread.

As some revolutionary societies consolidated and a much greater percentage of the population learned to read and write, people began to produce more of their own stories. And social institutions began to validate them.

Cuba, throughout its thirty-year-old revolutionary experience, has done a great deal in this respect. As a result of the literacy campaign of 1959, the vast majority of Cuban adults learned to read and write. After the campaign, Fidel Castro suggested to a black woman more than 100 years of age that she write about her life in slavery, during the pseudo republic, and under socialism: he insisted no one could tell it better.

Of course learning to read and write is one thing. Possessing the confidence, skill, and energy to tell one's story is another. As far as I know, that ex-slave woman never did write the book Fidel urged her to. But Cubans of both sexes and from many ways of life did begin to reclaim their collective memory. It's something that happens in revolutions. And the Cuban revolution supported this explosion in the retrieval of an entire national identity, as has the Nicaraguan revolution and other working-class movements for change. In 1971, Casa de las Americas, Cuba's extraordinary Latin American cultural institution, added *testimonio* (oral history) to the categories of novel, short story, poetry, theater, essay, and children's literature in its prestigious annual literary contest. The year before, Rodolfo Walsh had been one of the contest's judges. He had written *Operación masacre*, based on his research (and resultant solving) of a crime against Argentinean workers in the mid-fifties. That book, from the era of Juan Perón, was among several that popularized the new literary genre.

Cultural imperialism is as widespread and insidious as its economic, political, and military counterparts. U.S. anthropologists like Oscar Lewis went to Mexico, Puerto Rico, and Cuba and tried to tell Latin Americans their own stories—and to tell their stories to a waiting world, always avid about defining "the ways of the natives." In the metropolis, Lewis's *Children of Sánchez* (about working-class and marginal Mexicans) was widely acclaimed. But when the man who saw things through his prism of "a culture of poverty" went to Cuba with Ford Foundation money to tell the islanders' stories, the Cubans threw him out. They felt that he was distorting who they were, as well as reneging on his promise to train local people in oral history skills.

I don't think it's surprising that many of the next oral history titles to emerge from Latin America were written by and about women. The second wave of feminism had exploded across our collective consciousness. Women in the "developing" as well as in the "developed" countries began to understand the unique ways in which we've been robbed of the knowledge of our foremothers; and how our lives today are trivialized, ignored, or invalidated. We began to remedy this colossal lack by talking to each other, convincing our sisters that their voices are important, insisting they be heard.

Books like *Permit Me to Speak* (Domitila Barrios de Chungara's story of a Bolivian miner's wife as told to Moema Viezzer) and *I, Rigoberta Menchú* (a Quiché Indian woman from Guatemala telling her story through Elisabeth Burgos Debray) were forerunners, along with some of my own early efforts: *Cuban Women Now, Inside the Nicaraguan Revolution: The Story of Doris Tijerino, El pueblo no sólo es testigo*, and *Sandino's Daughters*.

Rigoberta Menchú's original tongue is Quiché. Already in her early twenties, this Indian woman decided to learn Spanish specifically so she could tell her story to the world. People are becoming aware of the importance and the power of their words.

All this work was essential. But it wasn't enough. The more we tried to reclaim and retrieve our history, the more obvious the inherent problems became. Questions arose, questions of ethics, of responsibility, of power and control. We began to understand that knowing our foremothers was not simply a question of researching a mistold or ignored history, and finding the women who'd been left out. Where would we find them? Our history itself was skewed.

We quickly knew that it wouldn't work to ask who the women erased from the earliest stones or codexes were, who the women from the Middle Ages or Renaissance had been. The very concepts of Middle Ages and Renaissance are male-defined. In order to retrieve our women's lives, we have to *revision* history itself.

The same has been true, of course, for native peoples, working people, people of color, and others whose identities are subsumed and subverted to stereotypical classist, racist, and sexist models.

Among our most exciting poets, most notably the women, many work diligently to recreate the voices—and thus the lives—of historical figures desecrated or absent in the more traditional texts. In this country I'm thinking particularly of Muriel Rukeyser, Jane Cooper, Adrienne Rich, Audre Lorde, and Paula Gunn Allen. Poets who revive images of foremothers as diverse are Molly Brant, Rosa Luxemburg, Fannie Lou Hamer, Emily Dickinson, Willa Cather, and Ethel Rosenberg.

Our authentic people's voices appear more and more frequently, not only in the book or poem or article, but in other media as well. Think of the inspiration for, and the content of, some of our most vital songs, street and stage theater, dance, murals, poster art. The names of some groups have become household words: Teatro Campesino, Sweet Honey in the Rock, Taller Gráfico, La Raza Cultural Center, West End Press, Midwest Villages and Voices, *Sinister Wisdom, Ikon,* San Francisco Mime Troupe, Wallflower Order (later known as Crows Feet and Dance Brigade).

Other lesser-known but important works include a broad-ranging conceptualization of what may be considered within the oral history framework. There are murals like San Francisco's Our History Is No Mystery, which include replicas of news stories read aloud by passersby. That, too, is oral history.

Since the Freedom of Information Act (FOIA) made accessible the enemy's words about our lives, there are writers working with people's FBI files and using them to fill in some historical blanks. Oral history is nurtured, as well, by such sources as these.

There are neighborhood photo projects in which whole communities spin stories off exhibitions of pictures from family albums. There are ceramicists who retrieve and recreate our ancestors' markings and symbols. There are all manner of mixed-media projects involving voice, theater, music, puppetry, dance, video, and film. All may involve some aspect of oral history.

The AIDS quilt, spread over the vast Washington mall, with people saying aloud the names of brothers and sisters dead from the disease: who can imagine a more moving and powerful telling?

In a number of recent peoples' gatherings, people have been making what they call a fish bowl. Concentric circles provide a context in which an inner group, bonded by a common condition, speak their experience and feelings. Perhaps they are African Americans or lesbians or single mothers or women with disabilities. In an outer circle people listen and then repeat back what they've heard. This is oral history, in yet another dimension and use. Some academics today teach courses in cross-cultural life histories in which their students learn to tell their own stories. This is oral history as well.

Oral history, then, is the recuperation of a memory that has been taken from us. It is our essential voice, relevant and necessary to the ongoing task of remapping our homeland.

—Saint Paul, Minnesota
Spring 1989

Reclaiming Voices
Notes on a New Female Practice in Journalism

I'd been in El Salvador two weeks and I was walking home one day when I heard shots. There were tanks all along the block, and some fifty soldiers and police. They had mortars, machine guns, and they were attacking one house in particular. It was incredible, because they had all this trained on just one house, and the only thing you could hear coming from inside the house were the shots of a small caliber pistol. Then the shots from inside were heard no more. Everything grew quiet. The smoke cleared and the first group of policemen and journalists entered the house. There was a young man dead in the bathroom. And there was a woman, maybe forty or forty-five, wearing an apron and with a kerchief around her head. She was lying in a pool of blood ... I was the only woman in the group, and the only journalist from the U.S. who had stayed in El Salvador for more than a couple of days that month. And I just couldn't believe what happened next: the Chief of Police went into another room and got a machine gun. He knelt beside the older woman and placed it in her hand. "This was the weapon, this was the machine gun she used against us," he said. He got a box of bullets, unused bullets still wrapped in paper, and he threw them on the floor on top of her blood. "Those were her bullets," he said. And the international press took photos and they said, "Right, right," and they took notes: "... she had a machine gun, she was shooting at the Government Forces, terrorist, guerrilla" and so on.[1]

There was something wrong with "free journalism." To begin with, many of us were unable to correctly formulate the questions, much less pretend to evolve answers. We thought we came from countries where freedom of the press existed. We were supposed to be able to write and publish anything. Yet in the sixties and seventies when our hometown newspapers filtered back to us in Mexico, Cuba, and Nicaragua, much more often than not the news we read was unrecognizable as having anything to do with the reality we saw around us. Who had written those feature stories? What world did they inhabit?

Inhabit might have been the key word. While we who were also writing about these places lived in them, relating to situations of everyday life as workers or as mothers with school-aged children, most journalists came, stayed a few days in the local luxury hotel, and then left. Much of their "news" came from conversations over drinks at that hotel's Americanized bar. We guessed you had to inhabit a place to know it.

> [T]here were six women working in production here in Jibacoa. Today eighty-six percent of the women in this community are working. We owe this in great measure to the theater.... Our experience with the play about sexism was tremendous. We criticized the man who thinks his wife is a submissive object in the home, and we showed how women can't and mustn't accept that.... We dramatized cases we have right here ...[2]

But if you didn't understand the language, if you didn't speak Spanish, how could you really communicate? How could you listen? To report accurately on a given part of the world, we decided, you must live and work in that place, speak its language, get to know its people and their culture.

And that's when we began to understand the more subtle nature of free press. For many of us did live and work in the countries whose news we cared to tell. Many of us learned to speak the language, deeply involved ourselves in the culture, listened. But the truer our stories, the more they had to do with what was really going on, the fewer opportunities we found for getting them published.

Our knowledge and experience pushed us to take sides. We were no longer "impartial," and in punishment we were relegated to speak only to each other. In our country with its loudly-touted freedom of the press, we had no trouble seeing our work in print. But our voices were limited to publications like *Liberation News Service* or *The Militant*, *The Daily Worker* or *The People's World*, that reached several thousand readers at best. *The Guardian, The Nation, In These Times, Zeta* maga-zine, and *NACLA* are among the most professional and widely distrib-uted of our progressive publications. None are much of a threat, though, to a population of 250 million.

I'm not going to pursue further this line of very obvious analysis. It's been done a thousand times by historians, sociologists, social anthro-pologists, and political scientists, as well as many journalists. I'm more interested, here, in talking about another whole way of telling the story, a way evolved and explored mainly by women: the first-person narrative, testimony, or oral history.

In the late sixties and early seventies two important forces came to bear on the work of a number of women who lived in and wrote from Latin America. The first was a disparate but growing awareness of the relationship between U.S. government foreign policy and the reality of life for most people of the mislabeled Third World. Conversely, it wasn't difficult for us to understand why real news about these people did not, for the most part, find its way into the mainstream U.S. press.

The second important force was feminism. It exploded across our collective consciousness, catching each of us wherever in our own lives we happened to be standing. As women reevaluating our present, we began to realize we had a past, a history hidden or distorted, a memory we needed to retrieve—for our own health and well-being. As writers, as journalists, we gradually came to feel it was no longer satisfying to try to *write like the men*. We were no longer sure we accepted male criteria for what good writing, or accurate journalism, should be. We began to listen to our own voices, play by our own rules. The process was sometimes uneven, an ascending spiral rather than an immediate shift. Some of us wrote essays about our discoveries. Others were less analyt-ical, more intuitive. We learned to trust our—and each other's—analyses *and* intuitive powers. Our work changed.

> Social life, uh uh: none. It was a neglected life. The people were traditionalist, poor, peasants. There was a solidarity among the families, and a lot of camaraderie among the women. When one woman was going to give birth another one would be with her. The women didn't smoke or drink. Those who had a bit of food would help out another who didn't have anything, even in poverty. That's how we were. When I was growing up and even after I got married there was still no school here.[3]

We began to understand that our collective as well as our individual memories have been invaded, raped, erased. Recreating these memories has been an ongoing concern, taking place in many ways and in a number of disciplines. Listening—to ourselves as well as to our grandmothers, mothers, and sisters, and to women of different histories, ethnicities, social classes, and cultures—has been important in the context of this recovered vision.

A new practice of listening and telling is sometimes called oral history. Sometimes it's called *testimonio,* or testimonial journalism. Some people refer to it more simply as in-depth interviewing. Whatever the defining label, it has created a body of voice and image, a new resource literature—much of it from the so-called Third World and much of it from and about women. This new literature provides a whole other way of listening to and looking at life in places like Latin America.

Although the best of this work crosses genre lines, for the moment and for the purpose of these notes I'd like to consider it as journalism. And I'd like to look at some of the things that set it apart from journalism of the more conventional type.

In the first place, I've not casually called it a *practice.* This way of telling a story is not product-oriented like the traditional (male-defined) news story, balanced on "events" and portraying them as static. When we tell our stories, or make ourselves vehicles for others to do so, we aren't bound by the traditional disciplinary distance. We are not ashamed of having a point of view. And we offer process. We are interested in what was, what is, and what may be in the future. We are interested in *how* and *why* our informants did what they did, and what contradictions or complexities were a part of that.

We began to be clear about who did what, and to whom. People were not massacred. The army massacred them (or the police, or whoever). Battles didn't take place. Named forces waged them, against named victims.

It was at one of our first union meetings. A few of the key members were late ... so we started the meeting without them. By the time they arrived we had made a number of important decisions. I was supposed to report these decisions and started off by saying, "Well, comrades, this was a great meeting. We did all we had to do. We changed our executive in a diplomatic way." I was then informed that the word was democratic, not diplomatic. "No problem,"

I said. I never was one for shutting up. I always went right
ahead and made my mistakes so they could teach me how
it was supposed to be done. That's how I learned.[4]

We based our choice of informants on criteria different from the
usual journalistic guidelines. We didn't go to the spokesperson (too often
the spokes*man*), we tended not to ask officials. We began to do our own
thinking about who makes history, and noticed it is usually ordinary
working people, women, often children. We believed it is important to
present different views of an event or conflict. We went to people with
contrasting viewpoints and consulted as well the more traditional
sources. But we chose our central voices from those who were centrally
involved.

And memory was vital. It occupied a new, almost sacred, place
in our writing: in our poetry, prose, essays, journalistic efforts. Even in
our images: photography and other visual art forms. We came to understand how a retrieval of our own memory was essential, not simply for
the language of our lives, but for the very meaning of that language, the
nurturing of life itself. And so we gave thought to ways in which we might
uncover, discover, recreate the memories of those whose voices we
passed on. It was not a matter of remembering more. It was a matter of
remembering *differently*, unfettered by what men have deemed worthy
of recording, unaltered by male interpretation, uncluttered by the male
system of rewards for achievement according to their values.

We were bringing back our own voices. We learned to listen. And
we were unafraid to present our voices in all their unaltered richness,
with respect for culture, with respect for wisdom even when that wisdom
assumed forms as yet unnamed among us, with respect for language.
Language, for us, was not to be deconstructed out of its social history, in
the manner of Derrida. Language lives intimately linked to time and
place, and is informed by history and ideology, music and meaning. A
new and evolving understanding of language has enabled us to hear our
multiple voices and offer them (often in translation) to others.

As feminism pushed us to question our assumptions on all levels,
we tended to bring less of these assumptions, cultural or otherwise, to
bear on the way we conducted an interview. Most of us tried to practice
a humility and respect for people's differing histories, customs, dreams.
An honoring of our differences as well as of our commonalities became
a goal among feminist women; such an honoring naturally found its way
into our work as transmitters of our sisters' lives.

[H]ow to retain the vitality, and often beautiful simplicity, of Rigoberta's words, but aim for clarity at the same time ... I've left the repetitions, tense irregularities, and sometimes convoluted sentences which come from [her] search to find the right expression in Spanish. Words have been left in Spanish or Quiché ...

—Ann Wright, translator's preface

[M]y cause ... born out of wretchedness and bitterness ... radicalized by the poverty in which my people live ... the oppression which prevents us from performing our ceremonies, and shows no respect for our way of life ... it's not easy to understand, just like that. And I think I've given some idea of that in my account. Nevertheless, I'm still keeping my Indian identity a secret. I'm still keeping secret what I think no one should know. Not even anthropologists or intellectuals, no matter how many books they have, can find out all our secrets.

—Last lines of Rigoberta Menchú's narrative[5]

Just as we gave thought to how to present other women's stories, we also understood it may not be desirable, or even possible, for us to do this alone, assuming the role of unique or only scribe. Sometimes we worked collectively, attempting to free ourselves of the competitiveness so prevalent among our male colleagues. At times we felt it particularly important to involve the informant, facilitating the protagonist's role as writer and/or analyst rather than preserving that hierarchical position for ourselves.

Our work attracted people, often eager to tell their stories through us. In the mid-seventies, living in Cuba, I was approached by Dominga de la Cruz, an elderly Puerto Rican woman who had become a well-known figure in Havana. Often referred to as "the woman who picked up the flag during the Ponce Massacre of 1937," most people ignored her personal history preceding and beyond that historic act. Dominga asked me to write her story; "... so I can leave it to the young ones," was the way she put it. I felt moved, honored. Faced with an ongoing exile, saddened by years of oppression in her native Puerto Rico, I thought that encouraging her to involve herself in the research and writing might give Dominga stimulus and hope. And it did, to the extent that she was still able to take on those tasks. The attempt, inconclusive as it was, nevertheless made for a very different kind of book than the one I would have written had I been satisfied to do it in the more conventional way.[6]

Sometimes these efforts were more successful. I think it's important to say that we women who in the seventies began exploring the possibilities of oral history in Latin America, listened to men as well as women (to an infinitely greater degree than the men had ever listened to us). Naturally, as we perceived the ways in which we had been historically silenced, we were especially interested in reclaiming women's voices. But we were also interested in our brothers, particularly when they were from the working poor, peasants, or other neglected groups.

In Cuba in 1975 I began work on a book about an elderly farmer who, although he formally had no more than a third-grade education, wrote verse plays about life in the countryside and had organized a local theater group to produce them. *El guajiricantor,*[7] as he called himself, took a very active role in telling his story. He made his testimony more vivid with gesture, and even theater. He sent me scraps of paper on which he recorded his dreams. And he found working on the manuscript itself exciting. The form of that book was richly shaped by our collaboration.[8]

The different phases of listening, recording, and transmitting others' voices had become a new field—oral history—rich in experiment and producing its own discussion about ethics, responsibility, and additional creative possibilities. When I began, in 1969, on what would be my first book involving this approach,[9] I was all pragmatism, solving problems as they arose. Oral history was already an incipient discipline among U.S. and European academics, with its attendant conferences, journals, discussion, and techniques. In Latin America, several movements for social change had produced what they would call *testimonio* (a new form that crossed the boundaries of literature and journalism). But I didn't pay much attention to any of this. By that time I was living in Cuba, which, because of the cultural blockade, was relatively isolated from the latest literary trends. My first contact with the term oral history occurred when the Mexican oral historian Eugenia Meyer visited the island in the mid-seventies. To my surprise she told me that my work to that point was considered pioneering in the field.[10]

When I had been working in this vein for a number of years, however, I began to experiment more. Process was always an important part of this experimentation. I had begun by wondering how to use a tape recorder, how to record a voice without technology getting in its way; in short, how to put people who had never had contact with recording devices at ease in the presence of such machines.

Then I began to do my own photography. Now the problem was

compounded: how would I attend to the voice at the same time as I concentrated on the image; how to move between one and the other so as not to diminish either but enrich both. Later these issues arose not only in the interviewing, but in the subsequent work of editing transcripts and printing photographs.

I remember how excited I was when I discovered that "listening" again to a voice—evoking, recreating the person's actual presence through rereading the interview transcript—influenced the way I might print that person's image in the darkroom; and that the act of seeing, the way an image came up through the developer, also influenced exactly how I edited a transcript. This first happened during the making of *Sandino's Daughters*, and became much more conscious in later work.

> I went in (to the hospital room) ... Alma heard me arguing and began shouting, "Mom, here I am." So the doctor said "Look, it's against the rules but that voice deserves an answer. You can see her for a minute." He was impressed by how young she was. He asked me, "How did they bring her to the hospital? They say it was a bomb...." I went in to see her and I'll never forget it. I wasn't crying but I was done in. I didn't cry so not to upset her, right? When the doctor opened the door, she lifted her two stubs, wrapped in gauze, and said, "Look, Mom, I'm alive! You see, they didn't kill me. They dropped the big bomb on me but they didn't kill me. Life is what matters, so don't worry yourself...." There she was, her arms blown off, and she was already covering her tracks ...[11]

The learning process wasn't always limited to well-planned investigation and subsequent conclusions. On an invitation from the Vietnamese Women's Union I visited what was still North Vietnam in the fall of 1974. It was six months before the Vietnamese victory of April 1975. I didn't speak the language, so I had to conduct my interviews through interpreters. I remember once, at a divorce hearing in Hanoi, my translator—herself a young woman—burst into tears and found it impossible to continue speaking. She explained that the very idea of divorce so shocked and saddened her that she couldn't abstract herself from the proceedings. I learned about custom and culture that day, in a way I would not have had I stuck to straight or "impartial" reporting. My interpreter's manner itself taught me much about women in Vietnam.

I can reminisce about my experience, but I don't want to give the impression that I was the only woman doing oral history and using it in reporting of one kind or another—in so-called straight journalism, in poetry, or in prose. In Latin America there were many writers working in this way. Prominent among them were a number of women whose work has been central to a real understanding of life in those countries. They include the Brazilian Moema Viezzer, the Venezuelan Elisabeth Burgos-Debray, the Mexican Elena Poniatowska, the Cuban Nancy Morejon, the French anthropologist Laurette Sejourne, who has lived for many years in Mexico, and North Americans like Karen Wald and Medea Benjamin, among many others.[12]

Women have not only retrieved and recreated the memory of language, of the voice; they have also worked with visual images in a particularly relevant way. The North American photographer Susan Meiseles is noteworthy in this respect.[13]

But I will take discussion of my own work one step further, and speak of what can happen—what did happen to me—when U.S. government officials decide to retaliate against those of us who tell it like it is. When I returned to the United States in January 1984, the U.S. Immigration and Naturalization Service (INS) denied my petition for residency. They invoked the 1952 McCarran-Walter Act and initiated deportation proceedings against me explicitly based on the critical nature of my writings. In citing offensive or "subversive" texts, an immigration judge actually and primarily quoted from the women in my books.

In searching for reasons why I have been singled out in this way, I have come to the conclusion that central among them is the fact that I have transmitted the voices of ordinary people—perhaps specifically ordinary women—from countries the U.S. government must lie about in order to justify its outrageous foreign policy.

Through a systematic campaign of dehumanizing the people in "alien" nations, our government can keep us feeling those people are *other.* It's one of the ways they perpetuate racism and keep us apart. If we hear those people's real voices, there is always the risk that we will discover we are not so different. We may not have to hate them after all.

I wrote a poem, at the height of my struggle with the INS, which speaks from my conviction that central among my "sins" has been the transmission of people's voices, the recreation of popular memory. In this context, I feel that it's not only me but the women in my books who are under attack by the INS. I'd like to close with this poem, in homage to the women and their voices, and in homage to this new way of working which makes it possible for us to hear them:

UNDER ATTACK

Listen. These voices are under attack.

Ismaela of the dark tobacco house, Grandma,
a maid her lifetime of winters, granddaughter of slaves.
Straight to my eyes:
"my mama used to tell me, one of these days
the hens gonna shit upwards!"
And I'd stare at those hens' asses, wondering
when will that happen?
When we pushed the big ones down
and pulled the little ones up!

"For Mama, Papa, and Blackie" she wrote
on the poem she left to say goodbye.
Nicaragua, 1977.
Disappear or be disappeared.
Dora Maria whose gaze
her mother always knew.
She trembled at her first delivery,
then took a city fearlessly.

Rain and the river rising. Catalina
chases her ducks that stray.
"And my months," she cries,
on that platform with poles, a house
to do over and over.
"My months gone in the hospital at Iquitos
and the full moon
bringing a madness to my head."
Her body is light against my touch.
A woman's voice, parting such density of rain.

Xuan, my cold hand in hers,
evokes the barracks.
"Soldiers who were our brothers."
Night after night, village by village
Quang Tri, 1974.
Gunfire replaced by quiet conversation.
The work of women.
Xuan's history, too, is under attack.

Dominga brings her memory down
from the needle trade, Don Pedro,
her own babies dead from hunger.
"I want to tell you my story," she says,
"leave it to the young ones
so they'll know."
We are rocking. We are laughing.
This woman who rescued the flag at Ponce,
Puerto Rico, 1937.
Known by that act alone,
until a book carries her words. Her voice.

I bring you these women. Listen.
They speak but their lives are under attack.

They too are denied adjustment of status
in the land of the free. In the home of the brave.

—Hartford, Connecticut
Winter 1988

Notes

1. Ann Nelson, quoted in *Women Brave in the Face of Danger*, Margaret Randall (Freedom, CA: Crossing Press, 1985).
2. Testimony from Jacinta Odilia Orozco, *Cuban Women Twenty Years Later*, Margaret Randall (New York: Smyrna Press, 1981).
3. Testimony by Olivia Silva, *Christians in the Nicaraguan Revolution*, Margaret Randall (Vancouver, BC: New Star Books, 1983).
4. Testimony by Gladys Báez, *Sandino's Daughters*, Margaret Randall (Vancouver, BC: New Star Books, 1981).
5. From Ann Wright's testimony in the translator's note and Rigoberta Menchú's testimony on pp. 246-7 in *I, Rigoberta Menchú*, ed. Elisabeth Burgow-Debray (London: Verso Books, 1984).
6. *El pueblo no sólo es testigo: la historia de Dominga de la Cruz*, Margaret Randall (Puerto Rico: Huracán, 1979). An English language translation is as yet unpublished.
7. *Guajiro* is the Cuban term for farmer or person who lives in the countryside. *Cantor* is someone who sings. Che Carballo, the farmer in question, coined *Guajiricantor* to define himself as a singing peasant.

8. *Sueños y realidades de un guajiricantor,* Margaret Randall with Angel Antonio Moreno (Mexico City: Siglo XXI, 1979). Unpublished in English.
9. *La mujer cubana ahora,* Margaret Randall (Havana: Instituto Cubano del Libro, Editorial de Ciencias Sociales, 1972). Also published as *Mujeres en la revolución* (Mexico City: Siglo XXI, 1974) and as *Cuban Women Now* (Toronto: Women's Press, 1974).
10. By this time I had done oral history with Cuban, Vietnamese, Chilean, Peruvian, and Nicaraguan women, some of which was published in book form, other parts of it in magazines.
11. Testimony from Zulema Baltodano, *Sandino's Daughters,* Margaret Randall (Vancouver, BC: New Star Books, 1981).
12. Moema Viezzer gave us *Let Me Speak! The Story of A Bolivian Miner's Wife* (New York: Monthly Review Books, 1978). Elisabeth Burgos-Debray transmitted Rigoberta Menchú's testimony. Elena Poniatowska was the first to publish the story of what really happened the night of October 2, 1968 in Mexico City. Her book *La noche de Tlatelolco* (Mexico City: Editorial Era, 1971) is so far unpublished in English. Nancy Morejón recorded the stories of Cuban nickel miners, Laurette Sejourne recreated the experience of the ground-breaking Cuban theater group *El Teatro Escambray,* and also collected testimony by Cuban women (her work is so far untranslated). Karen Wald first shed light on Cuban education with her book *The Children of Ché.* Medea Benjamin has just published *Don't Be Afraid, Gringo—A Honduran Women Speaks from the Heart* (San Francisco: Food First, 1987).
13. U.S. photographer Susan Meiseles was among the first to record the Nicaraguan war, and her pictures are history in her book *Nicaragua* (New York: Pantheon, 1981), as well as in magazines throughout the world. The way she makes her images, and the images themselves, I would argue, come from a specifically female eye. In El Salvador she continued to make pictures, and produced a collection by the thirty photojournalists then most active in that country. Since, she has been photographing in the Philippines, Africa, and the Middle East.

How We Clothe and Wear Our Bodies

Cuban and U.S. Women's Adornment in the Seventies

In the late 1950s and throughout the sixties, North American women once again began collectively to rebel against the show-case constraints of patriarchy. By the seventies, this rebellion affected much of mainstream America so that fashion advertising was forced to take it into account and speak to the "hip" North American woman. "You've come a long way, Baby," Virginia Slims cigarettes told us. Ads directed at women shifted in this period from the sweet and demure alone to those hailing a more independent lifestyle; featured alongside the upturned eyes and batting lashes were now also the fast car, jogging gear, and the woman's attaché case. Those of us who today are in our forties and fifties remember women's protests: innovative and often courageous demonstrations against the assumptions in those ads, against the beauty contests and other blatant commodifications of our womanness.

Some of us burned our bras, or didn't burn them but simply refused to keep on stuffing or flattening ourselves into one more contraption that limited our respiration and reshaped us to the created needs of others. Many African-American women stopped bleaching their skin and ironing their hair; the afro became an accepted headpiece, and Angela Davis and others set new trends of elegance. American Indian women rebelled against Bureau of Indian Affairs (BIA) school restrictions and said yes to the adornments of their grandmothers.

Many women of different colors and cultures said no to the fashion industry—designed primarily by men and linked to those other industries of violence and built-in obsolescence. What we did to our bodies, our hair, the way we dressed, increasingly conformed to our rapidly changing views about what we were willing or unwilling to do in the name of the oppressor's pleasure.

During this same period, in Cuba, a people's revolution was moving into its second decade. Many North American women traveling to that island looked to our Cuban sisters for ideological leadership. After all, Cuban women and men were building a society whose new laws addressed the solutions to basic inequities suffered by women everywhere: unequal educational opportunities, unequal pay for comparable work, lack of day care, the need for reproductive and legal rights.

Yet the North American women frequently found the customs and goals of the Cuban women confusing; they struggled for a more just society, but ignored what we considered feminist issues. The Cubans often felt their North American counterparts prioritized culture above class and were imperialist in our effort to proselytize around issues which for us were products of a very different level of production, a different history.

I was in Havana throughout the seventies. I had lived in Mexico from 1961 through 1969, when intense political repression forced me to seek another home. Already involved in studying and writing about women's issues,[1] I knew Cuba would provide a context for looking at the situation of women under socialism. In late 1969, then, I moved to Havana, and my first project was the two-year study which resulted in my early book on Cuban women.[2]

A dozen stories come to mind. Among the heroic world-class cane-cutters of the 1970 harvest, there were women who could hold their own with any man. These Cuban sisters had strong and powerful bodies. They earned economic and social recognition for their excellence at a very tough and demanding job. And when interviewed, as they often were, by domestic or foreign journalists, they would pull off the kerchief covering hair teased onto rollers (and often dyed as well), remove a work glove revealing long painted nails, and tell the reporter: "I cut with the best of them. But I'm still a woman, still *feminine* beneath all this sweat and dust."

In this stance there was ingenuity as well as limitation. The rollers weren't obtained at the nearest five-and-dime store (beauty products were some of the first consumer goods to disappear when the United States launched its economic blockade). Cuban women replaced them with the cardboard rolls that came in toilet tissue, just as they replaced eye shadow with pastel chalks, and nylon stockings by doing what their North American sisters had done during the Second World War: take an eyebrow pencil to the backs of their calves.

In Cuba innovation of this type was seen as resistance, resistance to the hostility from the north. So, what the North American women saw as conformity to oppression, for Cuban women became their proud rebellion against it. In spite of extreme heat, vast reduction in the quantity and rationing of clothing, and sophisticated fashion available only in the occasional copy of a magazine from somewhere else, Cuban women continued to push and pull themselves into tight-fitting skirts and seductive sweaters. They continued to eradicate the hair on their legs, underarms, or thighs below the bathing suit line. They continued to prefer dresses to pants—except for field work or military duty—and whatever their job they were quick to tell you they were "still women," still *feminine* beneath it all.

Clearly, much of this conformity to a conservative "feminine" image was rooted in the strong Spanish-Catholic tradition which also retained such customs as the exaltation of virginity and the chaperone for unmarried women notably longer than their preservation in less Catholic cultures. As the Cuban revolution became more and more isolated—economically and so also socially and culturally—an insular resistance to freer attitudes intensified.

Dress was not something Cuban women had the time or luxury of analyzing as middle-class women in the United States did: while studying revolutionary theory or coming together for consciousness-raising sessions on a Saturday afternoon. Alongside their men, *las cubanas* had made their revolution and were desperately fighting extraordinary odds in their effort to keep it alive. Theory was born in the heat of practice, and an examination of the cultural implications of political and economic change was not considered urgent. In fact, the suggestion that such examination might be needed was often seen as divisive.

Society cannot progress, of course, perpetuating the oppression of any group, and the Cuban Communist Party, as well as the Federation of Cuban Women, came to see the need for a major rectification of much of their earlier analysis of women's place in society. This happened most notably in 1974, and will surely happen again—periodically—with whatever rhythm Cuban women are able to achieve in their unique history of change. Internationally, the traditional Communist Party position on women had long been that gender equality would naturally follow economic emancipation. In the seventies that notion was vigorously challenged, especially by women in the national liberation movements. The Cubans began to see that pervasive sexist attitudes affected social progress at a variety of levels.

Back in the early seventies, hair was another area almost devoid of a common ground. While the (predominantly) lighter-skinned Cuban women dyed, teased, and curled their locks, the darker-skinned with naturally springy hair ironed theirs until it was a parody of the forced page-boy or stark ponytail of late fifties society. The stiffly coaxed and sprayed bee-hive was popular among women of all colors.

I once got caught in a hair dilemma for which there seemed no easy solution: I had come to pick up my three-year-old at her day-care center, and I'd arrived earlier than usual. Approaching her classroom, I suddenly heard the teacher's command: "Okay, everyone with good hair line up over here; all the kids with bad hair over there!" She was readying the children for home, and was holding two different combs: the fine-toothed one with which she would groom all those whose hair was long and straight, the pick she would use on the ones with kinky crowns.

I was shocked at this teacher's use of the words *good* and *bad* to describe the nature of a child's hair. But the teacher was Black and I was white, and when I raised my issue with her she raised hers with me: I was a foreigner, what did I know about Cuban culture! And besides, "That's just the way we talk! *It doesn't mean anything!*" I should make it clear that this incident reflects a particular moment in Cuban cultural history. It is indicative neither of its goal nor of how things are done today. In the early seventies the country's day-care centers were still largely staffed by amateurs; the priority was for as many children as possible to have access to them. Today a Cuban day-care teacher must study for four years, and those studies include elements of psychology and pedagogy that would not allow the incident described above. I recall this story in my attempt to convey another attitude towards female adornment, undoubtedly rooted in the same patriarchal value system women are breaking down, in both countries, in different ways and at our differing paces.

Another transitional but telling incident revolves around a Cuban hospital visit, also in the early seventies. A friend had hepatitis; two visitors from the United States went with me to see him. One of the visitors was close to eight months pregnant and she wore a full smock-like blouse over maternity pants. But we were stopped at the door and she was told she couldn't go in; women wearing pants were not allowed into hospitals "because their presence might sexually arouse the male patients!"

No attempt at reasoning seemed to have any affect on the bureaucrat at the door, and the visitor wanted very much to see our friend. So, after nothing else worked, she simply removed her pants and entered the hospital—against no one's objections—wearing only the smock which barely covered her underpants! Again, this is a Cuban hospital regulation that was eventually abolished; they did away with it in their own time, when logic told them it was something like the old Massachusetts law that forbids bathing on Sunday.

There is probably not another country in the western hemisphere that worked so hard or launched such a massive campaign as Cuba did to help win freedom for the U.S. revolutionary Angela Davis. Yet the afro which was already her trademark came slowly to the island. Today many Black Cuban women have varying-sized afros, and I'm sure there are also many women with corn-rows, maybe even a few with dreds.

Hair length and style was an issue for men as well in the Cuba of the seventies. A decade earlier, Fidel Castro's guerrillas had come out of the mountains with their long hair, beards, and strings of amulets and beads. That look was a mark of having fought, a badge of particular honor and not encouraged in those who hadn't been in the *sierra*. In fact, the more staid European Communist model took hold and seemed to call for the clean-cut look: very short hair was a must for schoolboys and the socially acceptable style for older males. The *integrado* (integrated) or socially responsible Cuban man looked very much like an FBI agent or professional football player in the United States!

At one overzealous point in the sixties, young Cuban men whose hair was "too long" were actually rounded up and their hair forcibly cut; the "hippie look," as the Cubans regarded long hair and other stereotypical attributes of young people in the United States, was too reminiscent of the country that had sworn to destroy the revolution, and of the drug culture the Cubans had sent packing with U.S. crime syndicate lords George Raft and Meyer Lansky.

Homosexuals were also specifically and tragically discriminated against in this period; gay men (and women, although lesbians tended to be less visible, perhaps due to the residual invisibility of all women) were considered a "social pathology" and many with highly visible profiles—such as artists and performers—lost their jobs. Homophobia was, at least in part, a legacy from the pre-revolutionary tendency to identify gay males with the frivolous and decadent lifestyle so prevalent in the Cuba of the fifties, in spite of the fact that many gay men and women were and are revolutionaries.

In recent years there has been a consistent effort to deal with official heterosexism in Cuba, and life for gay men and women has improved. A widely distributed sex education book, *El hombre y la mujer en la intimidad (Men and Women in Intimacy)*, addresses homosexuality as a legitimate sexual preference. For the best analysis to date of gayness and the history of gay oppression in Cuba, see Lourdes Arguelles's and B. Ruby Rich's two-part "Homosexuality, homophobia and revolution in Cuba." [3]

Women in Cuba throughout the first decade and a half of revolution internalized these values filtered through the usual patriarchal double standard. I think it's important to correctly set in context those years and their attitudes: coercive and limiting on the one hand, righteously rebellious on the other.

As is still true, due to U.S.-imposed restrictions, Cuba saw little North American tourism in the seventies. Because of their commitment and solidarity (and because of the Cuban leadership's ongoing determination to distinguish between our government and our people), one of the U.S. groups to make the deepest impression was the yearly Venceremos Brigade contingent, men and women (mostly young men and women) who went to work several weeks in the cane fields or construction, and then toured the island in order to see something of the revolution.

And the revolution saw something of them, as well. These progressive North Americans brought with them home-grown stances regarding dress and adornment. The women most often wore no makeup, did nothing to their hair but gather it up or let it fall free, and pulled oversized brigade shirts over unrepressed breasts. Stories from the provincial villages near cane camps or construction sites brought on frequent discussion of all kinds. Were these North American women slovenly or free? Dirty (because they didn't bathe with what they considered the superfluous frequency of their Cuban hosts) or merely natural? Lazy or comfortable? Ugly or beautiful? Natural body odors vis-à-vis the scent of deodorants and lotions was another issue among the Cubans as a people, and Cuban women in particular. One or the other became, in fact, adornment—emanating from two ideologically different stances.

Even during the worst years of the blockade, when a shortage of parts left many neighborhoods with running water only a few hours out of twenty four, people in that tropical country managed to bathe several times a day. A generic deodorant was sold on the ration card, and people used it as lavishly as possible. Even on crowded city buses you would find yourself (to whatever extent this was physically possible) ostracized if you sweated and smelled. The expressions of repulsion were unmistakable, the alienation articulated in young and old alike.

I can remember being in a cane camp in the winter of 1969-70. Among forty-eight Cuban women, another foreigner (an Argentine) and myself were singled out by our volunteering sisters. They came in commission to suggest that our showering once a day seemed inadequate to them. They urged us to do it twice daily, like they did. Considering that fifty of us had to line up to use three shower heads, this seemed excessive to us. But we learned it was an important cultural issue.

Yet there were many ways in which our Cuban sisters were ahead of us in their concepts of bodily adornment. The double media message—eat and then starve to death—was nowhere on Cuban television. In fact, the low weight and stature equated with the country's heritage of hunger had given way to a vision of plump as synonymous with healthy. "*Se te ve bien gorda* ... You're looking nice and fat" was a frequent compliment. Only later, when the revolution got around to looking more closely at diet and disease, were people—women among them—urged to eat less of the nation's principle export (sugar), to exercise, and not to let themselves get overweight.

The adornments of age, well-earned wrinkles, sagging flesh, and graying hair, were also attributes revered in Cuba long before our own consciousness of ageism. Although the Cubans held traditional beauty contests long after progressive women in the United States rejected them as meat markets, they reveled in poor women and women of color being able to enter and win those contests; and many of them were not so traditional. These honored women in the countryside, older women who were rewarded for picking record quantities of coffee or single handedly running a cattle ranch or pig farm. Socially valued adornment included the signs of hard work, the wisdom of age. Traditional rewards were still forthcoming.

I had a particularly difficult but ultimately moving experience involving Cuba's largest yearly beauty contest. Cuban carnival ends the cane season in mid-July, and the 1970 harvest would finish with the traditional event: street dancing, abundant food and free-flowing beer, a parade in every major city, and a carnival queen elected to reign over each festivity. I was judging an important literary contest at the time. Along with film and TV personalities, the Havana carnival commission wanted a judge from among those of us involved in reading poems and stories. We were some fifty men, and a few women.

I was surprised and shocked when Haydée Santamaria, the great woman revolutionary heading the institution that sponsored the literary contest, asked me to join those who would choose the carnival queen. At first I thought of refusing. Participation went against everything I believed in. But I didn't want to refuse a request from Haydée, a woman

I so deeply admired and loved. She must have some reason to have picked me, I thought. And so I consented, fighting off a headache the whole time.

In order to be able to take on this task with a modicum of dignity, I decided to write a short essay, voicing my ideas about beauty contests and why I believed they didn't belong in a socialist society. When the press interviewed the contest judges, I handed them my statement. It was given prominent coverage in the following day's paper. A year later, when I finally had the opportunity to ask Haydée why, among all the other literary judges, she had chosen me to take on that miserable task, she said: "The other judges would have been all too happy with the job. I knew you'd hate it. And I knew you'd find a way to try to educate against it. I was counting on you. We need to change these things, but the changes can't be imposed by decree; they must come through education, discussion, the developing consciousness of people themselves." The Cuban carnival queen contest did in fact begin to be phased out the following year.

If women during the seventies in the United States did not yet understand the beauty of age's markings, some of us did gravitate towards wearing apparel and adornments of ages—and peoples—preceding our own. It was a statement against the fashion industry, its manipulation of our tastes and pocketbooks. From the late fifties and early sixties we had begun to search for outfits of earlier periods, often finding them for pennies in the thrift shops. Flapper shifts, beaded bags, and ancient fur coats were especially popular. Today, as in so many other capitalist arenas, the corporation has caught up with the consumer. Vintage clothing has become a profitable business, and what used to cost us fifty cents at Good Will Industries, now costs $150 at Unique Boutique. Fur, old or new, is out—at least for the growing number of women in the United States who repudiate the killing of animals for sport and luxury apparel.

Some of us were (and still are) attracted by the great artistry of hand-woven or embroidered *huipiles* (the loose-fitting over-blouses made and worn by the indigenous women of Mexico, Guatemala, Peru, and other Latin countries). Wearing their art on our bodies seems to us to be a way of recognizing their genius as well as, in some cases, identifying with their dramatic struggles.

In Cuba the synthetic not-to-be-ironed fabric and the modern-day styles were always sought after: for comfort in lives that bridged a variety of activities, acknowledging extreme heat most of the year, and because appliances like washing machines and steam irons were still unknown in the majority of homes.

This brings to mind Cuban school uniforms, the daily unadorned adornment for all young people, boys and girls alike. The concept behind uniform dress in a society moving towards classlessness is clear enough; before the revolution fifty percent of Cuba's kids couldn't go to school. The immediate goal of a people's victory was that all children should have the opportunity. Dressing alike would eliminate differences between those who still had more and those with less. The "schoolhouse" might be nothing more than the shade of a large tree (although great numbers were fine buildings that went up rapidly all over the island). The early teachers might commit the kind of error our aforementioned day-care worker did. But school was primary, essential, and for everyone.

The first uniforms my own children wore in the primary grades included identical short-sleeved white shirts for boys and girls, and a rather heavy, unpopular, drill jumper or pair of pants, deep wine in color. I remember that the kids hated those outfits, especially the girls. They were unwieldy and had to be ironed—to meet Cuban standards of neatness—every single morning.

As the revolution progressed, school uniforms became more streamlined. Those attending the junior highs and high schools in the countryside wore lightweight perma-press shirts and pants or pant-skirts of a slightly heavier variety of the same material. No more ironing. There was pressure to "look right" by properly tying a broad necktie, and the young women were periodically reprimanded for using an excess of hair ornaments or costume jewelry. I never noticed that they paid much attention to those reprimands though, and whatever new bauble became obtainable in a country with so few consumer items, was soon the "in" thing.

In a climate like Cuba's, short pants—for boys as well as girls, for men as well as women—would have been ideal. We often wondered why these were considered socially acceptable in the cold northern European countries, and totally unacceptable in this tropical sauna. Beyond school uniforms, for which they could have been perfect, they would have been much more comfortable than the accepted dress for everyone, in every activity. While I lived in Cuba the dress code never included this possibility. In the period of strictest imposition of a certain norm, there was actually an unwritten law against wearing shorts in the street. I understand the prohibition was eventually relaxed, but that kind of easy apparel has yet to become commonplace.

In the tropics—in Mexico, Nicaragua, Cuba, and other Latin

countries—male formal attire demands something called a *guayabera,* rather than a jacket and tie. It's a lightweight short-sleeved shirt, worn outside the pants and often beautifully decorated with strips of same-color embroidery or tucking. It is considered fully acceptable for a man to use a *guayabera* as a formal suit jacket, in situations ranging from an affair of state to dinner in an elegant restaurant (and restaurant dress codes, especially in the more expensive places, are strict). Interestingly, and clearly a hold-over from patriarchal inequality, there is no such substitute in women's formal wear. In Cuban heat, in a country where air conditioning often does not exist or is broken, and in a society where a sweet-scented presence is so highly valued, women attending formal functions must adorn themselves in everything from nylon stockings and high-heeled shoes to lavish and unwieldy outfits.

Where does adornment become abuse, propriety confinement? In Cuba these dress codes always seemed restrictive to me, especially as they affected women. In the United States, great numbers of women no longer accept the confinement of girdles, bras, waist-pinchers, or shoes that throw our bodies unhealthily forward as we walk. Some might argue that it doesn't matter, we don't need those constraints when a much more massive and life-threatening objectification has us stuffing ourselves with gourmet delights and then engaging in anything from jogging to aerobics to self-induced vomiting until we disappear into a socially conditioned anorexia. Both situations speak eloquently of cultures in which a real female envisioning of our bodies has yet to overcome the mixed messages of male objectification.

We speak critically and sorrowfully of our Chinese sisters whose feet were once bound as a sign of beauty. Yet our sitcoms and commercial advertising are rife with images of the mature woman proudly holding on to her size-six figure. The very use of the word *figure,* for body, provokes some interesting analysis. When will we stop seeing ourselves as a one-dimensional cutout, inevitably assessed first as a pretty object?

Many of us puncture our ear lobes—today with rows of tiny holes—and some of us even pierce our noses in order to stud them with adornments of one kind or another. Yet I can remember the bewilder-ment, if not the scorn, of many North American women towards our Cuban sisters who painted their nails, teased and dyed their hair, and painted stocking-seam lines the length of their legs.

The use of adornments that either perpetuate a patriarchal idea of what we should look like or assume this gender identification on other terms (like the popularity of neckties and other male dress symbols among butch women) always raises complex issues. Do these practices denote similar or very different attitudes? And, what does it mean to gain our freedom from male domination by being *as much a man as any man?* Clearly, these questions demand different answers in different times and cultural contexts. Perhaps the only certainty I have gained throughout a lifetime of witnessing changing patterns in both Cuba and the United States, is the knowledge that things are very often not what they seem to be.

I am as rebellious of constraints as anyone of my background and generation. As a young woman I pushed the limits of class and propriety by shocking staid relatives with my black stockings and wild eye make-up. In those days my best attire came from the Salvation Army. As I grew older I continued to reject the fashion industry's use of my body as a moneymaker, but I went with the handmade products of my sisters to the south (I still love the apparel art and adornments of Latin American Indian women).

Later I gave up the painting and the dying, and still later stopped wearing anything but flat-heeled shoes. I shaved my legs and underarms in Cuba—out of respect for cultural difference—but joyously stopped doing so as soon as I returned to the United States. Recently, I've even been able to take occasional defiant pride in a scraggly beard, every hair of which I once removed with agonized desperation.

I also developed an understanding of the different issues facing Cuban women, their differing priorities and tastes. And I made it my business to try to explain the context of these differences to my North American sisters when they came to Cuba and commented, puzzled, on what they saw. But I know it took me many years to really internalize the fact that people's conservative or progressive nature is not determined by how they adorn their bodies.

It was in Mexico City, during the turbulent fall of 1968, that a woman sporting every conceivable stricture of male-imposed female "beauty" came to visit. Her face was a painted mask, her hair dyed and teased into a perfection of curls almost as high again as her facial profile. Her short body was tensed into the latest fashion, she almost wobbled on spike heels, and her finger nails were long and painted crimson.

I knew this woman by reputation; she was a revolutionary of stature, an economist, someone who had lived through several struggles. What she had to say about what was happening in Mexico proved both astute and compassionate. I remember being in awe of her experience and humanity, all the while wondering to myself how she could stand to dress the way she did, how she could bear to push and shove her body into those sacrificial patterns of artifice and compliance.

Years later I was to know this woman better. And I would follow her particular dignity to one of the most heroic deaths I've witnessed. To the end she looked almost the same, ever so slightly changed by time but with a presence that made her physical presentation utterly immaterial. She was a revolutionary because of who she was, not because of how she dressed.

I do not want to imply that because the inner person is the more important, the practices of adornment—particularly those that objectively subdue or demean—are not. I don't believe this at all. But I want to say that the meaning of dress, adornment, custom, cannot be separated from its cultural context. Just as the *afro* or corn rows, the *huipil* or comfortable shoes, are symbols of certain ideals, so are the multiple restrictions of a fashion-crazed society a measure of the way women (especially) are oppressed.

U.S. women's perspective on dress and adornment is as culturally bound as Cuban women's esthetic is culturally defined—by class, race, sexuality, age, and local tradition. There are practices that are clearly unacceptable—such as the bound feet; the definition of hair as bad or good; media coercion to overeat, starve ourselves, and then exercise in expensive gyms; the creation of a female image which depends upon an industry rooted in man's objectification of woman. These will be dealt the death blow by women ourselves as we move through our respective cultural histories to a place of real and creative freedom.

There are restrictive practices that can sometimes be turned around, so they may provide a space for the victim to act against the real enemy. Such is the Mid-Eastern veil, the ample apron worn by market women in El Salvador, the religious habits of many Nicaraguan nuns. All have been used, and powerfully, to hide the weapons of change. And there is the new image of woman, adorned in each culture as we feel more comfortable and creative, coming—each at our own pace—into a world where we ourselves set the terms and give meaning to traditions, old and new.

—Albuquerque, New Mexico
Summer 1988

Notes

1. *Las mujeres,* an anthology of writings from the North American women's movement, Margaret Randall (Mexico City: Siglo XXI, 1970).
2. *Cuban Women Now,* Margaret Randall (Toronto: Canadian Women's Educational Press, 1974). On the same subject: *Cuban Women: Twenty Years Later,* Margaret Randall (New York: Smyrna Press, 1981).
3. "Homosexuality, homophobia and revolution: notes toward an understanding of the Cuban lesbian and gay male experience, Part II," Lourdes Arguelles and B. Ruby Rich, *Signs, A Journal of Women and Culture* 11: 120-36, August 1985.

Living About Life

Recently I had the opportunity of viewing two new half-hour TV specials, part of a series to be aired on this summer's Public Television. In fact, in line with that aura of "impartiality" for which U.S. establishment media would like to be known, both are scheduled for the same evening, back to back. This is of particular interest when you've seen the films.

One, "Knocking on Armageddon's Door," is a reportage piece about Survivalists. Survivalists and Soldiers of Fortune (who claim deep differences on camera although both concern themselves with welcoming a nuclear holocaust and dedicating their present-day lives to preparing for it.)

"Living With AIDS" is the second film. In it Todd, a twenty-two-year-old gay man, dies of the epidemic disease. We are privileged to be shown some of the effects his approaching death has on him during the last months of his life, and *his* effect on the supportive San Francisco community that helped him live and die.

The protagonists in the first film claim that they are about life: survival, resistance (in many cases dependent upon the killing of others), a "winner's" attitude and activity. Although the stance of each person interviewed is perfectly clear, the ideology of the person making the film is somewhat less so. People speak for themselves, but the aura of shallow sophistication so increasingly characteristic of contemporary U.S. public broadcasting work allows viewers to feel strengthened in whatever beliefs they themselves may bring to the film experience. What this is likely to mean today, after eight years of Reaganism, is the validation and confirmation of values previously considered extreme in their conservatism, or fanatical pseudo-patriotism.

And so we see an annual Soldier of Fortune gathering in which paramilitary counterinsurgency recruits in full battle gear take aim at a line of automobiles on a ridge. The man giving the orders (whose perspective on the establishment media is that it is Communist with a capital C) yells "Let's pretend those are newsmen from ABC, NBC, CBS, and all those other left-wing terrorist groups!" The targets go up in flames. The crowd cheers wildly.

In other scenes we get a look inside a Survivalist bomb shelter, complete with indoor plumbing, four separate bedrooms, and supplies which include a year's food for sixteen people and 3,000 gallons of water. Thoughts of homelessness are inevitable.

Long-time promoters of the Survivalist mentality explain how, after nuclear death, civilization could be reborn "right here in Arkansas, where 350,000 armed hillbillies stand between the enemy and us[!]" They talk about being in the history books, all of them getting to be important, only people like themselves making it through.

There are spinoffs, like the interview with a couple who run a Survivalist store. From between her tight, repressed lips, she mentions their lines of books: titles on how to use different types of weaponry, how to take revenge: "Something for every situation," the husband interjects. At the film's conclusion, a large percentage of its viewers will, I am convinced, be looking for where to sign up.

Many would say the second film is about death, the socially (and by now, hysterically) feared death from AIDS. The media hype around the disease has already set into motion a chain reaction of elitism, superstition, terror, hate, homophobia, and other unchecked prejudices upon which years of faulty education can only hope to have a dubious effect. But this film is very much about life, and the extraordinary sacrifice and caring with which an entire community honors its waning moments.

Todd is an amazingly sensitive and courageous young man. He and his most recent lover, Bob, meet after he has already been diagnosed with the disease. They've never had a really ordinary relationship, Bob explains, as he tells us how he was attracted to Todd, among other things, for his courage. "We learned that love was about more than just sex," he says, and the camera lingers on a particularly moving scene in which Bob caresses Todd's head and the dying man slowly reaches up to grasp his lover's hand.

These two men, one physically strong, the other growing inevitably weaker, learn to care for one another in circumstances in which the simplest tasks—heating up a TV dinner, each embrace—take on dimensions many of us will never have occasion to experience.

We are privileged to be able to share Todd's dignity and struggle, his observations, the last few months of his life; and to feel its profound influence upon his friends and supporters. The successful lawyer who after work each day shops for and prepares Todd's food. The masseur who speaks of his gift of touch (and caringly shows us that gift on Todd's emaciated body). The woman hospice worker who tells us that deaths from AIDS, like those in a war, come so quickly one upon another that they don't permit assimilation. She nonetheless explains how each successive AIDS death has given increased meaning to her life.

All these people bear witness to the ways in which a truly healthy community, faced with official indifference if not scorn, explores the ways in which it can create life from a plague of dying. This film, which is so specifically about a fatal disease, is really about living in ways that help every viewer to live better.

I wonder what it means that in our society a film about survival is so very much about death, and that a film about dying is so pregnant with renewal. Perhaps it is the logical extension of how our thought processes are continually being turned around (stimulated by the media's betrayal of images and language).

A couple of decades, and any history is easily rewritten. Memory itself is under attack. Vietnam becomes a war of heroism. Jane Fonda publicly says she's sorry. Three Mile Island and Bhopal are forgotten in the cold war anxiety over Chernobyl. (The Soviet practice of waiting to publicize an event until they are sure of the facts is pointed to as further "proof" that theirs is the system in which such horrors are most likely to occur.)

But today it no longer takes decades, or even years, to recast an event, to make it into something it is not or keep it from being perceived for what it is. The media can distort the *meaning* of an incident practically before our eyes.

The U.S. government shoots down an Iranian passenger plane in the Persian Gulf. We, who are always given the news on time, are asked to swallow one contradiction after another as the story unfolds. Two hundred and ninety people are dead. The plane is flying outside the commercial flight path, then it is reported as inside. It emits one kind of signal, then another. The captain of the U.S. warship who gave the order to fire on the plane couldn't locate it in a public flight log, yet a TV commentator tells us it took him exactly thirty seconds to find it there.

Two hundred and ninety people are dead. We won't offer *reparations* because the word implies a guilt we refuse to own, but *humanitarian support for the victims* will make us appear generous. (And this handling of the affair is oh so good for the Republicans as their presidential campaign heats up.) As news of this disaster begins to give way to the next media sensation, the United States accuses Iran of tossing altogether unrelated bodies into the Gulf waters and then photographing them *for effect.* Yes, indeed, we know how a studied (mis)use of images and words can increasingly make us believe that up is down, right is left, in is out, great is small.

So it should not surprise me or anyone else that a film about death be mistaken for one about survival. Or that a Hosanna to life be presented to us as a study in death and dying.

What this prompts too few of us to ask, though, is what the particular juxtaposition of these two films tells us about the overall state of our culture. While we knew the major networks were controlled by commercial advertising, some of us once took refuge in public "listener supported" radio and television. We depended upon it to give us a less biased view of the world. Under current administration pressure, gradually or not so gradually, this greater impartiality seems almost to have collapsed.

We learned that many public television channels decided the film "When the Mountains Tremble," about the plight and struggle of Guatemalan Indians, was "too ideological" to show. All the while more and more works with a conservative point of view are being passed off as neutral. (Current American language usage may be the only place where the word *ideological* is commonly taken to mean a left or progressive ideology, rather than the simple expression of an idea or set of ideas, whether left, right, or center.)

And this makes it easier to understand how one layer of linguistic or imagistic falsification builds upon another until the lies they feed us lodge themselves upon a perfectly prepared terrain. Our memory itself is altered. We no longer question the origin of such distortion.

What does it mean, for example, that the word *magic* has been coopted to describe the performance of an expensive automobile engine, that the adjective *revolutionary* has been transformed to describe a deodorant or microwave oven? How are we supposed to assess principles when our President refers to criminal bandits as *freedom fighters* and calls himself a *contra*? Or when the Attorney General, whose record shows him to be unethical at best, can get away with telling the public he is resigning because he "has been cleared of any suspicion of wrongdoing?" How is our ever absorbent subconscious supposed to deal with this constant barrage of images and words created to convince us that *wrong* is *right, lie* is *truth*, we need this and *cannot live without* that?

How do we truly rid ourselves of racism before a small screen on which African Americans are portrayed as dumb boxers, funny old men, or cute youngsters adopted into white families—but rarely as thoughtful human beings with a rich cultural heritage? How do we grow beyond sexism before a box that offers objectified women as bait to sell cars or as having the know-how to get a husband, and to achieve sweet breath and anorexic waistlines? How do we build a world that understands all forms of love when every soap opera and sitcom presents heterosexuality as the only acceptable kind, and gay women and men appear only in token, stereotypical, or ridiculed roles? How can we hope to learn respect for the wisdom and beauty of age, when our models are ageless at best, at worst forever young? And how are any of us—African-American, Latina, Indian, Asian-American, Anglo, unemployed or underemployed, middle-income, poor or homeless, differently abled, female, male, gay, straight, old or young—able to relate to our differing but real needs, when the characters who people such favorites as Dallas, Falconcrest, and Miami Vice are presented as middle America?

The human face and gesture inevitably evoke emotion. And in most decent people emotion tends to produce a measure of compassion, sometimes even empathy. That's decidedly dangerous where deception and distortion are the goals. And so we have statistics, those supposedly neutral and foolproof measuring rods.

But here again distortion is easily built into language itself. Consider the following: even such a solid example of establishment authority as *U.S. News and World Report*[1] is willing to expose gross deception in major polls. (Today the medium is the message, to such an extent that the very magazines that deceive us can bolster their impartiality status by running an exposé like this.)

Under the title "The Numbers Racket: How Polls and Statistics Lie," this article explains that polls taken at the same time and among the same groups of people but which phrase their questions in different ways, always draw different conclusions: About *contra* aid, if those polled are asked what they think of "aiding the rebels in Nicaragua to prevent Communist influence from spreading," fifty-eight percent are for it and twenty-nine percent against. But if they are asked what they think about "assisting the people trying to overthrow the government of Nicaragua," only twenty-four percent are in favor and sixty-two percent are against.

Similarly, regarding the issue of abortion, those polled about "a Constitutional amendment prohibiting abortions" showed twenty-nine percent in favor and sixty-seven percent against. On the other hand, if polled about "a Constitutional amendment protecting the life of the unborn," fifty percent said they would favor that while thirty-nine percent would not. Wording was equally essential in determining people's feelings about social services. A poll asking if "we are spending too much, too little, or about the right amount on welfare" showed twenty-two percent to be of the opinion that we spend too little. But when the same question was worded "are we spending too much, too little, or about the right amount on assistance to the poor," sixty-one percent thought we spend too little.

And so it goes. Language misleads, then poll "results" claim an authority which further misleads and influences. And men with sufficient charisma and financial control over the machinery of mass media win "landslide" victories to positions that do indeed exert control over what we think, what we do, and how we (and generations to come) will live our lives. Of course an important part of the very nature of this deception is the fallacy that we are free to decide for ourselves, determine our life's course, and work in a system in which our real needs are respected as well as met. Isn't that what democracy is all about?

Having said all this, I do not believe the picture is a totally bleak one. In spite of the complex, pervasive, and ever more entrenched means by which capitalism manages to forge us in its own classist, racist, and sexist image, people's culture is a powerful force. And it's a force with which the enemy rarely contends. It can be oppressed and repressed, but it always rises, sometimes from a veritable ash pile of exhausted energies.

"Living With AIDS" is one example of our defiant culture, and its airing on Public Television this summer attests to the fact that our culture is not only very much alive but that it is still capable of reaching broad audiences. Of course we possess a powerful and multi-faceted cultural expression! (Think, for a moment, of our music, our literature, our art, our cinematography, theater, dance....) And of course these expressions are capable of reaching broad audiences; we can build upon our own reclaimed memories to call up the art within, and also make use of the technology which enables us to share that art with millions. Those of us unable to acknowledge this, need to do some retrieval work of our own. People's culture empowers those to whom it is directed, and those who make it. Our people's expression is clear not only in films like "Living With AIDS," but in the best of our music, literature, art, awakening consciousness, and coalition organizing.

We live in a place and in a time where complexities of vision and of growth often enable us to "dismantle the master's house" with our tools *and* with his.[2] Because of the daily and complex assaults upon our memory, because of the depletion of our vital energies, we need to work our way backwards even as we move ahead. For we must decode the ever more sophisticated conspiracy of distorted imagery and language. Searching for our roots, questioning every one of the system's assumptions about who we are, and recognizing our basic needs signal useful roads towards reassessment and empowerment.

With our own tools again in hand, we can insist that *only life is about life*. Our words and our acts will be an unmovable testament to ourselves, and to what we are able to create.

—New York City, New York
Albuquerque, New Mexico
Summer 1988

Notes

1. *U.S. News and World Report*, July 11, 1988.
2. Audre Lorde warns that "the master's tools will never dismantle the master's house" in the essay of the same name in *Sister Outsider*, Audre Lorde (Freedom, CA: Crossing Press, 1984).

The Human Face
of Revolution

F or those of us living in Latin America and concerned with political struggle throughout the decades of the 1960s and 1970s—and particularly for those of us who are poets and writers involved in the endless polemics around the responsibility of the intellectual in the battle for social change—the Salvadoran Roque Dalton was both a mentor and a comrade. A mentor even to many older than himself, because his questions always seemed to push just a little farther, their answers based authoritatively on his own experiences of theory and action. A comrade because in Roque a willingness to attend to whatever problem, an availability for whatever task, were constants throughout his life. Beyond the usual definitions of intellectual, activist, poet, philosopher, is that rare space where certain women and men live, exceptional people for whom any of the labels by themselves are totally inadequate. Roque occupied such a space.

He came from the smallest country in Central America, *el pulgarcito* (the little finger, or pinkie) as he called it, yet the whole world was his context for analysis. He always said his father descended from our famed desperadoes—the Dalton Gang—and that his mother was a poor working woman who had only briefly gotten involved with the man. (In his book *Taberna y otros lugares* Roque shares some childhood memories of meeting his father.)

Roque's poetry was powerful and also humorous—a combination which is not frequent enough. In his essays he tackled major issues with a mixture of insight, confidence, and humility rarely found in polemicists. Two other prominent qualities set this writer apart: he was an extraordinary listener, and he knew how to laugh at himself.

Those who knew Roque at different periods in his life speak of the brilliant student at a Jesuit University in Chile, the bohemian instigator of experimental theater and poetry festivals in Central America, the long-time member of the Salvadoran Communist Party, the founder (with others) of the organizations that would one day be capable of launching all-out people's war in his country, the relentless researcher of Salvadoran history, the fine journalist, the prize-winning writer, "the only Latin American poet who ever escaped a firing squad because the prison cell in which he was being held cracked beneath the shudder of a providential earthquake." (This last description is something Roque himself often repeated.)

Those who knew him better may remember the husband and father, the imperfect drinker and sometime womanizer (Roque inherited the traditional Latin assumptions in this regard but began, towards the end of his life, to come to terms with many of them). We remember the untiring writer, the man who refused special foreign food rationing privileges throughout his years in Cuba, the extraordinarily kind human being, the intellectual totally unafraid of exposing his own process in the context of shared discussion and debate.

Some of what Roque published during his lifetime strained the limits of the "acceptable"—in several quarters. Some of what he wrote proved uncannily visionary. Some of what remained unpublished at his death—but has since been made available—was prophetic, important both to literary history and to the history of Latin American political struggle.

El turno del ofendido (The Turn of the Offended One), published by Casa de las Americas, Havana, in 1963, is certainly one of the most beautiful books of poetry to come from that continent during the decade of the sixties. Several books of verse later, in 1969, his *Taberna y otros lugares (The Tavern and Other Places)* won the prestigious Casa poetry prize. It's a tougher book, more experimental in form, and deals with a collage of concerns ranging from childhood memories to the international political scene.

In the months before his death—back in El Salvador after a long exile, and involved in the underground struggle there—Roque circulated poetry written (in the style of the Portuguese poet Fernando Pessoa) under five pseudonyms. More than an arbitrary choice of covers, he actually developed five lifestyles, five ways of taking on the world, five poetic voices belonging to Vilma Flores, Timoteo Lue, Jorge Cruz, Juan Zapata, and Luís Luna. They were all students of one kind or another (Roque was speaking to the student movement, great readers of poetry), including a woman who "abandoned law in order to devote herself full time to the organization of a textile factory"; and they were all "born" between 1939 and 1950. When, after Roque's death, these clandestine poems, as they've been called, were finally published in book form, one could trace the poet's ongoing commitment to dealing with a whole series of continued and pertinent concerns: sexism, the spiritual side of Marxism, the peasant ideology, and the dialectics of struggle, among others.

And Dalton, when he was murdered by extremist members of his own political organization (May 10, 1975), left a poetic manuscript close to 800 pages long: *El libro rojo de Lenin (The Red Book of Lenin)*. In it the poet reaches his own heights of metaphor and polemic, craft and connectedness. A version of this major work has finally appeared in Spanish (published by Editorial Nueva Nicaragua, Managua) and is currently being translated into English.

This, all too briefly, was Roque Dalton the poet. There was also Roque Dalton the essayist; his long piece *Regis Debray y la crítica de derecha (Regis Debray and the Criticism from the Right)* being his best known work in that area. The French journalist and political polemicist Regis Debray theorized about Che Guevara's idea of a guerrilla nucleus, and after Che's defeat and Debray's imprisonment the right was quick to prove it wrong, hoping to dispose of the baby with the bath water. Dalton wrote incisively about the contradictions inherent in the attack, as well as about the *foco* theory itself. He also produced significant work on the history of El Salvador, the lessons Vietnam had to offer to the struggle in Latin America, poetry and political militancy, and on a variety of cultural themes. He wrote brilliantly on César Vallejo, the Peruvian mystic communist poet whose work changed the language of literature in Spanish.

And there was Roque Dalton the novelist. Shortly before his death he finished *Pobrecito poeta que era yo ... (The Poor Little Poet I Was ...)* which seemed, again, like a prophecy when it appeared posthumously. This is the book in which the author explores his generation of intellectuals in El Salvador, their privileged position vis-à-vis the greater population, and their response to the dramatic events which in that country have become the bread of every day.

Although Dalton lives as an inspiration to poets, political people, and cultural workers in this and other countries (The Roque Dalton Cultural Brigade in San Francisco's Mission district came on the scene almost immediately following Roque's death in 1975), his work was much slower to become accessible in English. Some of his best known poems, like "Headaches" or "OAS," were translated and anthologized while he lived. Curbstone was the first U.S. publisher to bring out a book by Dalton: *Poetry and Militancy in Latin America* (two essays, one in prose, the other in verse, translated by Arlene and James Scully in 1981). It wasn't until 1984, however, that a sizable collection of his poems was published in the United States.

In that year two books appeared: *Roque Dalton Poems*, translated by Richard Schaaf and again made available by Curbstone, and *The Clandestine Poems*, from Solidarity Publications (later New Americas Press in San Francisco, and now defunct). This last is a bilingual edition; the Roque Dalton Cultural Brigade took it on as a project with Jack Hirschman doing the initial translation work and Barbara Paschke and Eric Weaver involved in editing.

Roque Dalton was no longer a mysterious revolutionary figure, known by an elite few. He had become a contemporary Central American writer whose work had finally been made accessible through the commitment and energies of two small U.S. presses. But Dalton's most important work was still unavailable in English.

El Salvador is a country that's been on and off our media's front pages now for more than a decade—on when a dramatic event catches the attention of this country's news makers, off until another such event. The intensity of the conflict there—especially since it claimed the lives of the nation's Roman Catholic Archbishop, four North American religious sisters, a photographer for a major U.S. news magazine, six Jesuit priests, their housekeeper and her daughter, and tens of thousands of others—cannot be avoided by even the most ignorant and uncaring. But what does the U.S. public really know about *el pulgarcito*? Most newspapers lump events in one Central American country with those in another. Distinctions seem unimportant. And stories that are front page one day, disappear the next. As is our wont, until it is much too late, middle America will probably not care very much about what's going on in a place so "remote" from our fast food and ever upward mobility. Our capacity for making it through dinner while watching the five o'clock news has not been achieved without a pretty thorough conditioning.

Even those of us who manage to care, know little Salvadoran history. We remain ignorant of the fact that the first soviets in this hemisphere were established in that tiny country, or that in 1932 the dictator Maximiliano Hernández Martínez massacred 30,000 farmers and working people in order to put down a genuinely popular rebellion. Well, generations of Salvadorans also grew up without any knowledge of that holocaust; it was simply erased from their school texts. And if we in this country neither know nor care about what's happening in El

Salvador today, why should we know or care about what happened there half a century ago? *Miguel Mármol*, Dalton's major work, enables us to know and to care. It made it possible for his fellow Central Americans to know and care when it was first published in Spanish by Costa Rica's Editorial EDUCA (1972). Then it exploded like necessary wildfire throughout the countries of Latin America. Inside El Salvador copies smuggled into the country were passed from hand to hand. From this source, as from others, people retrieved their history, a collective memory so long denied. And it became an important part of their identity of struggle.

Miguel Mármol, born in El Salvador in 1905, is a shoemaker, trade unionist, revolutionary, founder of the Salvadoran Communist Party and alternately a member of its Central Committee or resigned/removed from that body. He was one of the leaders of the peasant-worker uprising which was so brutally put down in 1932, and miraculously survived the firing squad death which claimed almost all of his comrades. In his eighties, he remains, today, passionately and actively involved in his country's struggle for survival and justice.

In the mid-sixties, Roque Dalton and Miguel Mármol met in Prague. Dalton was living in exile, and editing the Latin American edition of International Magazine (the theoretical journal of the Third International). Mármol was passing through, coming from the Soviet Union where he had attended a meeting of trade unionists. The two men got together one night and Dalton—the listener—heard some of Mármol's story. Immediately he knew how important it would be to tell this story to the world. Characteristically, that's what he did.

Miguel Mármol, the book, belongs to a literary genre that came of age in Latin America with several powerful people's movements for change: among them, the Cuban Revolution, the Sandinista revolution in Nicaragua, and the struggles taking place in Argentina, Uruguay, Chile, Guatemala, and El Salvador. *Testimonio* is the Spanish word for a literature closely linked with the oral history beginning slightly later to be practiced in this country. Latin American predecessors include Rodolfo Walsh's *Operación masacre (Operation Massacre)*, and more recently Domitila de Chungara's and Moema Viezzer's *Déjame hablar (Let Me Speak)* and Elisabeth Burgos's *Yo, Rigoberta Menchú (I, Rigoberta Menchú)*.

Miguel Mármol told his story. Roque Dalton listened. Mármol relied on memory, going back to his childhood, speaking of his life in a matter-of-fact and more or less chronological way, offering his own analysis of events. Dalton, already an expert in the events described by Mármol, contributed pertinent questions, insights, arguments, and observations. He also of course did the invisible work implicit in any powerful testimony: the cutting, the pasting, the editing that produces a readable whole without betraying any of the important complexities.

Dalton is the intellectual, Mármol the worker whose pragmatism has informed his analysis of politics in action. "You're asking me if everything I've done and experienced was already written in my destiny?" he starts, in response to Roque's initial question. And he answers: "Only an academic would ask that kind of a question, and it makes me think of that song about 'what might have been and never was...!' "

The original manuscript had much more detailed analysis than the final version in either Spanish or English, many more pages of Roque's interpretation of Mármol's story, perhaps of interest only to scholars and political theorists. Dalton's introduction in the published version does an important job of situating the storyteller in time, place, and culture—political as well as national. But Mármol is also given the chance to offer his—sometimes conflicting—analysis, and there are letters from him regarding process, as well as the much more recent interview appended by the English translators.

The great Uruguayan writer Eduardo Galeano has said, "The lives of Miguel Mármol, master of the art of resurrection, are the most perfect metaphor for the history of Latin America." No question about it: here is a life that challenges the most extraordinary García Márquez character for its magic realist impact, while at the same time providing vital political testimony for those interested in Central America, past, present and future.

The result is a book that is high adventure as well as history, political analysis, and the poignant first-person account of one man who—like hundreds of thousands all over the so-called Third World—have committed their last breath to their people's liberation. This is an exceptional book. Some will find every word of interest, traveling in and out of treatise upon treatise, appendices, and footnotes. Others will read it as a novel, skipping the more weighty ideological discussions and concentrating on the human being, a man who—finally—tells his story to the world. And if, at some point, Hollywood proves less reticent than the commercial publishing industry, we may yet have a film—about the man who crawled out from under his executed comrades, donned his best friend's "brand new tan hat," and fled to a hiding place from which he would continue to fight.

I recommend *Miguel Mármol* as literature; it's a long-time classic in Latin America and much overdue here. But I recommend it even more as history, as a door open onto the real culture and struggle south of our shattering borders.

Dogmatism and rigidity seem to be the hallmarks of insecurity, a quality so heartily bred by our ongoing social distortions. In fundamentalist or other conservative rigidity we lose sight of our very humanity, our capacity to reason and discern. In the rigidity of the left we often lose sight of process. *Miguel Mármol*, the old-time but non-traditional Marxist, reminds us of our process—creative, sometimes brilliant, vulnerable, often imperfect. It is only by remembering these parts of ourselves that we can continue to move towards the reality of justice and equality we all so desperately need.

—Albuquerque, New Mexico
Summer 1987

Invasion as Metaphor
in America

Here's a first novel that's fast reading but long staying. It starts off with the narrator's first-person childhood memories. Our protagonist is Marietta, Miss Marietta, and finally Taylor, depending upon what period of her life we're talking about. You think this is great: something for light consumption on the daily commuter train, or to be absorbed in the pleasure of a steaming tub. And this is certainly a book that may be read in just such places. But it's not simply another trashy (read: delicious) piece of fiction. You are thoroughly hooked by the time you realize Barbara Kingsolver is addressing and connecting two of the most important issues of our times.

The Bean Trees is about invasion. Invasion, not as it is probed and theorized about by political thinkers, psychologists, or academics. Invasion of the psyche and of the body as it is experienced by middle America. And not middle-*class* America, but real *middle* America: the unemployed and underemployed, people working in fast food joints or patching tires, Oklahoma Indians, young mothers left by wandering husbands or mothers who never had husbands. In this novel you travel from Kentucky to Arizona and never even have to brood over the sophisticated complexities of New York, San Francisco, or Chicago.

The novel's protagonist, Taylor, knows nothing about the wars in Central America or about how the U.S. government promotes those wars and then rejects their victims, until she becomes friends with Esteban and Esperanza and accepts the fact that some people work fast food or assembly lines; others have used tire shops that double as sanctuaries.

The Bean Trees is hilariously funny. You laugh out loud. I literally fell off my chair. You turn the pages and wheeze, empathetically amazed and delighted by the characters who people these pages; by their perceptions of themselves, the world, and by the decisions they make for their moral as well as physical survival.

Before she renames herself Taylor, our heroine makes it through high school with the support of a brave and truly loving mother. She remembers one special teacher, whose chief claim to local fame is that his nails are clean. He becomes her key to a first real job: analyzing blood, urine, and feces at the small town hospital. This enables her to save $300 for an old Volkswagen: her ticket to the world. She leaves her provincial destiny behind, and hits North America's roads.

Pace-wise, or in some of its rhythms, *The Bean Trees* has something in common with Jack Kerouac's classic *On the Road*. But its meaning is exactly the opposite. Kingsolver's characters don't opt for dropping out of society; they are desperately trying to survive within its confines; some of them hope to make it better. For unexpected yet believable humor, made from the most painful cultural observations, it takes me back to William Eastlake's *Portrait of the Artist with Twenty-Four Horses*.

But it would be misleading to try to compare Kingsolver with either of these male authors. In style and vision, she has written a book all her own; and with a deep female consciousness that feels like bedrock when set against some of the preachier, more explicitly feminist works. Attempting to define this published, yet brand-new author, Georgia Cotrell's *Shoulders* comes to mind. Kingsolver's prose style has something in common with Cotrell's use of language. She also shares that writer's curiosity about a given (although different) social group, her integrity in shying away from surface judgments when looking at complexities and contradictions, and her explorations of non-traditional family situations.

Two lines of narrative eventually converge in Kingsolver's novel. There is our heroine, telling her story with the quiet unsophisticated irony of a tough and travelin' Kentucky woman. Much of this book is about identity, and she leaves home bent on getting herself a new name. She decides she'll take the cue from wherever she happens to be when she runs out of gas. "I came pretty close to being named after Homer, Illinois, but kept pushing it. I kept my fingers crossed through Sidney, Sadorus, Cerro Gordo, Decatur, and Blue Mound, and coasted into Taylorville on the fumes. And so I am Taylor Greer," she announces early in her story.

And there is an alternating chapter third-person narrative: the voice of Lou Ann, also from Kentucky but already a sometime Tucson resident, whose rodeo riding husband Angel Ruiz loses what sense of self he may once have had when an accident with his pickup takes off one of his legs below the knee. Irritable and dissatisfied, he leaves Lou

Ann before their child is born.

Taylor's VW breaks down the first time in Oklahoma where, along with repairs enough to get her on the road again, she acquires a child of her own. An Indian woman presses a silent baby of indeterminate age and origin into her arms. The woman retreats, leaving Taylor no choice but to continue on her way, now the adopted mother of this mystery bundle. The child seems slow in her responses; Taylor dubs her Turtle.

Her car dies definitively in Tucson. From then on, it's Taylor as a sudden mother, trying to make it for two. And Lou Ann with her little Dwayne Ray. *The Bean Trees*, on one well-fashioned plane, is the story of how these two poverty-level women find one another through want ads and mutual need, how they aid each other by pooling their meager resources and sharing a house, and how each helps the other go on surviving and learning about what life means.

The end of the scene in which Taylor and Lou Ann join fortunes is worth repeating here. The former has answered a house-to-share ad placed by the latter: "Lou Ann hid her mouth with her hand. 'What?' I said. 'Nothing.' I could see perfectly well that she was smiling. 'Come on, what is it?' 'It's been so long,' she said. 'You talk just like me.'"

And these two apparently different women are immediately compatible: "Within ten minutes Lou Ann and I were in the kitchen drinking diet Pepsi and splitting our gussets laughing about homeostasis and bean turds. We had already established that our hometowns in Kentucky were separated by only two counties, and that we had both been to the exact same Bob Seger concert at the Kentucky State Fair my senior year."

Lou Ann has been carefully programmed to ask permission for breathing. Many of us will recognize in her that part of ourselves that has trouble believing that we do anything well enough, are ever good enough, or belong anywhere—even inside our own skins. Taylor offers Lou Ann a piece of her life-earned philosophy, this one about men: "... one time when I was working in this motel one of the toilets leaked and I had to replace the flapper ball. Here's what it said on the package; I kept it till I knew it by heart: 'Please note. Parts are included for all installations, but no installation requires all of the parts.' That's kind of my philosophy about men. I don't think there's an installation out there that could use all of my parts."

This is also the story of Mattie, Mattie of Jesus Is Lord Used Tires, and the occupants of her labyrinth second floor: people like the nervous young priest on the motorcycle; and Esteban and Esperanza, who come and go in the night. After a short stint frying up fast food at Burger Derby, Taylor rebels and goes to work for Mattie, a knowledgeable woman who drinks coffee from a white mug decorated with hundreds of tiny rabbits having sex in hundreds of different positions.

Contrary to others with whom Taylor comes in contact, Mattie can tell right away that Turtle is a girl. And Taylor begins to learn about Mattie's world: "Mattie's place was always hopping. She was right about people always passing through, and not just customers, either. There was another whole set of people who spoke Spanish and lived with her upstairs for various lengths of time. I asked her about them once, and she asked me something like had I ever heard of a sanctuary. I remembered my gas station travel brochures. 'Sure,' I said. 'It's a place they set aside for birds, where nobody's allowed to shoot them.' 'That's right. They've got them for people too.' This was all she was inclined to say on the subject."

Nothing more is said at that point. But, if we didn't get it when we experienced Taylor's shock at discovering the damage suffered by Turtle's victimized body, by this time we can be sure that this is a tale about something more complex than two uniquely ordinary women making their way in the world.

There are endless delightful moments in this book. A typical Kingsolver scene happens when Taylor is introduced to Lou Ann's cat: " 'You wouldn't believe what your cat is doing,' I said. 'Oh yes, I would,' Lou Ann said. 'He's acting like he just went potty, right?' 'Right. But he didn't as far as I can see.' 'Oh no, he never does. I think he has a split personality. The good cat wakes up and thinks the bad cat has just pooped on the rug. See, we got him as a kitty and I named him Snowboots but Angel thought that was a stupid name so he always called him Pachuco instead.' "

As is necessary to any decent novel about ordinary America, fundamentalism as a leitmotif surfaces every once in a while. Taylor hits Oral Roberts country on her trip west, and the knowledge that she can always call 1-800-THE-LORD keeps her going through many a near desperate time. Towards the end of the story, a fully confident Taylor decides more out of nostalgia than anything else to dial the religious help line:

> The line rang twice, three times, and then a recording came on. It told me that the Lord helps those that help themselves. Then it said that this was my golden opportunity to help myself and the entire Spiritual Body by

making my generous contribution today to the Fountain
of Faith missionary fund. If I would please hold the line
an operator would be available momentarily to take my
pledge. I held the line.
'Thank you for calling,' she said. 'Would you like to
state your name and address and the amount of your
pledge?' 'No pledge,' I said. 'I just wanted to let you know
you've gotten me through some rough times. I always
thought, If I really get desperate I can call 1-800-THE-
LORD. I just wanted to tell you, you have been a Fountain
of Faith.'
She didn't know what to make of this. 'So you don't
wish to make a pledge at this time?' 'No,' I said. 'Do you
want to make a pledge to me at this time? Would you like
to send me 100 dollars, or a hot meal?' She sounded
irritated. 'I can't do that ma'am,' she said. 'Okay, no
problem,' I said. 'I don't need it anyway. Especially now.
I've got a whole trunk full of pickles and baloney....'

Kingsolver's is a sharp-edged humor because it tells a human but
never trivialized story. Taylor doesn't read about the brutal sexual abuse
of children in a book. She discovers it the first time she bathes Turtle.
And her knowledge is confirmed months later when she takes the child
to a pediatrician and listens to him tell her that the terrified little girl she
has imagined is perhaps a year and a half is probably closer to three.
"Sometimes they just stop growing," he says.

Two profoundly related versions of invasion, the sexual invasion
of a child's body and the political invasion of a nation's sovereignty, come
together and unfold in this story of ordinary people who understand both
realities as they touch their own life processes. It is also a story about
racism, sexism, and dignity. It's a story propelled by a marvelous ear, a
fast-moving humor, and the powerful undercurrent of human struggle.

Something happens in *The Bean Trees*. It's one of those old-
fashioned stories, thankfully coming back onto our contemporary literary scene, in which there are heroines and anti-heroines, heroes and
anti-heroes, ordinary humans all. They go places and do things and
where they go and what they do makes sense for them—and for us. There
are also surprises in this book. There is adventure. And there is resolution, as believable as it is gratifying.

Barbara Kingsolver, herself a Kentuckian living in Arizona,
clearly knows of what she writes. Her prose is effortless and lovely, her

structure easy, her evolutions warm and deeply satisfying. Invasion, as historic metaphor for sexual abuse and sanctuary, is not new with this novel. It has surfaced, over the past several years, in poetry and prose, notably by some of our most important women writers. Here it occupies a new territory, that of the commonplace, mostly undramatic, always warm, and sometimes funny story; told and lived by commonplace people, most of them women.

Trite as it may sound, reading *The Bean Trees* bolsters my belief in a politically isolated but essentially generous American people. The system will continue to hype us with words and images that systematically distort our sense of world and self. But as long as we retain the capacity to see and feel, as long as the connections are made in our lives (with or without the attendant intellectualization), and as long as books like this one are written to help us recreate our common memory, we will be able to leave worthy lives to those coming along behind us.

—Hartford, Connecticut
Winter 1988

Down Dangerous Roads

I.

I first met Judith McDaniel when *Sanctuary, A Journey* was just an idea, bits and pieces of a manuscript, fragments of experience still searching for the form which would ultimately link them together. Judith was driving through Albuquerque on her way to Tucson, where the 1986 Sanctuary trials were taking place. She stopped by to see me. We took a walk into the mountains behind my home. We talked. There were connections: Nicaragua, an ongoing participation in struggles for justice and peace.

Judith spoke very little about how she would make the creative links that give birth to a book, but I had no doubt the book was there. In the following months, as we shared a publisher and our books were due out at the same time, we also shared an anticipation akin to that of expectant mothers. I had occasional glimpses of her progress, but later, the book finally in hand, I told Judith I was surprised it had happened only now. I didn't mean I was surprised she had not written such a book before this, but that nobody had done so.

Divide and conquer has become a cliché in our society, but it's important to remember that it still works. By exploring commonalities we forge connections that give us strength. *Sanctuary, A Journey* is a book that pulls from a vast array of sources one common thread. These sources are alcoholism recovery, an insistence on breaking through the disinformation barrier (with one's life, if necessary), feminism, solidarity, internationalism, spirituality, a desperate quest for peace, the circle of witness, and an ear to the earth. Judith McDaniel's metaphor and vehicle for all of this is *sanctuary.*

This is a book of righteous despair, and also of visionary hope. A book in which we are prodded to move from the intimate to the general and back again; to reclaim our own dangerous (empowering) memory and risk life instead of death.

McDaniel has long been a member of the Religious Society of

Friends, the Quakers, for whom bearing witness is a daily, familiar (and useful) experience. "Witness, I learned again in my life," she tells us, "is a circle." Two of the explorations in this book are her own as a Witness for Peace traveler to Nicaragua (one of the group that was captured by the *contras* in October 1985 and forced to march through the Costa Rican jungle long enough to wonder if any of them would emerge alive); and the U.S. sanctuary movement, certainly one of the most powerful grass-roots struggles bearing witness in this country today.

The exuberant strength of this book lies in its power to make connections. Judith describes a woman in her weekly Alcoholics Anonymous meeting talking about Central American refugees who had sought sanctuary in the apparently removed confines of Albany, New York. Woven into the woman's story of her decision to volunteer as a monitor for the refugees is Judith's own story of capture and psychological torture. "I had not doubted Pedro's witness," she writes of one of the Central American refugees, a worker for the Human Rights Commission in San Salvador, "but hearing it in this new context—when my own life was in danger—made me know its truth in a different way." From these and other parts she makes a continuously renewable whole: "If other lives are changed by the hearing, and others feel moved to act differently, there will be new witnesses to that experience." And Judith's own history of struggle brings her to see that "This circle [of witness] is one of the primary reasons the women's movement in the United States, indeed in the world, is not dead, in spite of the many obituaries prematurely written for it."

In a coherent movement between poetry, poetic prose, the clearest essay style, and fragments of her personal journal (written on the San Juan River which separates Nicaragua from Costa Rica), McDaniel writes of the 1983 Seneca Women's Peace Encampment, Sanctuary, Central America, Big Mountain, Liberty Weekend as seen from a shelter for homeless women near New York's Times Square, a writer (myself) fighting deportation because of the critical nature of her writings, the meaning in walking, and the danger of memory.

Walking and *re-membering* are leitmotifs of this book. In the section called "Learning to Walk," McDaniel takes us step by step through her own history of walking. She tells a story to which many women will relate: being forced into oxfords (to support the feet!), trying "pointed toe heels" as a later measure of independence, hiking with the Girl Scouts, marching on the Pentagon. "Walking keeps me connected to the earth," she says. And later:

Once I walked into someone's work of art.... This year I
walked into a theater piece prepared by the universe.... I
found myself walking into an Alcoholics Anonymous
meeting one night when the fog had settled into my chest
and head to stay.... I have walked myself into a less safe
life. I walk on unsafe streets and in unsafe jungles. My
heart has walked me into unsafe loving along the way,
loving has made me use everything I know. Mostly I walk
to get where I want to be.[1]

Dangerous loving, dangerous living. But not for danger as an end
in itself. The section called "Dangerous Memory" is the climactic one, I
think. In the poem of the same name McDaniel retraces ground introduced in earlier pages, but here the essence has been distilled; we return
to images and ideas by this time familiar, with the renewed demand that
we take them seriously, hold their mirrors to our own lives. In the third
part of that poem, after retelling the story of her experience of political
capture and what that meant in her life, she says:

Home once again, I walked out alone
nearly every day that first week. Or:
still floating just above my body,
I watched me walking out alone. The eighth day
I met my mother, dead eight years.
As she walked toward me I peered
into her face. She was crying and smiling
at the same time. I had questions
to ask her but we did not speak.
I wanted to know how I could go on
living with so much shame:

  I mean
with the memory of the children sitting
at their desks in the school that was
only a roof ...[2]

The memories are from her own childhood and from the witness
she has borne in Central America. The shame is from her own childhood
—the destructive relationships that repeat themselves in substance abuse
and endless questions—but also from what she has seen beyond our
borders, her knowledge of the intimate connections between our system's
greed and the oppression of people both there and here.

In feminism we have retrieved our vulnerability and our strength, with shame for neither. One of the most important ways in which we pass this among ourselves and to others is through a revelation of process. We will no longer accept the patriarchal objectification of ourselves as product. We will *be* process. In "Saved from Complacency" McDaniel writes:

1.
This is not about myth
it is about conscious choice.
Yes the pipes froze
and burst one winter
yes sometimes we traveled
on opposite sides of the bed
instead of seeking the warmth
of the center
yes hard work
yes the cars not starting
at thirty below
yes the two mile walk in
when the plow was late
and yes the warm fires at night
the sun cracking a snowscape
the lilacs in spring
I wore that life like a skin
something I settled into forever
never saying *one day this will all be memory.*

2.
I wasn't prepared for how hard it was. You can tell
yourself in advance, look, this is going to be hard
so you've got to take care of yourself, but then
there is the gap between what you know and what you
remember to do. And sometimes you just don't know
what to do. After mother died, I remember my father
saying, I hear people telling me to take care of
myself but I don't know what that means. Do you
know what it means? Then—it was easy for me to tell
him—but now I don't know what it means at all.
I decided to leave ... [3]

Grief can be a cushion," she admits in the same poem. But she rejects that cushion, because, together with so many of us, she has built a commitment to risk. She has built it experience by experience, memory by memory, grief by grief, joy by joy. She tells us about the risk repeating itself over and over in the life of the alcoholic who has made the decision to recover, the feminist who understands class struggle, the woman who knows that white skin is always privilege, the lesbian who has made the choice to be out in a heterosexist world, the person who has placed her internationalist body on a critical border and dreamed herself to the other side.

In "Dreaming Back" she tells us:

> I dream back through the opening of
> each day of my life   each story
>
> about to happen ...

And she uses the dream to set the context for the entire book:

> For a month before going to Nicaragua, I had a recurring dream. I was in a village in Central America with some friends. A group of peasant women came by the house we were staying in and asked us to walk up the road with them. We knew the walk was very dangerous and my friends urged the women not to go. I was putting on my shoes to go and walk, feeling very angry with those who would not go. And they were angry with me. They said they were afraid and I was being foolish to go. In the dream I told them, "If I cannot walk up this road, then I am afraid of the kind of life I would have to live."[4]

This is a book about anger, and the consequences of anger. About risking and the consequences of risking. About loving, and the consequences of understanding that to open oneself to love means embarking "upon the walk from which there is no return" (as the Navajo and Hopi resisting at Big Mountain teach).

It is in the very last part of the book, "Traveling Through Big Mountain," that McDaniel brings the threads of her anti-racist, anti-classist, anti-patriarchal, anti-desecration, and anti-death consciousness and action to their most finely-honed statement. There are no easy answers, and she is not looking for tidy conclusions. She visits the hogan of Katherine Smith, one of the four keepers of the Navajo sacred earth bundles:

As a white person, I have almost no idea what that (to be one of the four keepers) means. But as a person who cares about the earth's survival, I approach Katherine Smith, keeper of the earth, with awe and reverence. And despair. Because here is one elder woman—joined with other men and women, it is true, but they are so few—who is in opposition to all the forces of a modern technological capitalist society which says she is anachronistic. Life isn't that way anymore, those forces say, she has to change. And Katherine Smith says no. Katherine Smith says that it is we who live in this other society who are anachronistic, that is, out of time. The earth is time, all time. She says that if we destroy the earth, we will cease to exist.[5]

II.

Judith McDaniel's book *Sanctuary, A Journey* was what brought me to Judith the person. When it was published I wrote the above review, and I wanted very much to get to know the woman who had succeeded in pulling those pieces together. I had my first opportunity on the occasion of the American Booksellers Association meeting in Washington, D.C. It was May 1986.

A book of my own, *This Is About Incest*, had appeared through the same publisher and at the same time as Judith's. We were both struck by certain similarities between the two. In the first place we were dealing with difficult issues, issues we knew might be hard to hear for precisely the people we were trying to reach. But the issues themselves were connected: the invasion of basic human rights, whether the rights of a body or a country. And what happens to a person—in both cases, a woman—when she rediscovers or reassesses events; what happens to her and to the people around her.

Both books deal with memory, the real dangers inherent in reclaiming it and the even greater dangers waiting to ensnare those who don't. And each book, in a different way, makes connections between the most intimate personal event and the larger political context. The personal and the political: a connection so frequently spoken of but so rarely made in the course of most human lives.

Nancy Bereano, of Firebrand Books, suggested that Judith and I do a joint reading in Washington. Sue Goodwin of the Washington School agreed. Both sponsored the program at a large church. Now I recreate the dinner Judith and I shared, the night before that reading. Both of us wanted to try to do something more than the usual two-set combination; we wanted to be able to alternate readings from our books in such a way that we would be able to transmit to our audience the deep connections we felt. And there we were, over a meal at the old Taberna, trying to get to know one another better and figure out the reading at the same time.

We quickly decided we would allow the audience to participate in a reading we would give to one another. Judith said she wanted to begin with a particular section, and I immediately thought of a section of my own that tied in with or expanded upon the issue she was dealing with. From then on it was fairly simple: one of us would begin to speak of a poem or prose passage; the other would excitedly respond. We found we wanted to take people on a journey, through our questions first, then deeply into the events that had provided some of our answers, and then lighten things up a bit, offer hope, finally leaving people with some questions of their own—and the courage to look for answers. We decided we would end with my reading a poem of Judith's and her reading one of mine.

When we said good night I felt that the promise of our New Mexican walk was fulfilling itself in the best kind of friendship, a real collaboration in the work. Somewhere around three a.m. I remember waking in my hotel room and realizing that a particular moment in the proposed reading might better unfold with a substitution in the material we had chosen. In the morning I called to share my concern, but it was Sunday and Judith had already left to attend her Friends meeting. Later she told me that she, too, had woken around three, with similar questions. In fact, she had made a substitution of her own. We were definitely on the same wavelength.

Our reading that night was everything we had hoped it might be—and a good deal more. The full house, peopled by friends and others who happened to be in town for the American Booksellers Association convention, was as moved as we hoped they would be. More than one told us we ought to take this reading on the road, and we were enthusiastic about the idea. Both of us travel frequently to read our work; why not try to improve on this initial collaboration and design something we could do together.

And so we did. But the results were not what we expected. Judith and I have done a lot more talking about our books and their messages. We have given two or three joint readings (those are all the joint invitations we've had, although neither of us have any trouble scheduling individual readings). We continue to feel that the combined format is important. And we've had to ask ourselves why it's been so difficult for us to schedule this collaborative event, and why—with the exception of that first magic evening—it's also been difficult for our audiences to hear it.

For me, a key to these questions came out of an experience in Hartford, Connecticut. I was teaching there, and Judith lives not far away, in Albany. We saw an opportunity to do our reading, and Readers' Feast—the wonderful community bookstore in Hartford—was quick to extend its facilities. We knew the audience would be much smaller than in Washington, but we believed those attending would be interested and responsive.

We were perhaps a bit more than halfway through the event when a voice from the audience broke the mood we'd so carefully created. It was a woman, later identified as someone who is frequently disrupting and rude. She shouted: "When are we going to take a break? I can't stand much more of this ..." and she waited a moment, clearly hoping others would second her complaint. When no one did, she insisted "... no one here is brave enough to say what they're really feeling." And she got up and walked out.

This Is About Incest is also a journey. It begins in a therapist's office, where I choose to confront a phobia that's been with me for as long as I remember. Working with one memory to get back to another, I uncover the sexual abuse of my maternal grandfather, many years dead. The blocked event begins much further back, of course, when I was so small that my only viable defense lay in blocking the terror of what I could not prevent with the development of a phobia I was better able to handle. My only possible survival mechanism had thus become my greatest terror.

The book chronicles this journey as straightforwardly as possible. I describe it, step by step, and offer not only the words as they found their way into prose and poetry but also family pictures, some of them modified by current consciousness, my grandfather and me at the time of the events, my painful struggle to unravel all that I had for so many years denied—even to myself. I wanted to give process rather than simply product. I reproduced, as faithfully as I could, the unfolding of what had been done to me, my reclaimed memory of that, and what I might do with that memory now that it is once again my own.

I was not saying this is the way it is, for everyone but *this is the way it was for me.* By sharing the experience, I want to tell others that they need not be afraid of their own journeys. Painful as they will be, they will always lead to greater personal freedom, an empowering sense of relief. But I didn't want to stop there. A confession wasn't enough. I felt it was important to link what happens in the body with what takes place upon the land, what abuse of power can mean in a single life and what exploring that teaches us about abuse of power when wrought upon groups, or nations. An individual's inability to remember damages that person's identity in much the same way as a people's collective identity is damaged when our history is taken from us, our real heroes and heroines erased, the events literally sheared from our collective memory.

Reclaiming a single memory is not unlike the reclaiming we do as women—or as African Americans, Latinas and Latinos, Native Americans, lesbians, gay men, working people—when we search out and revive that of which we have been robbed. The political implications in all these journeys have much in common.

And so I made that book, and struggled with my family to be able to come to the point where publication was possible. I began reading the poems publicly, in the readings with Judith and also, much more frequently, alone. And the overwhelming expressions of gratitude I received, from people who came up to me after a public appearance or wrote to me about the book, urged me to concentrate on how useful this sharing could be to others. Not surprisingly, I had neglected what happened to *me* every time I let strangers in.

The jarring incident at Readers' Feast and the surprising lack of interest in Judith's and my joint reading led me to reexamine what's really involved when you make difficult connections and ask others to consider making them as well. Our dominant culture, with its multiplicity of scientifically contrived controls, subjects us to a constant conditioning from which escape appears impossible and, if attempted, may be exceptionally uncomfortable. The messages are subliminal and absolutely clear: the more you assume the "virtues" of no-think, no-feel, no-speak, the more likely you are to enjoy what society seems to be offering: health, happiness, work, sometimes even power, an acceptable mate, and 2.3 children. Conversely, to the degree that we challenge what we're told is normal or natural, we risk not attaining the success we have been taught is necessary—not only in order to make it in this world, but simply in order to survive.

Risk: perhaps the key word in Judith's book and in mine. And probably the centerpin of what brought us together. Thinking about what happened when that woman interrupted the wall I had so carefully built between my pain and my audience, I realized that if I wanted to reach more people I had to risk myself more. I couldn't continue to separate my experience from my offering to such a degree. I had to be willing to let people in.

The following month, a group of women at Smith College invited me to read from my incest book. I found myself going about the reading in a new way. I did not read to the people seated before me; I talked to them, gently, explaining almost as if I had been in a small room with a few good friends the various stages of my struggle. It was a softer reading, a more open-ended offering. Vulnerable to the kind of dislocation I had just experienced, I chose to make myself more accessible rather than shut myself off from the possibility of it happening again.

I was working through the fear by bearing more explicit witness; again, I was learning from Judith's experience—and so many others—as well as from my own. The survivor of incest, like the survivor of rape and other abuses, must succeed in making her own body a sanctuary where invasion can never again be perpetrated. It is not unlike the struggles of a small nation, attempting to free itself from the abusive control of a larger, more powerful, one. And lessons evident in either struggle are useful when confronting the other.

And so the successive movements of art-in-life engender their own questions, their own solutions. When art and life are assumed head on, the worn-out dilemma about art imitating life (or vice-versa) gives way to a situation where the lines between art and life become less and less defined. Seamlessly, form and content really do merge.

We must risk in order to make the connections. We must no longer be afraid to reclaim and honor memory—in its most terrifying as well as its most gratifying forms. Let every battlefield become a sanctuary, where the rewards of personal and political truths may flourish.

—Hartford, Connecticut, Fall 1987 and
Albuquerque, New Mexico, Summer 1988

Notes

1. *Sanctuary, A Journey*, Judith McDaniel (Ithaca, NY: Firebrand Books, 1987), pp. 47-50.
2. Ibid., pp. 108-109.
3. Ibid., pp. 23-24.
4. Ibid., p. 9.
5. Ibid., pp. 164-165.

Exiled in the Promised Land

Marcia Freedman and I have never met. I have somehow missed her in all the places we might have inhabited together—all the conferences and forums, the cafes and living rooms. *Exile in the Promised Land* is also the first of her work I have read. Still, after reading this book I feel that we know each other well. In spite of very different backgrounds, in spite of searches that have gone in dissimilar directions, there is much in this book that is instantly recognizable to me. And it resonates in places that are often hidden—even from myself.

I could start by saying that we are both from Jewish families. Yet this leads more to difference than to commonality. Freedman's parents gave her a Jewish secular tradition: her father's struggle for justice was as much about being a Jew as it was about being a Communist; and the holidays were culturally if not religiously important. I received no such active tradition from my parents. They changed our last name, explored several Protestant denominations throughout my childhood, and (out of self-hate? a sense of alienation from their own parents?) removed themselves from most everything Jewish. I participated in my first Seder as an adult (and then it was a feminist Seder). Still, who knows? I have always felt that my emotional ties to Judaism inform my lifelong struggle on behalf of justice.

Marcia Freedman and I, close in age and regions of origin, both left the United States in the same decade. Her reasons may have been more consciously political than mine, but we probably shared some illusions—and also some courage—in our search for a *promised land.* For Marcia, who had a family tradition which very much included her identity as a Jew, Israel was a logical destination. I went to Mexico, then Cuba and Nicaragua, drawn by peoples whose liberation struggles depended, in the first place, on a radical disengagement from my government's control. Surely, we were both driven by visions of more just societies—societies where we hoped that new social as well as economic relations would produce the world we wanted—for ourselves and for our children.

Neither Marcia Freedman nor I would have called ourselves feminists when we left the United States. For both of us, however, feminism would play an essential role in our engagement with the countries to which we traveled. And we both became deeply involved with women's issues and women's work in those lands of our choice. I studied the mobilization of women, pursued oral history, and wrote about my sisters in Cuba and Nicaragua; Marcia was elected to public office as a foreign-born woman in Israel, helped found that country's contemporary feminist movement, and was part of the struggle to establish the first battered women's shelters there. (One of the many important things about *Exile in the Promised Land* is the fact that it provides detailed information about the Israeli women's movement, its politics, leaders, frictions, achievements.)

Both of us came out as lesbians after years of primarily relating—both personally and politically—to men. Freedman recognized herself as a woman-identified woman while still in Israel; I wasn't ready to do that until I returned to the United States. Our feminism would also signal choices that themselves had a great deal to do with our eventual decisions to come home. (Our concepts of *home,* I think, also have something in common. Neither of us says the word easily, and for both there is, finally, a notion of *other* when speaking of the birth country as well as of the chosen land.)

The difficulty with which Marcia Freedman and I have moved from birth home to chosen home and back, is at least partially informed by our experiences of feeling *outside* in both places. This is about being female, feminist, lesbian. It is about being socialist. And it is also, in whatever complicated ways, about finding ourselves the victims of xenophobia—in countries where belonging, in the political as well as in the cultural sense, is terribly important to a sense of self.

But let's go to the story. Marcia Freedman, with her husband Bill and their daughter Jenny, settled in Israel in 1967, just three weeks after the Six Day War. Her father had been a Communist labor leader, a moving influence in her life. Later he would commit suicide. Marcia's childhood included the shadow of McCarthyism as well as the thrilling images of people's struggle. Immigration to the Jewish homeland was a conscious homecoming for this couple; the dream was part of a collective memory, vividly alive:

Among the early Zionists, there was a radical minority, men as well as women, for whom Zionism was a utopian vision. They called not for the establishment of a state, but of a new social order in which sons no longer obeyed their fathers or wives their husbands, equality between sisters and brothers, free love. Instead of family, community. The children parented by all, marriage an anachronism. Jews would relearn how to live as whole human beings by returning to the land and laboring to rebuild it ... a state would only interfere with the process. The women understood their role as crucial to the process. "We create the homes that will create the homeland," they said.[1]

Into this social order which was very much a State, onto this new/old land, the Freedmans moved into an apartment in a complex with other families who became community to them. Marcia and Bill taught at the university, he was called up briefly in the 1973 war, she learned to keep house, shop, cook, and attend to their daughter's school within the context of this other culture. Indeed, her task was to "create the [home] that will create the homeland." And then, perhaps as much a result of the particularly Israeli electoral process as a response to her own energy and commitment, Marcia was elected to the Knesset. A woman in a fiercely traditional patriarchy, a U.S.-born arrival in a rigorously nationalist state, became a member of the cumbersome Israeli parliament. This alone would have been a fascinating story:

> I entered the Knesset, in January 1974, just three months after the Yom Kippur War, with my contradictions intact—distrust of authority and a belief that the social-democratic Jewish state embodied the values I'd been taught at home. I was soon disabused.[2]

> Unique I was. My opinions, my frames of reference, my age, my accent, my size, and my sex conspired to differentiate me from everyone else. Above all, I was identified with a movement [feminism] that seemed to terrify my colleagues. I would never have to worry about being coopted.[3]

But this was not to be the only story. Several years before, on a 1968 visit to the United States, contact with some of the recently written classics had opened Marcia to the new feminist movement. As with so many of us, the ideas percolated and took root. Then they exploded. In the fourteen years she would live in Israel, this Jewish woman from New York would help found the modern-day feminist movement in her chosen land; run for a seat in the Knesset and win; fight hard (and more often than not, lose) on issues such as Palestinian and women's rights; turn her back on traditional party politics; separate from her husband; identify as a lesbian; find herself rejected by some of her sisters as well as by all of her jobs; see her daughter—temporarily rebellious and angry—off to an escape in the United States; and eventually leave Israel, no tidy endings to her dream.

Freedman's book is much more than a courageous history we can reference as we ask the burdensome questions. Its major contribution, for me, lies in the fact that it reveals just how important the relationship is between *racism or nationalism and gender oppression* on the one hand, and the *survival of social responsibility* on the other. For in the wake of the recent events in Eastern Europe particularly, some of us have felt that the purely economic explanations, important as they undoubtedly are, are not enough.

We wonder if the worker states in disarray do not owe their downfall, at least in part, to the fact that issues like racism, nationalism, sexism, and heterosexism were never considered basic to the transformation of society. Cultural problems like criticism and dissent were too often swept under the rug; so often that generations of potential thinkers have been sacrificed, and the joy of participation turned sour. *Exile in the Promised Land* is a testimony to the fact that the marginalization of women's issues and other so-called superstructural concerns in Israel represented that country's abandonment of socially responsible ideals.

If this formulation seems tentative, the relationship between a narrow nationalism and the survival of a just way of life has been around much longer. Israel is the promised land for, among others, those who survived the terror of the Nazi Holocaust. Yet almost from the moment of her arrival, Marcia draws conclusions from her witness of an ever more deeply entrenched occupation of Arab lands. With her outsider's eyes, she is able to see the Palestinian people as they organize to fight back:

> In March of 1976, the pattern that in 1987 became known as the *intifada,* the Palestinian uprising, emerged.... The predictable but long-in-coming revolt of the Palestinians ... is now a reality. The Israeli government still refuses to negotiate with the Palestine Liberation Organization....

The handful of stone-throwing children have become armies of stone-throwing children. The few hundred Palestinians in Israeli jails have grown to six thousand.[4]

For the author, bearing class and national as well as gender witness brings inevitable consequences:

> I was already infamous as a militant feminist in a country where the liberation of women was seen as a threat to national security. I was an upstart immigrant who went too far too fast. By coming out, in 1975, in favor of a two-state solution, I became more notorious and more isolated, *even within the feminist community*.[5]

The above emphasis is mine. Freedman's commentary on the problems of women struggling together is no less interesting than her commentary on the sexually mixed global political scene. As her own story unfolds, she addresses complex issues within the women's movement from deep personal experience. Her account of loyalties and jealousies, among feminists as well as political comrades, is interesting and useful history.

Sometimes, though, her analysis of feminist politics seems overly psychoanalytic:

> [W]e were helpless victims of a dynamic whose only precedent we experienced in infancy. In patriarchy, the only women we perceive to be powerful are our mothers. We learned to identify with and to reject them, and they us. The residue is the need for unconditional approval and a lasting expectation of betrayal. Feminist politics begin with these unconscious, infantile expectations ...[6]

I would rather believe that feminist politics begins with a primal memory of wholeness, that our analyses then transform that memory into the realization that women can and must rebel against the suffocation of patriarchy.

Freedman, a woman in her early fifties, in whose life many U.S. women of her generation will find immediate parallels with their own, is wonderfully poetic in her descriptive skills. Recalling the celebration of a witches' sabbath, she evokes a scene filled with sensual beauty:

> [W]e were trying to create our own rituals. I lit a candle to welcome the Sabbath Bride. We called her Ashtoret,

the Caananite Goddess who, the Bible says, was worshiped by Solomon in the Temple at Jerusalem. I placed my hands over the candle, thumbs and forefingers together. The silhouette on the ceiling was a graceful vulva, flickering in the rhythms of the candle's flame. We all watched the shadow dance on the ceiling. Everyone saw the shadow of Ayala's hand, approaching and then stroking the shadow vulva. She made love to me for the first time there on the ceiling, openly and unashamed, as the others watched in fascination.[7]

In Freedman's book there is also important retrieval of the symbol and meaning of the Hebrew lexicon. Throughout this story, there is a return to the roots of language. When, shortly after Marcia and her husband arrive "the Israeli government [announces] the permanent annexation of Arab Jerusalem [which] the newspapers [call] ... reunification," Marcia speaks of historical determinism. And then, "The primary concern of a society of survivors," she says,

is bitachon ... The Defense Ministry is *Misrad Ha'-bitachon,* and a child who is insecure is said to lack *bitachon.* You can have or not have *bitachon* in someone, confidence; you can buy *bituach,* insurance; and you can express something *b'bitachon,* with certainty. Security, defense, insurance, confidence, certainty. It's all the same thing in Hebrew.[8]

It is no coincidence that many years later, the hard lessons learned, the feminist bookstore and women's center which is Marcia's last Israeli project is called *Women's Voice.* Voice, as a necessary precursor to change.

But Freedman's writing is also filled with examples, like the above, of her love and understanding of Israeli culture, of things Jewish; and of the beauty of the land—sound, color, light. Her capacity to see and hear, her curiosity and growing understanding of a complex people and their place, is never compromised by her understandable personal bitterness, which she also explores with honesty and compassion.

Much earlier in the book, we are told about *L'alot artzah,* ascension to the land. The Freedmans came to Israel "in a moment of optimism that was fleeting and never to return."[9] The dream of a pioneer state, the kibbutzim movement, a sacred history—it was all still alive. Going through that initial airport immigration process, Marcia was asked for her father's name and ("instinctively covering my political tracks—my father was a Communist, and I was a child of the McCarthy era") she gave it in Yiddish: "The Clerk wrote it down. [She] became Marcia *bat* Feivel Shrage, Feivel Shrage's daughter."[10] A foreboding of what would follow.

During her years in Israel, Marcia Freedman witnessed ever broader encroachment on, and occupation of, the Arab territories; and an intensified persecution of the Palestinian people. At the same time, she embraced feminism and it embraced her. And she made the connections. If it was her commitment to justice and her innate abhorrence of an exclusionary nationalism that first led Freedman to question Israel's abandonment of the ideal of peace for an ideal of nationalist survival, it was her developing feminist consciousness that helped her identify the betrayal of a movement's stated socialist principles.

Later, speaking about the resolution which came out of the U.N.-sponsored International Women's Conference in Mexico (1975), Freedman addresses the racism/anti-Semitism dilemma which continues to trouble our own women's movement:

> Jewish women "came out" and proclaimed their Judaism, as well as their loyalty and support for the state of Israel. ... no one discussed the merits or demerits of the charge of racism. The Jews of the dispersion agreed with the Israelis that the charge was no more than thinly veiled anti-Semitism. Some American Jewish feminists charged that the women's movement itself was anti-Semitic. "These are men's politics," I wrote to friends. "We mustn't buy into it. Both sides are killers and both sides are racist. That is the nature of nationalism. As feminists we have to oppose it everywhere, even among ourselves."[11]

She knows from experience that narrow nationalism is male politics, and also that "the Arab-Jewish conflict always played a decisive role in the development of Israeli feminism."[12]

Coming home to the promised land was a long cherished dream for Marcia, and becoming an exile there was a drawn-out, complex, and intimate tragedy. The book's structure as well as its exquisite writing and unrelenting honesty allow us to immerse ourselves in this woman's personal struggle as it weaves its way in and out of a public life.

This writer's description of her marriage coming apart beneath the weight of change will also ring familiar: the young wife typing the graduate husband's dissertation, while she kept house and "most of all

... tried to keep him happy and content. Everything changed in the 1970s," she writes. "My sudden leap into activism opened us up to ourselves and to the unequal nature of the compact between us."

After her election to the Knesset, the marriage began to unravel: "[we] lay in bed, night after night, side by side, not touching." When Marcia finally brought herself to ask her husband why he wasn't interested anymore, his response was surprisingly articulate and honest: "Since I've learned to respect and admire you as a person," he said, "I can't relate to you as a woman."[13]

The same feminist issues are central to the larger picture. As a member of the Knesset, Freedman finds few legislators, even from her own party (the newly formed Citizens Rights Movement), who are willing to lend their names to her struggles to better women's lives: for services, for reproductive choice, for the recognition of battering as a social problem, and against the patriarchal dogma of the rabbinical courts. Even among the other women in office—and there are pitifully few—she has little real support.

After a first term, battle-weary and no longer a novice, Marcia must decide whether to run again. Another successful campaign would mean victory for Israeli feminists as well as political legitimation for herself; "I'd be a *mensch*," a good girl, she says. But, she counters her own arguments in favor, "I wasn't changing the world; I wasn't living in my body."[14] This, for me, is the pivotal moment in Marcia's story. This is when she leaves traditional politics and returns to grassroots organizing:

> Before, during, and after the Knesset years, the women's movement was home, an ideological, emotional, spiritual, and political home.... The women's movement was never large enough to be a constituency, nor was it organized enough to be a political base. But it constituted the only public space in which, most of the time, I felt at one with myself.[15]

For those of us for whom capitalism is not the system which best serves human need, recent world events have posed insistent questions: What went wrong with socialism? How could it have failed? (How could it have failed *us*?) But was that really socialism? These are questions of the heart, emotionally strafing, deeply troubling. The intellect's questions are much more complicated, and every bit as troubling.

We always knew that the socialist experiments, born into a world of unrelenting hostilities, were also and each within its own historic framework threatened by economic error and the weaknesses of human spirit. In most cases these experiments were indelibly marked by the old system: classist, racist, nationalistic, sexist, ethnocentric, heterosexist, too often accommodating to their own weakest links.

But the other questions don't go away: Where does all of this leave the yearning for a truly participatory society? Has the term *democracy,* coopted so often and by so many, lost it's real meaning? And what *is* its real meaning? Is power always a corrupting force, the patriarchy an inevitable trap? What kind of life—indeed, what kind of a planet—will we be able to leave to our children and grandchildren?

It is in the context of these questions, in the context of recent developments—in the Soviet Union, Eastern Europe, Nicaragua, and our own United States, as well as in Israel and for the Palestinians in the occupied territories—that reading Marcia Freedman's *Exile in the Promised Land* becomes a moral imperative. Not simply an extraordinary personal memoir, a fast and thrilling read for Jewish women and for others, but a book that sets before us, in the story of a woman's insightfully told life, a weave of these questions translated into the everyday stuff of identity and community, memory, political hopes, relationships and mothering, war and peace, the destruction or survival of humanity itself. Marcia Freedman's book further bolsters my conviction that until our movements for social change fully confront the issues of gender, nationality, race, and sexuality—as well as those of class—such movements are doomed to failure.

Exile in the Promised Land gives us a great deal. It is at once a thoughtful feminist memoir, a passionate chronicle of struggle, an exciting lesbian coming out story, and a moving tale of mother/daughter love. It is also much more than all of these. In its exploration of some of the larger political questions, it takes risks and signals important connections.

The difficult map of identity/exile/home charts the terrain upon which Marcia Freedman goes deepest yet offers fewest answers. Perhaps it cannot be otherwise. In our politically compartmentalized world, the insider/outsider issue of identity in place may be the last frontier. Fourteen years after immigrating to Israel, her life unalterably changed, Freedman decides to return for good to the United States. But leavetaking and return, arrival and loss, are not resolved. Her book ends:

> This time, boarding the plane that would take me "home,"
> I had to say goodbye to hope as well as despair. A year

earlier, I had a rush of expectation about a new life in California. Now the tears streamed down my face. Though life in Berkeley was pleasant, though I was beginning to relax and heal, though I found not only a lesbian but a Jewish community that were welcoming and supportive, California was exile. Permanent exile. Israel would always remain my home.

... Daily contact with Israel's present is only depressing. The most dire of my predictions are realized in ... headlines. Half the country is depressed by the events of the day and the feeling that the course of events cannot be stopped. The other half moves relentlessly toward the extremist right wing of Israeli politics—nationalist, racist, violent, and more xenophobic than ever.

I follow it all ... in close touch, but removed. I organize Jewish women's peace activities here, to bridge the gap. But it doesn't. I left, and I will remain cut off from my home forever.[16]

—Hartford, Connecticut
Spring 1990

Notes

1. *Exile in the Promised Land*, Marcia Freedman (Ithaca, NY: Firebrand Books, 1990), p. 131.
2. Ibid., p. 81.
3. Ibid., p. 80.
4. Ibid., p. 109.
5. Ibid., p. 108.
6. Ibid., p. 186.
7. Ibid., p. 209.
8. Ibid., p. 34.
9. Ibid., p. 32.
10. Ibid., p. 28.
11. Ibid., p. 180.
12. Ibid., p. 52.
13. Ibid., p. 122.
14. Ibid., p. 155.
15. Ibid., p. 171.
16. Ibid., p. 234.

'All the Different Characters That Populated My World'

Some Notes on the Teaching Experience

I.

My belief that we were just reading another poem about the "Other" was shattered when I was able to come to grips with the fact that I have been made to feel marginalized myself. Even though on the surface I managed to look like everyone else here, the facts of my class status and my ethnic origin made me feel different [and] as though I had to conceal these facts of my existence.... [Reading] Sandra Cisneros, I had a tremendous identification with her. I was reminded of my childhood and of all the different characters that populated my world. I realized that I came from the margin into the center, and that I could, in fact, go back and not be permanently sucked into the trap of assimilation.

The above is from a final paper written by a working-class woman student of Uruguayan origin for a course I teach called Eight Contemporary U.S. Women Poets. The scene is a mostly homogeneous white upper-middle-class campus, one of the many liberal arts institutions which—along with our state and city schools, community colleges, and vocational institutes—are responsible for educating those upon whose shoulders, intelligence, and imagination this country's future rests. The paper might not have been so extraordinary had it not signaled the beginning of this student's conscious retrieval of her ethnic and class identity.

In spite of important efforts to broaden the literary canon and make changes in a university curriculum that still miserably fails to adequately address class, race, and gender issues, today few English departments teach required courses in African-American, Native American, Hispanic, women's, or gay and lesbian literature, nor are these included in core courses in most schools. Without going into each of these separate literatures, one might easily argue that Black women are overwhelmingly represented among the best of our contemporary writers,[1] yet they are studied occasionally, if at all. Visiting professors or regular faculty may teach a course featuring *ethnic* material on a one semester basis. We need a new, inclusive, canon, primarily because we *all* learn from our many-textured cultural heritage. With the current canon it remains a matter of luck whether or not our students study any but white males, whether or not our students of color, women, and others have the opportunity of studying a literature in which they may see themselves reflected, in which they may find useful role models or otherwise validate their lives. This was the first time my student, a junior at a prestigious liberal arts school, identified with an author.

For the past several years I've taught my Eight Contemporary U.S. Women Poets course and other courses like it. I've focussed on women's work, because I know how essential it is to read the female in our history, and because the literary canon is still overwhelmingly dominated by men. Many literature students take courses in which all the poets—or novelists, or fiction writers—are male. Sometimes the token exception is Emily Dickinson (and more often than not she is taught as a reclusive oddity, rather than as the brilliant and passionate lesbian she was, a woman who lived at least one hundred years too early, trapped by oppressive familial and social circumstances, freed only by her pen).[2]

From the wealth of material available, I cover eight poets because the number works well in a thirteen- or fourteen-week format. It allows for some breadth in terms of race, culture, sexual preference, age, and writing style; and combines a representation of at least some of our many voices, validating the origins of at least some of those students who will take the course.

This non-traditional variety in the authors I choose is the first thing that surprises many of the students who read the syllabus. It is a terrible reality that in a social order in which anyone who is not white, male, middle-class, "ageless," or young is *other,* my course focusses on *female* poets. But I would not be satisfied if those women represented homogeneity in other ways, for example, if they were all Anglo, or if they spoke in traditional genres about traditional subjects.

For my own enjoyment I change the list from year to year, but the last time I taught this course, two poets were Indian (one Navajo, the other Creek), two African-American, one Mexican American, one Jewish, and concerned with that identity in her work, three Caucasian, five from the working class, three lesbian, six mothers. One took her own life. Their birth dates ranged from mid-twenties to late fifties. North American poets all, for the United States—the canon notwithstanding—is a great mix of class, race, ethnicity, politics, sexuality, psychology, and culture.

But I want to get back to the quote with which I began these notes. The student who wrote it looked Anglo, spoke English without an accent, and exemplified the studied lack of pretense exhibited by most of the young women from wealthy families on this particular campus. Until she came out[3] as a Uruguayan immigrant who was studying at this school because her father's job as one of its janitors enabled her to do so, no one in the class would have guessed that she was—by virtue of being an immigrant—different from them.

Indeed, like so many young people in this country, my student had worked from her earliest school experience to be indistinguishable from her peers. She'd received the message early, no doubt from her struggling family as well as from friends and acquaintances: in order to succeed in the United States as a young Latin American woman, she would have to learn to blend in, to forget her Uruguayan roots, to remember not to mention her father's job as a janitor on campus; in short, she would have to deny her own existence.

It may be interesting here to note that in the class discussion that followed the process of remembering initiated by this young woman when she read a Latina woman's short stories, more than a few of the students said they thought it was harder to "come out" as a working-class woman than as a lesbian on this particular campus. I'm not sure I agree with the assessment, but it certainly speaks to the extent to which class oppression permeated my classroom and the campus in general.

Among female faculty of working-class origin, I have spoken to many who find their experience ignored, devalued, and even ridiculed within the "sacred halls." It is frequently easier to "pass" than to demand class recognition and respect. Sadly, making it through to a tenure-track position has often required rejection of working-class roots at such a deep level, that the woman herself has become estranged from her culture.

Although the poets we studied represent a broad mix of backgrounds, this was an expensive private college and the students themselves seemed fairly homogeneous. In a group of fifteen, there were only two older returning women students and—until the Uruguayan immigrant's testimonial—there seemed to be a single woman of color (African American). But wait, were the rest really all cut of such a similar mold? As the semester unfolded and we got to know one another, several revealed their working-class origins. One did so rebelliously; two more hesitantly, uncertain of their classmates' response. A couple were on full scholarships. Discussing the different poets' lives and work provided the context for some poignant admissions about how difficult it could be to be working-class or non-white—different in any way—on such a campus. More importantly, it enabled us all to reconnect with the wisdom and power of this previously ignored aspect of our collective identity (memory).

I've spoken only of women in relation to this course. That's because only women enrolled. In my five years of teaching Women's Studies, American Studies, Literature, and Writing at U.S. colleges and universities, it's been my experience that *all* courses about women poets, or with titles like Women and Ethnicity, Third World Women, Feminist Theory, or Women, Class, and Race, draw women students almost exclusively. Sometimes there are one or two brave men, often none. We (teachers of literature, academics in general) have progressed very little—in academia as well as outside it—in recognizing the importance of women's thought and creative production *as* a part of general education. Much less do we understand that unless we begin to include appropriate numbers of women in the curriculum, our whole sense of (literary, cultural, scientific) history will continue to be skewed.

Students have told me how their male friends often scoff at their choice of a course like Women's History, ridiculing the idea that there even is such a thing. I believe that a course on unlearning racism, sexism, and homophobia must be required at the freshman or sophomore level at all schools. The discussions which pit mainstreaming[4] against a strong Women's Studies component are missing the point as far as I'm concerned. I think we need both, and urgently.

Women's Studies, hard won on campuses in the early seventies, is not simply a restructuring of content, a retrieving of women's history, thought, and culture, a re-visioning of knowledge. The particular pedagogy that has been developed within the discipline—with a focus on personal empowerment through non-hierarchical structures of learning—is specifically female and also informs my way of teaching. While women in the United States were reclaiming their identities and many of those in academia were fighting for women's studies as a necessary discipline, I was participating in my own liberation- and female-centered struggles in Latin America. Later I will talk about how those struggles inform my teaching today. Suffice it, now, to say that I make essential connections between teaching and what I learned in the popular movements in Mexico (1961-69), Cuba (1969-79), and Nicaragua (1979-84).

In all my classes—Women's Studies and others—my students and I sit in a circle. Most class periods begin with a time in which we can check in with one another, sharing experiences that touch on issues dealt with in the course—or anything one or another of us is moved to put out there. Sometimes a student wants her classmates' praise for a job well done; occasionally she may need support in time of trouble. By devoting twenty minutes or a half-hour at the beginning of a three-hour class period to this type of exchange, we are able to create a safe space, an essential precondition for both learning and teaching—yet a condition that is often overlooked throughout mainstream academia. I believe the creation of safe space is important for several reasons. If students don't feel safe, if they don't feel that they can exercise their own process of analysis and voice opinions without fear of disapproval or reprisal, learning itself is stifled. There must be room for discussion and for disagreement—with the professor as well as with each other. A truly safe space can only be made by everyone involved. Students must know their ideas will be respected. Discriminatory remarks, cynicism, and trivialization are never tolerated in a class of mine.

Further on, my student's paper reflects the impact that safe space can have on an individual's ability to think critically, imaginatively:

> What kept me from stagnating and choking on the academic aspects of feminism and merely "talking the talk" was the atmosphere of acceptance and informality that existed in our classroom. By shying away from the traditional academic models for holding discussions and allowing ourselves to be human before anything else, *a subjective distance between the poetry and ourselves was removed.* I have to admit that many times I looked forward to class because it did not feel restrictive or confining like most classes I have to take. The concept of a "safe space" allowed me to talk about myself and take risks that I would never have taken otherwise....

This atmosphere of acceptance and informality depends on the building of trust among the students themselves and between students and professor. Respect for one another's ideas is paramount. I've learned that it helps to adopt a few other non-traditional discussion techniques: one student may be asked to recognize another after speaking herself, the group may be asked for suggestions if a few students repeatedly take too much time and others remain silent, it may even be useful to invite the course participants to examine and comment on workload and course requirements.

My pedagogy here has important links to the experience of collective effort and criticism/self-criticism practiced in the Cuban and Nicaraguan contexts and to my more recent U.S.-based experience with the power of feminist psychotherapy. When a genuinely safe space for teaching and learning is created, a collective energy is released and the results can be contagious.

I do not believe in altogether eliminating the teacher/student hierarchy. As long as the power relationship based on book knowledge or years of work and life experience exists, as long as most college systems require grading, it would be dishonest to pretend that students and teachers share equal power. In fact, with thought, such hierarchy can be useful. The easy informality of first-name exchange and informal discussion does not obviate the fact that the professor brings to the course a knowledge and experience the student is only beginning to acquire. We must be willing to assume responsibility for our teaching role, be prepared to pass on our memory—collective history, questions, concerns, and partial answers—and to be present to receive their responses, to hear their reactions, and to encourage their aspirations.

I try not to compare students with one another or force them to compete. Competition, often destructive competition, is generally considered "natural" in our society. I prefer to encourage each student to try to fulfill her or his own potential. This is something I learned in Cuba, where *emulation* was socialist practice, as opposed to competition which is such a centerpiece of capitalism. The way it works is that a collective—students, workers, whoever—discusses their common needs. Together they decide upon goals and help each other achieve them. Comradeship and mutual aid replace an atmosphere in which individuals succeed at the expense of their classmates, with the consequent feelings of inadequacy and hopelessness.

Methodology, while important, is not enough. Content is primary. Elemental in assuring respect for a multiplicity of class, racial, and cultural perspectives is the teaching of work by poets who themselves come from diverse classes, races, and cultures; who speak from and of diverse perspectives, who push past the sterile homogenization so often cherished in academia to put forward a more provocative and complex vision of the world. Only by knowing this work are we truly educated in North American literature. It is not simply a matter of studying *the Other.* It is also about *remembering our names,* knowing ourselves.

Students need to know they can fulfill themselves and contribute to society not in spite of but *because* they are women and/or people of color, lesbians or gay men, unique in their abilities and in how they see the world. A professor can help to teach this self-knowledge by unearthing role models, teaching their work, and recognizing them as valuable contributors to our common culture.

My student's paper continues:

> There was definitely a risk involved in telling the class about my background.... Out of fear and anger I decided to come out ... until we reached Sandra Cisneros I did not feel a deep connection to any of the poets.... She provided a missing link for me—what it means to be yourself (*una Esperanza*)[5] and what it means to be yourself within the context of boundaries (of a particular kind of family, the Hispanic culture, the immigrant experience, the perverse class and social structure of the United States, around men)....
>
> [The ways] I have of breaking down the distance between myself and others is writing and drawing. But it was only in this class that I realized that none of my characters or subjects has ever been anyone from a marginalized group. I have always *chosen* [emphasis mine] to play to my audience in putting together characters—so it follows that I sold out on many occasions to what I thought the workshop wanted to read. The most important thing I learned in this course is that I had been doing this without any conscious thought. I had heard of the expression *mind-rape* in Mary Daly's *Gyn/Ecology* but I never thought that it could exist in such a pervasive and dangerous form—in myself.

This woman, just waking to a recognition of the terrible pressures under which a classist and racist society has forced her to live and function, still phrases her conditioning as "choice." I hope that over the years she will understand that she did not *choose* to write only white and middle-class characters into her stories, that the "choice" was made for her, years before her parents began their survival struggle in one of the poor Hispanic ghettos of a major U.S. city.

In order to *get out*, in order to make it into a good college that could promise white-world and ruling-class acceptance, she was forced early to deny herself. From preschool on up, an educational system disrespectful of difference pushed her to conform. But she is on her way now. All it took was one crack in the armor. With the beginning of self-recognition comes relief and a new attitude towards life, a new energy:

> I had to begin to question everything in my life. I felt as though I had been awakened from a stupor of zombifica-tion. Somehow, I had completely forgotten years of my growing up. Conveniently, I had wanted so badly to fit in, that I forgot myself. Now I can actually talk without shame about where I am from without a feeling of being a victim.
>
> ... I have seen evidence this semester that my per-ceptions have changed in my studio arts work. I have seen a difference in the way I perceive the world. My touch with charcoal is bolder, not so contained and shy. I am not obsessed with perfection in shading, and I recognize that being raw is fine sometimes....
>
> It was only when I was able to see myself in another woman in an Advanced Fiction Workshop that I take, that I realized that I had, in fact, really begun to change my views, and to trade shame for self-acceptance. This young woman is Asian, yet she is ashamed that her parents are immigrants. She prefaces every story she writes with a note about how it's not autobiographical. Then she gets upset when the class cannot follow the story because she has not stated that the characters are Asians who believe firmly in the values of home, family, and tradition. It is sad that she has to assume the ethnocentricity and an-drocentricity of her audience. I saw so much of myself in her.

Because of a participatory learning experience, rooted in a course whose content recognizes and respects difference as well as connection, this woman has a new perspective on who she is. And she is able to see, in another student, the same desperate attempt to "white herself out" that, only weeks before, had been her own socially imposed prison.

Paulo Freire[6] and others have taught us about the desirability of students playing an active role in their learning process, and also how important it is that the material studied be approached in the context of the students' lives. These lives are disparate and rich with difference: from the urban ghetto to the Midwestern farm community, from the single-parent mother to the member of an alcoholic or sexually abusive family, from those who early know they are lesbian or gay to those whose fathers insist they be what they were not (or what they are), from the immigrant from anywhere to the native person proud of an identity preserved against historic odds. Connections are essential in a world in which *dis*connection is the fabricated order of the day.

In all my classes I try to provide an alternative to the current fragmentation and condensation of information (or misinformation)—on a psychological as well as political level. Teaching, for me, must question product (the inadequate canon, which excludes and therefore invalidates most of who we are) as well as process (obsolete "educational" structures, in which students are taught to mimic out-of-context and largely useless material rather than seek out information, consider it within its sociopolitical framework, relate it to their lives, and produce their own ideas about what they have discovered).

Some, already molded by twelve years of rote schooling, do not take easily to this approach. I have had a number of students ask me what they are "supposed to think" about an event or idea, or look confused when we disagree and it's clearly okay with me that we do. One student, in the same class with the author of the above-quoted paper, found it literally impossible to do her final on "any poet covered or issue raised in this course." She insisted I assign her a subject; when I did so, she accepted it gratefully, and wrote disconnected pages revealing a brilliant but tightly channeled mind.

II.

Early in 1984 when I came back to this country, I thought a good deal about what kind of work I could do that could meet two goals—earn a living as well as give something back to society—goals which (because of where I had lived for the previous quarter century) weren't easy for me to separate. I had no experience as a teacher, except for sporadic poetry workshops or informal on-the-job training in one or another of many employments. In fact, my educational and work histories themselves were pretty non-traditional.

I had been bored in the stifling fifties, and eager to get out and explore the world, I quit college in the middle of my second year. Thereafter, and in a number of countries, I waitressed, wrote for a bullfight magazine, worked in the office of a feather factory in New York City's garment district, danced flamenco in a Spanish club, was an ill-fated secretary, worked with refugees, developed my skills as a midwife in Mexico City's misery belt, edited a bilingual literary magazine, translated and interpreted, worked with media in Nicaragua's young revolution, and did a great deal of political organizing.

And I always wrote. By the time I came home, I had published more than fifty books—of poetry, essay, oral history—many of them about the lives of the people among whom I'd lived. In the ten years preceding my return, I'd also begun to do photography. But my words and pictures were, unfortunately, not something I could expect to keep me financially solvent. I tried to think of some work which would support me while enabling me to share the truly privileged experience I'd gathered in more than twenty years in Latin America. Teaching immediately came to mind.

College-level teaching seemed appropriate for several reasons. My publications and life experience would, I imagined, provide the equivalency of a degree, thus allowing me to work at the university level, whereas a teaching certificate would be needed to work in primary or high schools. Then, too, I felt a real connection with these young adults: old enough to be aware of social and political issues, yet young enough not to be completely set on the popular course of *don't think, don't make waves, and believe that things will get better* (sad product of the Reagan years).

Once I'd decided that college teaching was what I wanted to do, finding a job wasn't easy. I didn't have the traditional degree, and with most of my adult life spent outside the U.S. job market I also lacked the requisite know-how that comes with years of networking among ex-schoolmates, writing resumes, interviewing. As a woman, as well as someone who had been away long enough so that even a credit card or money machine seemed strange, I certainly didn't have access to the "old boy network" or the sophistication that goes with it. But the women—and some of the men—I knew had developed alternative networks of their own. I am indebted to them for helping me begin one of the most satisfying adventures of my life.

Over the spring and summer of 1984, fresh from the emotional stress of the U.S.-financed and directed *contra* war heating up in Nicaragua and still uncertain as to how smooth my homecoming would be,[7] I had the help of a number of wonderful friends who worked in academia and knew that what I had to offer would be valuable to those I might teach. Tony Oliver, who up to his untimely death headed the University of New Mexico's program of Continuing Education, got me started. My then husband, Floyce Alexander, was supportive and encouraging. I remember especially his helping me write the first resume I ever had, from the vague memory of years when much had been accomplished but little written down. My friend Ann Nihlen, at that time still untenured in UNM's Department of Educational Foundations, took my books to people in positions of influence, helped me make contacts, and linked my skills with possible openings. When the time came, I was not afraid to tell Ann I couldn't remember having seen a college syllabus, much less could I imagine how to write one of my own.

Fortunately, there were others back then who believed in my ability to teach, including members of the UNM search committee who hired me for my first course—Third World Women (a title I didn't invent or entirely agree with). Over the next several years, I was an adjunct professor with the UNM Women's Studies Program, its departments of American Studies and English, and Continuing Education. I taught Latin American and U.S. literature, writing, courses on race, class, and gender, and a course I developed which has become my favorite: Women and Creativity.

I didn't want to teach *about* women's creativity, but to explore —with women students—the ways in which the patriarchy has blocked our creative powers, identify and work through those obstacles, and find ways to free the powers in each of us. (And I don't consider creativity only as it refers to the arts. I believe survival itself requires of women our full creative powers.)

In my experience in academia, I learned what those with a longer involvement already knew. Women, minorities, and artists on campuses across the country fill the adjunct positions which institutions increasingly use to cut their budgets in the areas of faculty security, advancement, and benefits. Faculty positions that are not tenure-track, or that are part-time or occasional, have no job security, do not receive benefit packages, and do not offer any degree of educational continuity. Thus, a school may pay lip service to being an "equal opportunity employer," but numbers rarely tell the real story. We need to ask how many women and/or minority faculty members are tenure-track or have tenure, how many will be there next semester or next year, how many are treated the same as their male counterparts when it comes to time off for scholarship and extra funding. The propensity for hiring *irregulars* in adjunct positions, grossly unfair to the entire educational process, probably provided the leeway that allowed me to work those several years at the University of New Mexico.

I took on as many courses as I could get, usually two and occasionally three a semester. My students liked the way I taught, and I felt increasingly at home in the classroom. Friends who were in the profession were generous with pedagogical advice; and as I slowly lost the fear and sense of intimidation which came from never having graduated from college myself, I was also able to learn, as I have during my entire life, by doing.

In the spring of 1987, I was invited to interview for a visiting professorship in the English department at Trinity College in Hartford, Connecticut. I was hired, and taught there in 1987-88. That led to an ongoing relationship, through which I've returned to Trinity and will do so again. Invitations were forthcoming, as well, from Oberlin and Macalester colleges, and the University of Delaware. I was no longer an adjunct, but neither have I been able to get a permanent contract with any one school. At first it was my immigration case that impeded such an offer. But even though I won the case in 1989, I still have more than a few strikes against me: I am fifty-three years old, a woman, a lesbian, have socialist feminist politics, hold no degree, and—perhaps most significantly—passionately believe in teaching students to engage with the world, develop their own political principles, and explore a variety of life options.

Most teaching doesn't seem to be about that. Or perhaps it would be more accurate to say that teaching that is about that is considered suspect in most U.S. institutions of higher learning, and that the professors who engage in it do so out of enormous courage and at great personal risk.

In these times of serious economic crisis everyone feels impelled to hold on to the security, real or imagined, that comes with adhering to the conventional. For professors, that may mean not questioning a canon although it is both antiquated and biased, or not being willing to participate in redesigning a program that is grossly inadequate. For women and minority professors the pressures to conform are obviously much greater than for white men. For students, faced with parental expectations as well as with a narrowing job market, it may mean just wanting to get through and out without asking too many questions. Some of those students who follow this seemingly painless path, and those who drop out altogether because they cannot take it, will end up on the streets—members of our rapidly growing homeless population. But this fate doesn't bother the fundamentalist proponents of *back-to-basics* education, because they want a more selective process of higher learning, not one that is more democratic.

One of the most frightening aspects of contemporary education in this country is its absolute lack of historical reference. Ancient history, and history that ends a generation or two before the student's lifetime, is taught without questioning the class, race, or gender biases of bourgeois historians. When it comes to a student's own history, what has happened during her or his lifetime, the picture is worse. Popular media reflect textbook error; students of mine show routine ignorance of the rise of European fascism, fifties McCarthyism, the issues involved in our war against Vietnam, the long succession of U.S. government attacks upon countries that dare to become independent of its control, the Civil Rights Movement, the struggle for women's rights, what really happened in the sixties.

If you do not know your history, you lose essential memory. And you cannot know yourself. If you remain ignorant of history, you cannot hope to affect change in society or even in your own life. A part of our tragic inheritance from the Reagan years is this terrible erasure, a manipulation of words, concepts, images—in education, media, even literature—that serves to disconnect us from ourselves. Some of us can fight back with salvaged or retrieved memories. Today's college students were not even teenagers when the Reagan era began. They need conscious educators to help them remember.

III.

I am convinced that our future—and the future of our planet—depends upon citizens who possess memory and history, who understand the intersection of race, class, gender, and other cultural issues in their lives, women and men who know their place historically as well as in their society and community. We need people of our full national range: of differing races, ethnicities, sexual preferences, ages, and degrees of ability, who are proud of who they are. This pride is nurtured, among other ways, when who students are is validated in what they study. Only with a changed curriculum, a less antiquated and restrictive canon, will we be able to share our identities from equal positions of strength and respect.

In a highly technological and fragmented society, where we are confronted in our earliest years by fragments of ourselves (breasts, thighs, lips, teeth, the seductive expression of fear—all used to reaccomodate our sense of body image, sell an automobile, limit our options, and wage unnecessary war), an important part of the educational process must be the retrieval and reassemblage of those pieces. The proverbial mind/body split must be a subject of classroom as well as therapeutic concern. I have found journal writing to be a place where this healing process can take place.

And so I would like to close these notes by focussing on the use of student journals in my particular pedagogy. Years of oral history work, especially with women in Latin America and Vietnam, inform my belief that the personal narrative provides an extraordinary window through which we can retrieve memory, understand process, engage in self-examination, and begin to inhabit that place where feelings and reason may reconnect and be valued.

The following excerpts are from students' journals in different sections of the course, Women and Creativity, as it developed on several campuses. Because of the nature of the course, only women's journals are represented here. I must note, however, that I have used journal writing as a part of literature courses and others—with men as well as women—and sharing them always enriches the learning process.

In my teaching, participants keep a journal in which they comment on assigned readings and the connections they are able to make to issues in their lives. I collect the journals weekly, and three or four times during the semester make up a composite of entries, keeping them anonymous and giving expression to repeated issues from varying and sometimes contradictory points of view. These composites are then given back to the students who read them collectively, using their own words as a basis for discussion.

Not all students immediately grasp the journal assignment, especially in places where their previous training has been traditional. I must emphasize, often repeatedly, that this writing will not be graded, that it may range in length from a few lines to several pages, that I am interested in feelings as well as ideas. I've had the same problem with the concept of a *reaction paper* (four or five pages of a student's reaction to a book; no, not a description, not a formal analysis, but rather, "What did you think and feel when you read it?"). When students become accustomed to the journal, though, they find it to be a liberating process.

In some ways what follows is a replica of the journal session, although I have chosen the excerpts from different groups of students; and with this essay rather than with a classroom experience in mind. As you read this selection of fragments, perhaps it would be useful to imagine that you are sitting in a circle, in a room full of mostly young women of differing backgrounds and needs, joined in their womanness, often as well in their pain, and—more arbitrarily—by the fact that they have elected to take this particular course at this time. We are trying to get to know, and learn to trust, one another.

I have arranged the excerpts in a way I believe will engender useful discussion. Someone in the circle reads the first entry. Perhaps there is silence, perhaps discussion. Time is allowed for both. Then the next student in the circle reads the next piece. The process builds and acquires a presence of its own.

In Women and Creativity, journal writing and the discussion it can provoke prove to be powerful parts of the learning process. I share these entries here because they speak of what can happen when the canon is inclusive, the educational process encourages making connections between books and life, the teacher/student relationship is played out in a context of respect, and a safe space is created.

*　*　*

I am glad that I have mentioned my troubles with speaking and writing. I don't have to pretend that it isn't happening. I hope that now I will be able to move around/ beyond/with/over it. To help with that, I chose to write this instead of typing it. The shapes of my letters are sometimes the only part of myself that I can give to my written work. Each word that I put on this paper is carefully chosen and weighed, sometimes I forget what I wanted the sentence to say. Already my shoulders are tense ...

*　*　*

A block causes many deaths. My major block in any classroom is that I slip away, creativity first. *My* may remain, but the me-ness of me is gone. Even in this journal entry it is desperately trying to escape. *This won't be acceptable, it doesn't make sense, you're wandering way off track, she won't want to read it.* Maybe not, but I will ...

* * *

A fear that I cannot find a cause for: why people say things about me [because] I am so backward that I can't even talk in a class and I can barely write for one and it seems like the only people who understand are the other non-talkers and we're not saying anything. I was in a class last semester where I felt more and more deviant for being quiet. And a problem. I hope that doesn't happen in here. It seems to be something fundamental with me. I can't *just say something.*

* * *

I woke up this morning in physical pain. My body and my thoughts have been arguing this week. I've been trying to convince myself to pick up the old *fat* feelings. Why is weight such a big deal? When I went home people kept saying, "You look so skinny!" I have lost weight since this summer. Now all of a sudden I feel like maybe I can play the game and win. Maybe I can be thinner. Thinner than everyone. It scares me. I'm trying to validate the voice that says, "Honey, don't listen, don't buy into that." So my body this morning was reminding me that I cannot leave her. She is not separate ...

* * *

I felt thrilled and relieved leaving class last week. For the first time in my experience a women's studies class and professor want the personal experiences included in a journal, rather than the usual emphasis on academic critiques of feminist theory ...

* * *

I loved the film "One Fine Day." But I am bothered by the emotion I feel when seeing something like that. It feels like I am opening a can of worms. I see pictures of women who were and are strong, who have faced oppression. I want to own the history of women as if it were mine. I don't want to be cheated. When the Women's Political Caucus had its national convention in Albuquerque a few years ago, they included a film series. One film I saw was about Rosie the Riveter. Seeing it was like finding my mother after thinking myself an orphan.... Feeling powerful because you know (at the moment) that you can change things, that you're part of a *whole* group. It's addictive ... feeling connected.

* * *

An idea occurred to me last week as we were discussing the poetry of Ai and Audre Lorde. Some people in the class liked the fact that some of the poems were obscure, that meanings were not clear and thus open to interpretation. I did not—and do not—and began to wonder why I've never been able to enjoy this type of poem. I realized that I've always been suspicious of double meanings and unclear wording, and traced this back to my earliest memories of being tricked by words: my older brother's promise of "presents" that turned out to be assaults on my body, "rides" that turned out to be traps I could not escape from.... It dawns on me that there is a whole class of experience I have never opened up to—the subtlety of a poem, the abstract images in paintings, and who knows what else! Unexpected meanings hold no joy for me—a sad commentary on the dulling effects of incest.

* * *

I read Tillie Olsen's *Silences* today, and I'm feeling the reverberations. She wrote about *using* a text "in the deep sense that writers use the discoveries of other writers as a step toward their own growth." I am discovering the layers of a story I recently lived. In a sense I am still living it. Let me try to tell it to myself, because soon I will have to explain it to an official committee....

My writing teacher, Dr. ——, begins the critique [of my story] with "WE ALL KNOW THIS COMES FROM J——'s LIFE." He says it is very raw, subjective material. "I don't think J—— quite understands this story. She should write it in the third person, instead of the first person. It would help her understand." Then he goes on to talk about the story in the context that the character is me, even though the character's name is Claudia.

He says, "What did we learn from this story? We learned nothing. What does it say? Nothing."

The hardest story of my life to write, that I'm not necessarily happy with, and Dr.—— tells me it says nothing. I wanted to be mature, I wanted to accept criticism. I want to be a great writer someday, and I *want to work* to get to that point. I knew it had faults, I was super aware of the story's faults. But he was denying me the process to do a raw, subjective, or bad first, second, or third draft. He wasn't being professional, he was pulling a power game with me. You don't personalize fiction in a critique session. He hadn't done that to anyone else the entire three weeks, and everybody was writing personal things, all writers write personal things. He was punishing me in a vicious, destructive way for not smiling and putting up with his attitude towards me. I had threatened him and he was getting back at me.

He tells me I should make the story more "universal" rather than "particular." The following was the opening scene of the story:

> "Now a tongue can't do what a man can do," said my psychology teacher Mr. Sorin when he explained lesbianism to me. He stuck his tongue out of his mouth to demonstrate his point.
>
> It was 11th grade and I felt like I was watching a game show which always made me feel sorry for the contestants, the host, the audience, and myself.
>
> "Now," said Sorin walking up to my desk, "a finger can't do what a man can do." He gave me a knowing look and held up his index finger.
>
> "Two fingers can't do what a man can do."
>
> Sorin saw I was looking confused so he held up two fingers.
>
> I was looking frightened.
>
> "If you think this is difficult material," said Sorin, "just wait till we get to Freud." With that he gave a nod and walked back to the blackboard....

I was under the impression that manipulation through

media images was a fairly universal experience for Americans, especially adolescents. I was under the impression that mandatory heterosexuality for women was a universal female experience (or is "universal female" an oxymoron?) Not being listened to is a universal experience, it's the legacy of growing up female.

This criticism came from a professor who is implementing progressive changes into the English department curriculum. This in a way testifies to his personal vindictiveness towards me, or his absolute hypocrisy, or is it stupidity?

* * *

This is the first class I've taken that has what I would call soft edges, a class that incorporates its subject into the form of the class itself. I feel that the knowledge I acquire and the effort I put into the class will actually help me to grow in my understanding of creativity and lead to a change in my own behavior, specifically in performance and in being closer in touch with my own musical expression ...

* * *

The thing I like best about Adrienne Rich is that she realizes she cannot separate her politics from her poetry. "The moment when a feeling enters the body is political. This touch is political." To me, everything is personal and almost everything is political. Women are continually being denied benefits, opportunities, promotions, and equality, while men advise them not to take it personally ...

* * *

B's journal extract talking about social service as creativity was exciting to me. As an undergraduate, in an honors literature class, I was berated by the elitist teacher for training in social service. She told me that working with "mental defectives" was beneath any intelligent person, that academia was the only world of value. She made it clear that I had no value as a thinker or student unless I would switch my major to literature. Since that course, twelve years ago, I've dreaded all literature courses ...

* * *

At 16 I took my first pottery class. I immediately loved the clay. I felt happier, more whole, than any time in my life. The process made me feel more connected than anything I can remember. I always had a sense of a thousand women before me, kneading and slapping and shaping, making utensils.... My family thought my work bizarre, ugly and awkward. My mother told me that I was just like her—that neither of us had ever had talent. So I put my work away in a box in the closet and got on with good Catholic girls' college prep school. But I thought a lot about that primacy, that sensuality, that connectedness. And I didn't find it in any other activity ...

In college my live-in lover discovered my pots. He was an artist and he loved my work. He saw its earthiness and, their connection to shapes in nature. We displayed the pots around our house and other artists saw them and liked them. Nobody even conceived that I had made them. So I enrolled for a college-level pottery class. He enrolled too. He thought it was cute that I'd take art.... I spent more time in the ceramics lab—met more potters. Pottery started encroaching on home life. He didn't think that was so cute. A metal smith, he had no real affinity for clay. Trained to three-dimensional art, the assignments were easy for him and probably boring. I struggled. The wheel became my tormentor. I had a horrible time learning to center. He told me I didn't have the right eye, or the ability ...

Determined, I went to the lab one morning at six and pulled cylinders for twelve hours straight. Finally I had a pot that I loved. I ran home and pulled him back to the lab from dinner to make him see. He had to admit my pot was better than those he cranked out. He wasn't really happy for me. He didn't think I was so cute anymore. He became scathingly critical of me in every area but ceramics—our competition became more open in every area, our relationship increasingly symbiotic. Because he had years of art training, he had a great technical sense. I'd ask for help in finishing my work clearly—he'd do it for me, or withhold comment, but he'd never give me the constructive criticism or instruction I requested. I took one more course without him. The professors regarded me as his—cute—girlfriend. Some never learned my name. Since, I've taken private lessons from a woman and worked a lot on my own. Every so often I run into him. He's selling tires in Santa Fe and drinking a lot. He doesn't do art at all. I sent him an invitation to the women's show where I exhibited. He didn't come ...

* * *

In a health education class a few days ago, I went through one too many "barrier breaking activities," as they say in certain circles. I remained silent while the rest of the group commented on how swell this latest exercise was. Then I raised my hand and suggested alternatives to these instant intimacy packages. I described an occasion last semester when you had us write of our experiences with the *El Salvador* book,[8] and then read our responses to the class. I felt very close to class members as I listened to what they had written. I felt I knew them better through sharing our responses ... a single evening's exercise, not prepackaged and xeroxed into meaningless questions, that did a lot towards developing class cohesiveness.... No one in the health class responded to what I said. The next person was called on, and he passed out yet another xeroxed copy of a little game for getting to know each other. I think it's just too threatening for a lot of people to reveal themselves, so these little quickie exercises serve as pretenses for risk-taking and listening.

* * *

June Jordan always leaves me frazzled and upset. I have a tendency to keep the really important issues in my life just below the surface. Whenever the "big picture" becomes clearly in focus it is just too overwhelming. Facing what it means to be Black and female in this country is just too scary. But Jordan does not allow for denial.

Despite the bleakness she has a plan of action that I hope to keep in focus and share ...

* * *

The striking thing for me about the last class was the insight that I haven't been able to accept (or even perceive) a cultural or social explanation for my own silences, more striking perhaps because I'm supposed to be an anthropologist, one who explains behavior in terms of culture. Yet I'm not willing or able to see my own behavior in those terms. Instead I take on the weight of the world and blame myself completely for not being able to write. Seems melodramatic.

I'm beginning to see the relationship between my silences and those of other women, but only as a little crack in a big wall through which you can just begin to glimpse disjointed parts of landscape on the other side. Again, the really surprising part is that I haven't allowed myself to make these obvious connections before, as they apply to *me*.

* * *

Until now I have not learned how to be alone with myself when I am involved with someone. I stop creating when I fall in love. As if all my creative energy is offered up as a necessary sacrifice on the altar of "love." And then I am surprised to find myself empty, resentful of the time and energy I spend attending to the needs of my lover ...

In silence, once the waves of fear have passed, a great strength gathers in me. It glows and radiates like a sun of its own, using my body, my spirit as its tools of expression. I have a passion for creating, and I have been terrified of it. When it shines in my eyes it often frightens people, causing them to turn away. And so the choice: create or be loved. I refuse to accept this dichotomy any more ...

* * *

From among hundreds of such entries, received from student groups over a five-year period—and for the purpose of these notes—I have chosen particularly those that point to family or relationship abuse and manipulative "educational" experiences, because these constitute such oppressive obstacles to personal integration and creative freedom, and yet they are usually considered irrelevant to academic life. They illustrate the process through which some of my students—who have surely taught me as much as I have taught them—make the connections that push us all forward.

—Albuquerque, New Mexico
Spring 1990

Notes

1. I would include among them Toni Morrison, Alice Walker, Bernice Regan Johnson, June Jordan, Sonia Sanchez, Audre Lorde, Maya Angelou, Angela Davis, and Paule Marshall.

2. Some historians argue that the term *lesbian* is not applicable to women who did not call themselves that, by virtue of living in a period in which the option, however difficult, was not yet given social voice. I would argue that Emily Dickinson's long romantic attachment to her sister-in-law Susan Gilbert, her clear references to physical sexuality in the poems to Gilbert as well as in letters to other women—including Kate Scott Anthon—and her numerous written rejections of the Christian, i.e., dutiful and heterosexual, lifestyle, amply justify the characterization. Dickinson's lifelong commitment to women, the obvious pain she endured because her sexual choice was impossible given her time, class, psychological make-up, and culture, and a close reading of her poetry, all help to establish this reality. See *My Life A Loaded Gun, Female Creativity and Feminist Poetics*, Paul Bennett (Boston: Beacon Press, 1986).

3. This is the student's language, which also reflects common contemporary usage, especially as regards homosexual identification. I prefer *fully identified*.

4. Incorporating a female vision, work by and about women as well as from a women's perspective, into all disciplines in the existing curriculum.

5. Esperanza, a female name which translates as Hope, is that of the protagonist of Cisneros's *The House on Mango Street* (Houston, TX: Arte Público Press, 1988).

6. Brazilian Paulo Freire evolved a theory for the education of adult illiterates which is based on the conviction that all people are capable of looking critically at their world in a dialogical encounter with others, and that given the tools for such an encounter they can perceive their personal and social reality and deal critically with it. His most influential book on the subject of participatory education is *Pedagogy of the Oppressed* (New York: Continuum, 1989).

7. I didn't yet know that the U.S. Immigration and Naturalization Service would attempt to bar me from my homeland because of what they considered the subversive nature of my writings. As this became apparent, with the deportation order of October 1985, and my immigration case was a reality in my life, my teaching career as well as much else was immensely complicated.

8. *El Salvador* is a work of thirty photographers, text by Carolyn Forche, edited by Harry Mattison, Susan Meiselas, Fae Rubenstein (New York: Writers and Readers Publishing Cooperative, 1983).

Art as Information
Some Sixties/Eighties Parallels

Contemporary interest in the sixties comes not simply from our periodic fascination with anniversaries—two decades, a quarter century, thirty years—but responds to deeper parallel connections. Now, as then, we are clawing our way out of the strictures imposed by a period of repressive conservatism, dangerous conformity, and censorship with its offshoot, self-censorship. Now, as then, socially conscious artists respond with our work, passionately committing our creativity to change. Now, as *opposed* to then, electronic advances have given those in power the use of much more complex weapons against us.

Back when *IKON*'s first series was a clarion voice among the little magazines, independent publishing ventures, café readings, exhibits, performances and happenings of all kinds that together defined the sixties renaissance, the long death chill of McCarthyism had just begun to thaw. Great artists had been silenced by the anti-communist witch hunt, many of them permanently. Others were changed forever, after years of not being able to find work, publish, or speak. The consequences for our national intellect and creativity will probably never be thoroughly understood.

When things "get better," most of us tend to breathe a sigh of relief and happily retreat from dissecting events or the forces that shape them. How often has the U.S. electorate massively voted for those whose only solutions are a string of utterly empty promises? *Don't worry...things will get better. Just have faith,* campaigning politicians urge. *It isn't in our nature,* our profusion of dime-store psychologists tell us, to dwell on how things went wrong or on how to make sure they won't go wrong again or—more important—on the crippling effects such deformations may project into a future tense. The notion that such analysis doesn't come naturally to North Americans is most certainly produced and nurtured more intensely by our media images than by any rational look at our experience or by an assessment of our most profound feelings.

161

The McCarthy-era chill of the fifties didn't lift of its own accord; the energies unleashed by artists who dared to raise their voices created a dialectic that itself produced the *new* avant garde, one that vowed, once again, it would not be silenced. As is true with every struggle to throw off the forces of repression, those who demanded voice and space, those who insisted upon making themselves heard, brought many others into the dissident arena. These pioneers were the men and women for whom the witch hunters reserve such epithets as blatant, vulgar, strident, obscene, belligerent, angry, or just plain willful. These artists, in turn, provided context and courage for those to come.

Raw questions also surfaced in our art back then. Were they really any different from those which artists have always asked? In the larger sense, perhaps not. The major issues continue to be integrity, community, love, fear, death, contradiction, sorrow, antagonism, fulfillment. It's the composition of society, and how we perceive our relationship to it, that changes from generation to generation. The movement from fifties to sixties brought with it, among much else, a more open, cruder discussion of the contradictions between societal norms and human need. This new honesty, this willingness to lay bare our innermost landscapes—ugliness, abuse, need, shame, pain, revolt—became a central theme in our art. ("Airing dirty laundry in public ... Making things up ... Lying ..." our male-defined elders would say, when much later this search led some of us to write about battery, rape, incest, Satanic ritual abuse: the previously protected terrains of a patriarchal society.)

Neither did the sixties themselves happen in a vacuum. Remember that Ginsberg had to battle for the right to publish *Howl* as early as 1956, a precursor to similar struggles which would later be fought over such classics as D. H. Lawrence's *Lady Chatterly's Lover*, Henry Miller's *Tropic of Cancer*, and William Burroughs's *Naked Lunch*. (These, of course, are all books by men. Women's creativity and thought were still overwhelmingly absent from the literary canon and only the most "male" of them were on the best-seller lists. Black writers were only tokenly present. Gay and lesbian culture was still camouflaged or underground.

The late fifties produced those courageous women and men who would foreshadow the explosive decade: Beat and Black Mountain poets, The Living Theater, Action Painting, the Happenings and early performance pieces, Merce Cunningham—the list is long and an artist's position as forerunner or disciple may, in retrospect, be a matter of opinion. But by the early sixties individual talents had once again coalesced into movements. The little magazines were their most authentic and enthusiastic showcases.

In New York City, from February 1967 through the same month in 1969, a magazine appeared which was both within the context of the sixties literary renaissance and quite different from the other *littles*. This was the first run of *IKON*. In its first issue it described itself as "a magazine of information about works of art (literary, performing, visual) and about the process and problems concerned with art by those involved in that process." It shunned what its editor, Susan Sherman, called the "professional critic, the professional middleman, the professional observer. There is no longer a place for the uninvolved," she proclaimed.

IKON's seven sixties issues were true to that initial promise, becoming a forum for the most exciting and far-reaching *politically conscious art*, regardless of the medium. On its every page it declared that meaningful art and a consciousness of the world we live in are inseparable. And the magazine grew beyond its physical form. In late 1967 through 1969 there was also the *IKON* Store, a storefront next to La Mama on 4th Street between Second and Third Avenues.

Susan talks about that space where alternative books and magazines were sold, where they had a community mimeograph machine, where one of the first block associations in the city got its start, and where events and meetings of all kinds were frequent. The first meeting of Radical Lesbians took place there. In 1968, when the Weathermen split off from SDS, hundreds of people responded to a one-inch ad in the *Village Voice* and came to hear four of the "Weatherpeople"; there was an overflow crowd and Susan prevailed upon one of the speakers to hold a street-corner rally for those who couldn't get inside. At a benefit for the local Black Panther Party, two FBI agents were obvious—drinking their beer and eating potato chips, Susan says—among the 120 or so people who filled the locale. Much later, when the Freedom of Information Act (FOIA) allowed Susan to read her file, she realized how much of what those informers wrote they had fantasized or just invented for their pitiful weekly paycheck.

In the art of those times, a recognition of "the American" was essential. In painting, in music, in theater, and especially in literature we no longer looked to Europe. Europe, in fact, started looking to us. And so our eurocentric vision began, ever so slightly, to crack. In New York City, institutions like The Artists Club were born in an old industrial loft; where painters, sculptors, writers, musicians, and even critics came together to share ideas and concerns outside the confines of the establishment. A few blocks along East 10th Street, from Fourth Avenue over to Second or First, housed alternative galleries, some of which were artists' cooperatives.

The first Cedar Bar, on University Avenue near the corner of Eighth Street, was the scene of less formal discussion: Willem and Elaine de Kooning, Franz Kline, Milton Resnick, Pat Passlof, Robert and Mary Frank, Larry Rivers, John Cage, Alice Neel, and others held forth. Ornette Coleman's white plastic sax made sweet music at the Five Spot, Odetta sang at the Village Gate, and slightly further north and west, Julian Beck's and Judith Malina's Living Theater was a constant source of energy and inspiration.

I had come to the mecca of the art world from the provinces (Albuquerque, New Mexico) in 1957. So I knew that outside of New York City, artists' communities were also generating important work. Such work had a proud history where I lived, ever since the twenties when the Atchison Topeka and Santa Fe Railroad opened the southwest to people like D.H. Lawrence, Mabel Dodge Lujan, and Georgia O'Keeffe. And it was happening in California, Illinois, Minnesota, Georgia, and many other places—as yet unconnected with the metropolis. But the San Francisco and New York renaissances were surely the most visible and vocal. The Beat road map connected both coasts, and poets went "on the road," reading to one another, high on the mind-expanding (and in retrospect fairly harmless) artists' drugs of the decade.

Some of us dared define *America* more broadly: as including what we perceived as a culture of *Latin America*, and—although unevenly—of our own multiracial history. Some of us explored the roots of Latin American, African, and Asian artistic expression and developed working relationships with those continents' contemporary artists. After four essential years in Manhattan, in 1961 I would travel south to Mexico. There, with a Mexican poet named Sergio Mondragon, and immersed in a multinational group of young writers and artists, I founded *El corno emplumado / The Plumed Horn*, a bilingual literary journal that for the next eight years would bridge cultures and mark a decade. My contact with the first *IKON* and its visionary editor Susan Sherman dates from this period.

But I'm still talking about New York City, late fifties and early sixties. In 1959, Fidel Castro and a ragged group of bearded rebels had taken power on the island of Cuba. Some artists, as their predecessors in the thirties had done, broke from the peculiarly U.S. constraints that proclaimed art as "pure" or "beyond politics," divorced from social concerns. They visited or even lived in Cuba. (After her death in 1986, the Cuban period in the work of the great people's artist Rini Templeton has come to light.) In New York and in response to the 1961 U.S.-backed Bay of Pigs invasion of that country, African-American poet Amiri Baraka (then LeRoi Jones), Elaine de Kooning, Marc Schleifer, and myself authored a protest signed by hundreds of artists and writers.

We would need yet a greater historic distance from the civil rights movement, as well as from the Black, Hispanic, Native American, women's, and gay and lesbian movements that reemerged or would surface in the late sixties, in order for us to recognize cultural contributions defined not simply by our "generosity" but by these peoples themselves. In this sense, I knew then about the artists who had come from the east and became known as the Taos School (Lawrence, Lujan, O'Keeffe, and others), but wouldn't have thought to explore the work of New Mexico's San Ildefonso potter, María Martínez, or the makers of the storyteller dolls that were first sculpted by Pueblo Indian artists in the sixties. Just as there was more than a single culture in Latin America, Black and Hispanic cultures in our own country were never what a mostly liberal white male art world assumed them to be.

From fifties to sixties, art in its various contexts (as well as peoples' perceptions of traditional academic canon—history, literature, art, the social sciences) changed radically. In the transition from eighties to nineties we can see a similar shift, but now we also have our sixties history to help us understand current trends. The book-banning atmosphere of the fifties gradually ceded to the sixties renaissance, just as the tendency to retreat or pull back that was forced upon artists in the eighties gives way to the exuberance which today seems just around the corner. (Witness radical multi-media art itself, such as that made by Guerrilla Girls or Tim Rollins + K.O.S. Witness artists', writers', and musicians' enormous efforts to support the struggles of victims of colonialism and imperialism in other lands, as well as our own farmers, homeless people, and those with AIDS.)

Struggles to distort our cultural history (by some) and retrieve it (by others) follow a similar curve. Against the Allan Blooms and Saul Bellows of this world, we accumulate and unleash a fountain of energies that won't be stilled. Bloom's fundamentalist crusade for a return to "the basics" and against all indigenous faces of our culture is well-known. In the case of Bellow, I am referring to the Nobel Prize winner's derogatory statement in the context of the efforts to diversify curriculum at Stanford University, that "he did not know 'the Tolstoy of the Zulus; the Proust of the Papuanes.' "[1]

Poetry, fiction, and artwork that brought form and content into a single focus was at the cutting edge of that creativity expressed on the pages of the independent sixties press. Time and space also joined forces in new ways, or at least we were more conscious of how they affected one another. This could be seen in the pages of *IKON*'s first series, where the layout of each contribution creatively balanced meaning with visual impact. In what might seem to be a very different genre, it was also apparent in the varieties of ephemeral art that emerged throughout this period: a renewed interest in the found poem, body-painting created and washed away in a night, a new type of audience participation in experimental theater, Happenings with a single evening's life span, the role assigned to chance in performance pieces, "pop," and other expressions among the visual arts.

This sixties art was rooted in experience, in the present. The beginning of the decade was marked indelibly by the civil rights movement in the south. That extraordinary struggle by Blacks and whites affected American culture throughout the country. By midway through the decade, intense student protest ignited hundreds of campuses. And by the late sixties Vietnam provided the disturbing images on the evening news. Malcolm X, Martin Luther King, Jr., My Lai, Selma, the four Sunday school students in Birmingham: these were encoded into our national memory. The art rooted in these images, in these events, spurned preciosity and armchair observation—the experience itself was the thing.

Sixties art stood in defiance against the withering formulae of timid predecessors, as it began as well to search out and use the legacy of previously ignored forebears. In the following decade we would unearth our lost and unsung female visionaries (some of our strongest women poets began to retrieve these women's voices in their work). We would begin to read gay and lesbian voices *as such,* and artists who began to write or publish past midlife, battled disability, or dealt with other politically risky conditions. Later, with the advent of the AIDS epidemic, we would embrace a culture of life born in close proximity with death.

In that first run, *IKON* crossed several bridges; the men and women published in its pages explored magic, language, the latest psychoanalytic theories, and places like Cuba where a new society encouraged and supported its *cultural workers.* This concept of the artist as *cultural worker,* like the concept of the New Man, came from the experience of our Cuban brothers and sisters. Participating in a different social system, we nevertheless longed to be able to apply such ideas to our lives and art. In Mexico to a certain extent, and then in a much more comprehensive way in Cuba and Nicaragua where I lived from 1969 to 1984, I was able to know and work with artists whose relationship with the State was necessarily more urgent, more practical, and allowed for farther-ranging possibilities.

But it was never easy to sustain an independent bridge between writers and readers. I remember an incident in the mid-sixties around the publication of *El corno emplumado*. The Pan American Union, cultural arm of the Organization of American States in Washington, had bought 500 subscriptions to our magazine. For a struggling literary journal this meant economic security for at least another issue, then when we published an exchange of letters with a well known Cuban poet, an emissary from the Union traveled to Mexico to let us know that unless we stopped giving space to Cuban poets, those subscriptions wouldn't be renewed. By that time we were preparing our issue featuring an anthology of the new Cuban work. Of course we told our "benefactor" what he could do with his subscriptions.

Throughout the sixties, in *IKON* as in most of our other artistic forums, those published were overwhelmingly men. In looking at *IKON*'s first series, with an eye to selecting the pieces for this anthology, Susan and I remember how heavily weighted on the male side its contents were. The same is true of *El corno emplumado*, and the vast majority of other little magazines of those years. Even so, the fact that we were women undoubtedly, though still unconsciously, opened us more than other editors to our sisters' work.

We weren't yet feminists, but like the pre-"chill" people's artists of the thirties, the sixties intellectuals and artists saw ourselves as social beings. We were concerned with assuming social responsibility. This was something we talked about a great deal: the ivory-tower isolationism encouraged by the threatening fifties was giving way once more to a sense of community, and to the activism community engenders. As artists back then, we asked ourselves what our responsibility might be, to whom we owed it, and what kind of art it would produce.

This led to polemics, projects, and important artistic statements subscribed to by a variety of artists who might otherwise not have crossed formal or esthetic lines. The Angry Arts was a New York based movement of protest against the Vietnam War which involved writers, painters, musicians, theater people, and others. By 1969 and 1970, there were numerous collective readings by poets and writers outraged by the war. These took place in cafés and parks, and also in such academic forums as the Modern Languages Association's annual meeting.

Later, it would be a young Chinese-American architect, Maya Ying Lin, who would design the extraordinary Vietnam Veterans War Memorial in Washington, D.C. Much more recently, in Montgomery, Alabama, she built a memorial to the civil rights struggle. The Vietnam experience and the struggle for desegregation in the south (which, as Lin points out "[happened] simultaneously ... you never realize that overlay") profoundly affected a generation and its artists.

The freedom schools of the civil rights movement (Mississippi, 1964) inspired the concept of *free school* that began to challenge a stifling academy. *Free schools* and *free universities* sprang up everywhere. Poets and writers went out into the community; prison workshops and the Poets in the Schools programs were born. Lines from contemporary poetry and images from contemporary art began to appear on subway and bus placards, in architectural projects, and in parks.

Some visual artists looked to the great Mexican mural movement —or our own WPA (Works Project Administration, one of the U.S. government efforts to provide work during the depression years)—and the first neighborhood murals were painted, increasingly with the participation of people in the communities they served. When creative women finally came to the fore, monumental endeavors like Judy Chicago's Dinner Party pushed feminist art to a retrieval of our history. Later, Chicago's Birth Project would link the power of a visionary artist with that long-obscured women's art which had forever been regarded as craft: quilting, weaving, embroidery, fine needlepoint. A public discussion of process would be a part of this.

Sixties art literally wrote itself onto our bodies and our walls. The anonymous artist claimed his or her space. A more active class struggle, the powerful fight against racism, and the new feminist consciousness brought into clearer focus our rejection of the self image and falsely created needs projected by the establishment media. The results of this focus could be seen in such seemingly disparate manifestations of popular art as New York City's graffiti covered subway cars or the emphatically altered billboards that began to spring up everywhere: key words paired with blatant female seduction images ever so slightly changed, the addition of one more word to stop signs, producing "STOP WAR" and "STOP RAPE" on street corners across the country.

One of the exciting things about peoples' art in the sixties was that it revived attention to process. The Beat and Black Mountain poets moved out from Williams, not Eliot. Some went further, their new voices echoing Brecht, Reich, Artaud, Vallejo, Kollontai. Poets hitting the road

to share their work in lofts and cafés, the Happenings, the first performance pieces: increasingly the artist's process itself became his/her
product.

Later, with feminism and the explosion of women's art, this
exaltation of process became much more political. As women, process
had always been at the center of our unacknowledged experience. But
our process was shunned as meaningless, and in the bargain we were
denied its product. Strong feminist voices like Toni Morrison, Adrienne
Rich, Joy Harjo, Leslie Marmon Silko, Sonia Sanchez, Sandra Cisneros
and scores of others; women's music such as that made by Sweet Honey
in the Rock; powerful women's theater like At the Foot of the Mountain;
extraordinary women in the visual arts; all are pushing outward the
confines of the traditional canon.

Along with Black and Hispanic Studies, Women's Studies (and
much more recently and incipiently Gay and Lesbian Studies) fought its
way onto the country's campuses. Feminist magazines, presses, gallery
spaces, dance companies and theater began producing work that could
not be ignored (although many of the good ole boys continue to try).
Essayists like June Jordan, Alice Walker, Mab Segrest, Judy Grahn, and
Paula Gunn Allen bring female experience and the larger political picture
together in ways men have not. Women's and lesbian archives begin the
serious work of retracing and refocusing obscured history. The Lesbian
Herstory Archives in New York is particularly noteworthy. Women's and
lesbian oral history projects like Elizabeth Kennedy's and Madelaine
Davies's in Buffalo, unearth exciting stories—*herstories* in the new
vernacular. Scientists like Ruth Hubbard question not only women's role
in science, but—consequently—the nature of scientific work itself, and
thus what knowledge is. Feminism has changed the course of the work
of all these artists and scholars.

For movement women and artists, who in the early seventies
began taking over the independent publishing ventures and art spaces
our hard work had helped to create, process was not something to be
discarded, or so easily ignored. Our cultural institutions, which after
almost two decades have their own cultural identity and history of
struggle, stress attention to process as intrinsic to the product we wish
to nurture and preserve. *IKON*'s second series includes a number of
special issues: Women and the Computer, Creativity and Change, and the
Asian-American women's issue, in which this is particularly apparent.

IKON #9, "Without Ceremony," (an Asian-American women's
anthology) is worth noting, among much else, because of its several

community collages: conversations among different generations of working class Asian-American women discussing their struggle to balance tradition and rebellion in their lives. This is one more example of the emphasis on process. *IKON*'s first book, *We Stand Our Ground* (which combines the poetry of Kimiko Hahn, Gayle Jackson, and Susan Sherman), devotes its first twenty pages to a conversation among the poets. Here a Japanese/German/American heterosexual woman, an African-American lesbian, and a Jewish lesbian tell each other and their readers how family and society have influenced them, what it has meant to them to be women, engage politically, create, resist, write.

Entering the nineties, we gather and unleash our creative powers in the wake of another repressive period. Eight years of Reaganism in this country achieved epidemic homelessness, increased economic crisis even for the middle and upper-middle classes, cutbacks in social services and cultural programs, the reversal of many hard-won people's rights, a backlash of conservatism, a rigidity, false patriotism, and mediocrity in the arts with real parallels to the fifties. The media, technologically advanced as never before, succeeds in helping the elite to trivialize what is meaningful, to magnify trivialities, to rewrite history and even proclaim its demise. Fundamentalism, political as well as religious, has become the new ruling-class ideology.

But even as officialdom announces the death of unions and the consolidation of the electronic revolution, the final victory of capitalism, the end of history itself, the extraordinary power of people's culture resurfaces through inevitable fissures. Feminism continues to change all of society, not just women's lives. Labor struggles are revitalized. A woman, Geraldine Ferraro, runs for vice-president. Before she loses, and despite her class and skin privilege, she manages to address some real issues with intelligence. An African American, Jesse Jackson, runs for president and is visibly forced from center stage, but his new type of campaign suggests a renewal of truly participatory possibilities for electoral politics in the United States.

Some of the young artists of the sixties have earned a degree of power in the eighties and nineties. This, along with the general public's incipient resentment of endless media hype, may account for the fact that today, even among such a costly genre as commercial film, we can find outstanding examples of revolutionary art. Some titles that come to mind are "Pow Wow Highway," "Torch Song Trilogy," "The Milagro Beanfield War," "Born on the Fourth of July," "Do the Right Thing," and "Roger and Me."

Internationally, as the United States becomes the largest debtor nation—rapidly being bought out by Japan—a number of the governments in eastern Europe have been transformed, most of them in bloodless revolutions. The Bush administration welcomes these new governments into the "arms of democracy," indeed takes credit for much of the change. Most Americans' understanding of the Berlin Wall phenomenon, however, misses several key points. For one, no matter how inoperative or corrupt these regimes were, their own socialist histories produced criticism and change to a degree unimaginable in the United States. More important, Gorbachev in the Soviet Union has pushed for an opening on all fronts which has unleashed the power of critical thought, viable dissent from within, and basic human growth.

The week Rumania exploded, TV viewers were shocked by hideous television footage: unforgettable images of mountains of dead bodies. Seventy thousand murdered was one statistic repeatedly given. *Genocide* was the word used to describe what Ceaucescu's dynasty had wrought. When, before the dictator was summarily executed, it was suggested that the Soviet Union and/or Warsaw Pact countries lend military assistance to the Rumanian rebels, Gorbachev was eloquent in his response: "In 1968 we went into Czechoslovakia," he said, "and only last week we had to apologize. The era of large nations invading small nations is a thing of the past."

Even as Gorbachev spoke, Bush continued to focus on Cuba as the hemisphere's all-time villain and wage warfare of varying intensities against the peoples of Nicaragua and El Salvador, to name only three nations close to our borders. Then Bush and his Marines invaded Panama. Polls show eighty percent of the people in this country approved, or at least accepted the invasion as necessary. With the histories of our invasion of Grenada and our assault upon Libya, the media found it easier than ever to sell the U.S. public on this travesty of international relations.[2]

And here is where our creative use of image responds to and intersects with the system's media manipulation of those scenes which have literally become our lives.

The U.S. government has created a "drug war" in which anything goes. The plague of coke and crack in our neighborhoods, which began to be infested years ago when the CIA operated its Air America opium and heroin runs out of Southeast Asia, makes all *apparent* efforts to curtail this death seem welcome. Panama's deposed President Manuel Noriega, who got on the U.S. blacklist when he refused to continue cooperating with our CIA, was a made-to-order target. Here, image distortion has been particularly grotesque, even going so far as to confuse cocaine with corn *tamales*.[3] Noriega has been successfully vilified to the extent that most will agree: in the invasion of Panama *the end justified the means.* Even the more critical reportage makes no difference, that which details the U.S. role in creating Noriega in the first place. We can see it all, yet accept it all. Such is the power of today's media.

As I write I am thinking of the recent and startling revelations with regard to the media coverage of events in eastern Europe. Those seekers of democracy who assaulted and conquered the old order now freely admit key images were faked. In Rumania, bodies from hospital morgues were heaped and strewn in the streets to create those scenes of mass murder and justify the use of the word *genocide.* The reported "70,000 dead" in one city were in truth 200.[4] This disinformation was necessary, they—and even some among us—insist, to incite the people to maintain their insurrection against Ceaucescu's secret police. There too, *the end justified the means.*

In Czechoslovakia, a "student death," reportedly the result of police brutality against a peaceful demonstration, was staged to similar effect. The "student" even received a name, a family, people mourned him with lighted candles. But we now know there was no such student. Again, faked media images helped to bring down a government; the idea that *the end justifies the means* has become such an accepted part of our culture that this type of rigged coverage no longer even elicits protest.

Some of us are shocked. How can such things happen, we may ask. Sadly, we need not only understand how they happen, but that our own establishment media, our "free" press, is the master of such manipulation. The idea that an end can justify the means is, indeed, a basic tenet of a product-oriented society. The facile image, the idea sold subliminally with subterfuge and glitz, the product—always the newer, better product—takes precedence over process, which is ignored, if not totally erased. "News" gives information and disinformation. Art also, and essentially informs and disinforms. The old discussions which antagonistically positioned social realism and so-called *pure* art are no longer on our agenda. But artists and writers who are affected and moved by the central issues of our age, create from a consciousness of how imagery is manipulated as well as out of an energy aimed at change. We need our collective memory so we may know and give of ourselves. Art makes new leaps from and into life.

IKON, on the cutting edge in the sixties, reappeared in the eighties with a second series as essential to the creative avant garde. As feminist and lesbian culture challenged assumptions of all kinds, the magazine reemerged as a feminist literary journal, a forum for women's work. Written in large letters across the first cover of the magazine's second era: "We can and must create a new world with new forms, techniques and ideas."

And, just as in its first incarnation, *IKON* often baffled the purely literary and the narrowly radical by refusing limiting definitions, this time it again moved beyond confining paradigms. Not just gender, but race, ethnicity, class. Not only women, but sometimes men as well—for example in the powerful Art Against Apartheid issue.

In going back and retrieving some of the most exciting work from its sixties pages, this issue of *IKON* does more than honor a period of tremendous artistic power. It recognizes certain sociopolitical parallels. It reminds us, as creative beings, to think about the importance of raising our authentic and multiple cultures against the death-dealing chill of a Jesse Helms, an Ollie North. It urges us to step up the fight against the murderous corruption of our words, our images, and our lives.

—Hartford, Connecticut
Winter 1990

Notes

1. *New York Times*, January 19, 1988.
2. This essay was written before the U.S. buildup and aggression in the Persian Gulf. If unclear before, it is now abundantly so, that Bush has proclaimed himself the world's strongman to a previously unimaginable degree, and no longer pays even lip service to international law or norms of coexistence.
3. Photographs of the "cocaine" that Noriega was accused of possessing in his home were published in the mainstream media. Later, the cocaine was discovered to be *masa harina*, a pale-colored corn flour used to make *tamales*.
4. The major European newspapers featured stories about this hoax, although it remained almost unpublished in the United States. One January 27, 1990 article in *Le Monde* of Paris was titled "Le charnier de Timisoara n'en etait pas un" (No Such Mountain of Corpses). This is a translation of the article: "The images of mutilated corpses shown after the Timisoara massacre on television throughout the world are the result of a montage fabricated in order to incriminate Ceaucescu's Secret Police, according to

three doctors of that city who spoke on the private TV channel RTL-Plus. The doctors said 'revolutionaries' took the bodies of people who died of natural causes from the Institute of Legal Medicine and from the local hospital. They presented the corpses before TV cameras as victims of the Security Force. A woman shown with the body of a child on top of her—an image that was particularly dramatic—was in fact a woman who died of alcoholism. The doctors said the child was not related to her in any way. As far as the scars on some of the bodies are concerned, these were not provoked by torture as claimed, but by the marks of the autopsies which had been performed on the bodies."

Something About
My Pictures

1. Origins

In 1978 I was working as a journalist for a Cuban cultural magazine. Frequently they'd send me out to explore the history of a colonial village, or to cover an outdoor *peña*. Sometimes the photographer they assigned to go with me followed my mind's eye with his camera. More often, though, his (or occasionally her) camera had its own eye. Because I've always felt acutely respectful of other artists' creative process, it wasn't easy—in fact, it would have been impossible—for me to say, "Look, that's not it ... this is what I'm looking for."

I needed to learn to do my own photography. Although having to bear with another artist who was so often missing my point seemed to be the catalyst, I think my entering the world of visual images at the age of forty-two had its deeper roots in a problem of language. I'm a poet, and during the Cuban years I was writing in English while surrounded by people—colleagues, a readily available audience, even my own children—who spoke Spanish. Of course there was always translation, and a few of my poems were translated by some very fine Spanish-language poets. By that time I also wrote a great deal of prose in my acquired tongue. But poetry was my purest and most expressive art form, and language still posed a barrier to my direct, undiluted communication with the people I cared to reach. I'm sure I turned to pictures at least to some extent in order to bridge this distance.

On a 1978 reading and lecture tour of the United States, I bought a basic Pentax 35mm camera with a standard 50mm lens. My learning route involved helping to convert an unused bathroom cluttered with discarded junk into a working darkroom to be shared with a good friend. His name is Grandal, and he is one of Cuba's finest photographers.

Those of you who have never thought about what a quarter century of economic blockade can do to a small country, might try to imagine a land where food, health care, education, housing, and recreation are all equitably distributed, but where much else is necessarily hard to come by. I'm not implying that the art of photography was a luxury, to the Cubans or any of the rest of us living in Cuba at that time; only that there was a necessary hierarchy of priorities, and we all had to struggle to make our pictures.

We begged left-over film from tourists, answered friends who asked "What can I bring you?" not with the standard request for deodorant or blue jeans but with pleas for photographic paper. We learned how to make our chemicals from scratch. Sometimes what we could get didn't turn out to be enough. Often I'd go out to shoot with an empty camera, having to imagine my successes and failures. A 35mm lens was already becoming my favorite. We were lucky to be able to condition our darkroom at the ninth-floor apartment where I lived, and to have a bed sheet large enough to blot out fading city lights, because the door to our tiny laboratory never really shut completely.

I was a passionately involved student and Grandal was a wonderful teacher. It was apprenticeship in the old-fashioned sense: long hours of silent observation on my part, and, on my mentor's part, an almost total imposition of his way of doing things. My first serious projects were an abandoned shipwreck off the Matanzas coast, the popular photographers who worked with box cameras in the city parks, and the *fotingos* (a word which, in spite of its phonetics, has nothing to do with photography but refers to the 1959-vintage automobiles that ingenuity still had running on Havana streets). Dolls became of interest to me, then doorways. One of the few Cuban pictures that still moves me is a little girl with a pile of plastic shoes playing by the stairwell of a seaside housing project. When I began making pictures in the old Colón Cemetery, I knew I was involved with a subject that would stay with me for years.

It's not easy for photographers in this country to imagine the way we worked. The amber bottle story may give you some idea. When we mixed our chemicals, there were no plastic gallon containers available at a nearby photo supply shop; a single one-gallon jug made of amber glass shared by four photographers was our only possibility for storing light-sensitive developer. There were warnings and even threats about what would happen if one of us broke that jar. Where would we find another? Needless to say, I was the one with the bad luck; rinsing it out one night against a cement wash sink, it slipped against the crude tub and cracked. That was the night I understood that for all his harsh blustering Grandal really cared a great deal for me. He kept his anguish to himself. But our photography virtually stopped until we could talk a neighborhood pharmacist into relinquishing a replacement.

My photography might have benefited from a much longer stay at Grandal's side; I certainly felt I needed more time with the basics. But maybe not. In this kind of a story things generally happen when the time is right.

2. Oral History

Four months after I developed my first roll of film, I was off to Nicaragua to do a book on women in the Sandinista revolution. Interviewing women, listening to and recording their stories, had been a deep involvement of mine for close to a decade. It was logical that I should want to hear what my Nicaraguan sisters had to say, months after the end of their long people's war. Grandal was encouraging: "Shoot a lot," he said, "and send me all your film. I'll develop it for you and send you the contact sheets so you can see what you're doing wrong." Grandal meant well, but it wasn't an arrangement that appealed to me.

For three months in Nicaragua I borrowed darkroom space from five to seven each morning. There I developed my previous day's work, hanging the negative strips up to dry and returning late each night to print contact sheets and see how I was doing. The power of the Nicaraguan experience pushed me to bring my meager skills to an acceptable level. I lost some important shots, of course, but I learned a lot. I still print from those very early Nicaraguan negatives, and I often wish they were technically better. But I also know that doing it Grandal's way would not have pushed me to acquire the skills I needed, or to achieve the images I got.

It was in Nicaragua that I learned how to engage with a woman whose cultural relationship to both tape recorder and camera was often very different from my own. It was there that I learned to listen and see almost simultaneously. I had been recording people's stories for years, but someone else had always done the photography that went with those stories. Now I had to be able to probe a life while making sure I had images as well as tapes. It was in the process of writing *Sandino's Daughters* that I began allowing the way I'd edit a transcript to affect my images, and the way a series of images came up through the developer to influence the way I'd edit a voice. I was beginning to make what in my work would be important connections between the image and the word.

3. Making the Work More Useful

Over the years, especially working with other women, I've enjoyed watching my photographic images travel and grow and change. When North American artists Miranda Bergman and Marilyn Lindstrom came to Nicaragua to paint a mural on the Managua children's library, they were careful to consult with Nicaraguans on the final design. The Nicaraguans wanted the children in the mural to look like Nicaraguan children. I was able to provide dozens of throw-away prints for use in suggesting particular features from Matagalpa to the Atlantic Coast. Back in this country, as well, some of my images have made their way into Jane Norling's and Miranda Bergman's San Francisco Balmy Alley murals: my large, exuberant market vendor became a woman learning to write; one of my mothers holding a tiny picture of her murdered son now lives as well on that wall.

I'm always happy when one of my images becomes a poster for solidarity work or claims some other use in our collective struggle to counter the mass-media propaganda that would forever distort the faces and gestures of those we are taught to fear and hate. Of particular satisfaction to me in this respect is Esther Parada's juxtaposition of one of my portraits of the Nicaraguan revolutionary Nora Astorga with the *New York Times* 1978 portrayal of Nora as a Mata Hari figure (see "Woman to Woman: Our Art in Our Lives").

Another moment I remember fondly was when the Sandinista Children's Organization announced a contest for a photo image they wanted to represent Nicaraguan children. My young boy astride a cart loaded with bananas took first prize. I won a toy dump-truck, some Plasticene, a doll, and two rolls of 35mm film! I had shot that image in the Chinandega banana fields just two days after United Fruit pulled out in 1982.

That picture was in my recent retrospective exhibition at the Everhart Museum in Scranton. About ten days after the opening, I went to give a gallery talk, and had the opportunity of observing people as they viewed my pictures. Most visitors were enthusiastic; a great many comments taught me a lot. But two women stopped before the young boy and the bananas, and I heard one say to the other: "Now I know why I always wash my fruit...." Which only goes to show there is always more than one way of experiencing the same image!

During those first years making pictures, the central problem for me remained one of bringing my already considerable experience of thinking, seeing, and creating in one medium to bear upon my condition as a latecomer in this new one. My level of sophistication as an artist often suffered against my simple inability to approach a subject, or to develop and print a photograph the way I wished I could.

4. Art in Revolution

One of the greatest supports for this and other dilemmas was the seriousness with which both Cuba and Nicaragua regard the arts; the efforts made—under blockade conditions and, in Nicaragua, in a war-ravaged situation—to address the needs of the artist, as well as the general public's spiritual need for authentic artistic expression.

In Havana I joined the photographers at the Union of Writers and Artists. Coming together on Wednesday afternoons to criticize one another's work was essential to my early development. In Nicaragua I was fortunate to be around when that country's photographers' union was getting off the ground. Along with the community provided, the possibility for shows, and solutions to the problem of procuring materials, there were fascinating discussions among people who for the first time had control over their nation and their art. How may the two walk together? What needs, if any, does one impose upon the other? What children are born of this union?

I'm not sure I should call myself a documentary photographer, although in this country that's the label most critics seem to give me. In Latin America I did what is commonly called documentary work, but it always seemed to me that the sociopolitical situation demanded that. Here in the United States I'm drawn to a more studied statement, sometimes conceived and developed over a long period of time and then set up in a studio or other contrived environment. I think of what I do as chronicling; what I care to say with my art goes beyond the picture plane of a particular time and space. It seems to me that the demands of time and place are what change, not my approach to those demands.

5. Subject Matter

Women are always interesting to me. When I make pictures, whatever the time and wherever the place, images of women are always likely to be prominent among those I choose to make. In photographing women I am always also mirroring myself as I explore the lives of others.

Graveyards are not places of death but places of life for me, where the living make their statement by using the transition of loved ones who are gone. There is nothing like the absolute fact of death to evoke considerations about how we do our living.

Since my return to the United States in January 1984, I have worked primarily in four photographic directions. When I was recently arrived, I wanted to do a calendar, with images of women from Latin and North America. Eventually I produced work, a book (it was no longer a calendar) that I called *Women Brave in the Face of Danger*.[1] Women's bravery for me was not limited to a wartime trench or a "man's" job; simple survival, for women in a patriarchal society, implies danger. It requires tremendous everyday courage and creativity.

As a spinoff from photographing women, I continue to work with images of mothers and daughters, and often of mothers, daughters, and granddaughters. Generations of women intrigue me. What do we say to one another? What do we pass on, what do we hold back? I'm still making images of mothers and daughters, and probably always will. My first conscious picture in this ongoing series was a mother and daughter in San Pedro Norte, near the Honduran border of Nicaragua. There have been dozens since.

I continue, some might say almost aimlessly, to make pictures in graveyards. Almost everywhere I go, if I have time, I seek them out. I think I am making images of a particular social configuration, social norms, strata, our prejudices and sense of humor. A graveyard image might attract me for its architectonic or esthetic qualities, but I'm interested in the social commentary as well.

And then there is our search, as women, to become what we are. A catching up with ourselves. Intensely affected by the ways in which the media uses us, outraged by the fragmenting and manipulation, I have recently completed several series. The first, "She Answers Back," is a story. A young woman looks at and thinks about herself in the world. She catches for a woman's softball team. She has been asked to be a bridesmaid at her younger sister's wedding. Nineteen images move back and forth among themselves and move as well through one woman's coming to terms with her claim upon her own life.

Another series in this vein is "Mask: Cosmetic Mud." I use my teenage daughter, Ana, as a model. In these sixteen images she applies, makes faces through, and removes a mud mask used to cleanse skin not even dirty. Eyes, nose, lips, ears, are isolated through the mask and assume expressions unnoticed when they blend into a whole. As in "She Answers Back," I do my own fragmenting—a process I believe is notably different from the way the media fragments us.

Confronting and attempting to deal with an incest experience in my childhood, I found myself using photography in the actual healing process, as well as poetry and prose. The result was my book, *This Is About Incest.*[2] These images include old pictures from a family album; my grandfather—who was the abuser—and me stopped in the time of the abuse, remembering the moment of perpetration; as well as my adult self retrieving and crushing that memory, taking back its power. This is me doing oral history with myself as well as using my several creative forms to help work through a problem of personal invasion.

"Touch" is a series about tenderness, in which gender and race are blurred in the power of human touching. These are pictures of hands touching breasts. Are the hands also female? Male? Are one set of hands black, the other white? Reactions to such simple subject matter have been startled, often embarrassed. Since my return to the New Mexican desert and mountains, I have been experimenting a bit with infrared film. It seems particularly interesting to transmit the very special light working on land and landscape here. The Saguaro cactus, in its habitat outside of Tucson, Arizona, has been another focus of my camera's eye. I continue to travel to that magical area to photograph the cacti like great beings in communion with one another.

6. Mentors

I would like to speak of influences, and that's difficult. Precisely because I came late to photography, with maturity in another expressive form as well as simply in living, my influences probably come from a broader range of places than they might have had I traveled the more traditional academic route.

I grew up with art, with image. My mother was a sculptor; my father a cellist. Art was familiar and valued in my childhood home. I was deeply visually moved by the abstract expressionists in the New York City of the late fifties and early sixties. In my writing I was influenced by the Beat poets and the Black Mountain school. The particular hue and quality of light in New Mexico has been another important constant in my life.

Early photographic mentors were Lewis Hine, Dorothea Lange, Diane Arbus, and Robert Frank. Personally, I am indebted to photographers Grandal, Susan Meiseles, Jack Levine, Claudia Gordillo, Judy Janda, Colleen McKay, and Anne Noggle. Marxism and feminism are ideologies that continue to inform my visual and written work.

I am also deeply influenced by the insider/outsider aspect of my own life, having been born and raised in the United States, living in Latin America for twenty-three years, and then returning to this country at the particular time and under the specific conditions which now claim me.

7. Insisting on the Vision

A very important experience for me as a photographer was my 1988 retrospective exhibition at the Everhart Museum in Scranton, Pennsylvania. Although I had shown before—in Managua, Mexico City, Vancouver, Toronto, Washington, Milwaukee, and Albuquerque—this was my first really comprehensive show, and the first in which such a broad selection of my imagistic concerns had been seen in one place. Robert Schweitzer, who curated the exhibition and encouraged and inspired me throughout its planning period, made me think about my photography in new ways. I'm sure I owe a great deal of my future work to his sensitivity and support.

Time is always an obstacle to my work. Time to think, to wonder about the images and seek them out. Time to work in the darkroom, time to show people what I'm doing and look at the work of others. Anne Noggle once suggested that if I really want my pictures to succeed, I must give up writing; concentrate all my energies on the visual expression. She may be right. But I cannot do that. For better or for worse, I am a writer *and* a photographer; what I am able to produce will always be a hybrid: imagistic words, an eye which is perhaps too literary, sometimes requiring words to establish meaning. Working in this way has its advantages and disadvantages. But for me it is no longer a matter of choice. If I'm lucky, I will be able to make something of my own from the marriage.

By forcing me to fight an immigration battle, by challenging me for what I believe and because of what and how I express the way I see, the U.S. government daily robs me of creative time and energies.[3]

But I also know that in my creativity lies my greatest resistance to this "rape." My conviction is solid. To the strength and insight needed to create, I always dedicate my work in progress.

—Albuquerque, New Mexico, 1986;
Hartford, Connecticut, 1988; and
Albuquerque, New Mexico, 1988

Notes

1. *Women Brave in the Face of Danger*, Margaret Randall (Freedom, CA: Crossing Press, 1985).
2. *This Is About Incest*, Margaret Randall (Ithaca, NY: Firebrand Books, 1987).
3. This was written before I had won my case. Since its victory, the stress I describe has lessened of course, but the emotional backlash is still there. It will undoubtedly take a while for the tension of those years to assume a gentler level.

Woman to Woman,
Our Art in Our Lives

Jane and I did a painting, with collage elements from
many photographs of Palestinian women. It was a
tribute to those women, and one of the photographs
that I xeroxed and painted and collaged and worked
into the composite was of a woman, profile, in a scarf,
holding a baby ... for some reason it really looked to
me like you, reminded me of pictures of you in Cuba. It
was a proud, strong feeling photo, and as I struggled
(almost all night!) to finish, in that quiet and peace that
only comes in the wee hours in an urban place, I
drifted on thoughts of your life, your history, your work,
and how glad I am to know you, and to love you ...

The above is from a letter I received from a friend. She is a
wonderful artist and muralist, a woman whose feminist as well as
internationalist concerns consistently inform her art. Reading and rereading the paragraph, I realized it contained several of the sparks that
would finally push me to write a piece I've been wanting to get to for a
while now: something about the ways in which women's expression
often draws powerfully on other women's creativity; on how we share
each other's visions—attempting to push them further—from generation
to generation and also among those of us now who live and work in an
ever broadening network of female expression.

This single paragraph of Miranda's letter (my friend's name is
Miranda Bergman) exemplifies so many ways in which we make our art:
"Jane and I did a painting...." Communal creativity, in so many different
circumstances, is valued and nurtured. "It was a tribute to those
women...." In our art we frequently honor other women, often women
who continue to be historically ignored or silenced. "I xeroxed and
painted and collaged...." Women artists have worked on the cutting edge

of innovation, experimentation, and mixed media. And, finally, "as I struggled (all night!) to finish, in the quiet and peace that only comes in the wee hours in an urban place, I drifted on thoughts of your life...." The recognition and sharing of process, as well as the generosity of acknowledging connection, are among the most relevant aspects of female creativity.

As Miranda worked, she freely admits she used the nurturing presence of a friend's life. She is telling me that my life informs her creativity. On a deeper level, she is also telling me that my life is art. I want to write, here, about how women often take this process one step further; not only allowing a human presence to inspire us, but actually using another woman's art in ours, transforming and pushing it further in our own creative process. I believe this is a particularly female experience.

Before going further, I should say I don't believe this is an inherently female experience; that is to say, it is certainly not pro- grammed or explicit in a biological sense. We—women and men—are socialized to these ideas and praxis. Patriarchy, especially as it operates in the context of advanced monopoly capitalism, promotes a male-dom- inated model which induces extreme individualism, an unhealthy sense of competition, rampant aggressivity—the good-ole-boy syndrome.

There are men—artists among them—who have come to under- stand these issues and attempt to address them in their lives and work. There are also women—generations of them—who continue to internal- ize the conditioning that tells us we must mimic men in order to succeed. Class, race, and other conditions, as well as gender, must be factored into our analysis. What I am saying is that feminists are waking powerfully to the possibility —indeed, the need—of changing these relationships.

I want to write here about how many women who are artists revel in this particular creative sharing, and also about how specifically feminist are the mechanisms we employ. The act of taking an idea, an image, even a more fully evolved work of art by one and using it as the basis or jumping-off place for a work of art by another, is not only qualitatively different from the traditional male concept of artistic exer- cise: it is entirely antithetical to the male concept of what art is about.

Men have taught us we must be guarded and jealous with our work: unique, original, exclusive—these are male adjectives and for the most part denote the male perspective on artistic creativity. Original thought, pure art or art beyond politics, lines that are clean, impartial (when speaking of research goals, or journalism), "pure" theory (that is, theory that is not continually put to the reality test, but left in books for coming generations to revere): these words and phrases all belong to traditional male thought—in academia, publishing, the arts.

As long as we (women artists) were urged to believe that we must travel our roads to fulfillment by writing (or teaching or performing or painting or making photographs or music or whatever) "like a man" or "as well as the men," it seemed important as well to be unique, original, exclusive. It seemed necessary to play the clever word games, invest ourselves in the one-upmanship, move as far as we could from the roots of our meaning. We took pride in learning to be the devil's advocate, adept at spewing a convincing argument for any side of any question. We were forced to sell our passion and commitment out to rationality—with the male seal of approval.

Rarely were we considered by men to be unique or original because of our own personal or collective histories. And if we were, it was not called art—not by the critics or the marketplace or even by the mass audience, all of which are dominated by a male, white, and ruling-class conception of what art should be. What we did might be called, benevolently, "craft." Or it might be described (with derision) as committed, too personal. Strident is a word they seem to like. Women's art was and still frequently is labeled uncomfortably intimate, or raw. Embarrassing. The product had to conform to a vision patented by white, ruling-class men—more often than not translated into "the latest trend." And here product is another key word. In the male concept of art, the product is all important. For many women, process has now become central.

As we imitate men, we lose memory. Without the collective memory—our real history—we are denied our uniquely personal history as well. If we cannot remember the women who have gone before us, we cannot remember ourselves, our own lives. We are not whole. As we retrieve and recreate the memories, we recreate ourselves.

Most creative women of my generation spent far too much of our lives attempting to conform to male standards. As a writer, I can remember years trying to "write like a man," unaware that the more I attempted to measure up to male criteria the further I strayed from my self, my culture and vision. When—with the help of a movement of women—I began to make the connections necessary to a more personal search, I found that my anger at all the lost time was as intense as my relief at finally being able to bring body and mind together in my work.

Essential to this creative coming together of mind and body is a recognition of the importance of process. I'm not sure if we first tap this process in ourselves, and that frees us to go back and retrieve the history of the creative women who were our foremothers; or whether the retrieval of those women's energies is what ultimately frees us to tap into our own core vision. However it works, in a creative life the dialectics of both practices certainly nurture us from that moment on.

My friend Marilyn Lindstrom, a Minneapolis-based muralist, read a draft of this essay and zeroed in on the idea of creative foremothers. "Some of them are still alive," she told me, "like Meridel[1] who has such a terrific way of encouraging you before you are who you will be, and in that way helps you to become who she knows you'll be." Marilyn said that when she was much younger, she and Meridel traveled by Greyhound to an event some hours away: "I won't forget," she said. "I had painted a single mural, but Meridel introduced me to people there as the wonderful Minnesota muralist. She made me believe in myself. Women know how to do that. So many men won't even give you credit after you've done something; Meridel would give you credit before, and it was that faith, that certainty, that helped you know you'd be able to become the artist you had to be."

By contrast, who among us has not had an experience in which a moment of particular recognition or satisfaction has been diluted or ripped off by a male colleague or friend suddenly—unconsciously, we would like to believe—diverting attention to some minor need of his own? Marilyn spoke of the time she walked onto a stage to receive an award for a finished mural when a co-worker, a usually sensitive and supportive man, came up and interrupted the moment's intensity by asking her a totally irrelevant question; a social non-sequitur unless we analyze the discomfort many men evidently experience as they sense the shift in women's practice. "It's a whole other way of situating oneself in the world," Marilyn and I agreed.

When we unearth a previously obscured history, our own creative impulses begin to make more sense. We find voice for our ways of seeing, our rhythms. We speak to complex, fluid realities rather than to static ideals. Women troubadours in thirteenth- and fourteenth-century Provençal were less idealistic than their brothers, more concerned with the everyday contradictions in life and its relationships than with the "perfect love." Those almost forgotten female poets paid attention to their lives and the lives around them. And they spoke much more realistically of those lives in their poems.[2]

When the Russian political activist and writer Alexandra

Kollontai was banished into diplomatic service because her ground-breaking feminism made the male Bolshevik leaders uncomfortable, she wrote her feminist ideas into marvelous novels, including *A Great Love* and *For Love of Worker Bees*. The German revolutionary and essayist Rosa Luxemburg left us more than the brilliance of her economic treatises. In her love letters there is political commentary as well as passion—an early example of female expression in which intuition and reason not only exist together but nurture one another. Georgia O'Keeffe's painting defies all the male rules; it is fiercely female and monumentally universal. And she created it virtually alone, long before the support of a community of sisters.

More recently there is such an abundance of women artists whose ground-breaking visions cross male-defined lines that it is difficult to limit myself to the mention of a few. Examples from different media and genre would be Muriel Rukeyser, Adrienne Rich, Jane Cooper, Nancy Morejon, Paula Gunn Allen, and others (in their retrieval of our fore-mothers' voices in their poems); Harmony Hammond (especially with the advent of her bag and wrapped art); Judy Chicago (in her great Dinner Party and Birth projects); and June Jordan, Alice Walker, and Mab Segrest (whose essays are as personal as they are political, as political as they are personal).

Women were among the first to insist that the personal and the political are as necessary to one another and as interrelated as are form and content in the discovery of the early Marxist critics. When in the seventies the male-dominated papers, journals, publishing houses, art galleries and museums, theaters, and other spaces denied us access or told us we weren't producing the real thing, we broke away and created our own. Too often we realized we had been the ones doing most of the hard work that kept those male-dominated spaces alive. So we occupied them, sometimes taking them over completely in order to be taken—and learn to take ourselves—seriously.

Women artists, in the rich traditions of all these sisters, are creating a body of work that is female in deep and complex ways. We are creating a new language, recognizing the legitimacy of our experience as women. Men have told us: "One assumes that ..." We say instead: "I think" or "we believe" or even "we feel ... we know." We are beginning to learn how to refuse the passive "I was raped," placing responsibility directly with "he raped me." We name the aggressor as well as the victim, and so aid the victim in becoming a survivor.

Meridel LeSueur said something wonderful about women's

visions: "My feeling is that women have to really use their own language, which will probably be subjective ... [not] the sterile, analytical thing that has become a way of seizing your mind.... I think language has another function besides analysis. The other one is heat. I mean, language should heat you. You should rise out of your chair and move."[3]

Ours is the language of process, and paying attention to our process informs the language we make. In the academic world we tend towards active teaching. We are more interested in helping our students retrieve their own collective histories than we are in teaching them how to regurgitate neat little packages of thoroughly processed information. We want them to learn to think for themselves—without being afraid to honor their feelings or commit themselves to ideas. Indeed we encourage their passion and commitment rather than advising them to live on some unreal terrain of "pure" dispassionate reason (invented by men). Because of this we often do not publish our work in the "correct" academic organs, making it even easier for the male establishment to deny us promotion or tenure. And our publications or other creative expressions often assume forms which simply do not meet the criteria set forth by the male establishment.

A colleague and friend, a professor in educational foundations at a large university, spent years studying male and female stereotyping in grade-school children. With her findings she designed a board game, a "toy" with which children could express their feelings about these stereotypes and see that, as boys and girls, they could enter the fields of their choice. My friend had a hard time convincing those who ruled on her tenure eligibility that the creation of the board game was worth as much as a book, or even as an article published in an acceptable academic journal. Perhaps the fact that the board game was for children further devaluated it in the eyes of academia.

If we are poets, when we read our work in public we also evolve new ways of connecting with each other and with our audiences. Most of the new performance poets are women. In my own recent experience, my readings with Judith McDaniel are an exploration of this territory. Both our books deal with issues of invasion, alienation, responsibility, and creating safe spaces in which to heal and act. When Judith and I read together (see "Down Dangerous Roads") we don't use two separate blocks of time as if they belonged to each alone. We design a program in which the work moves from voice to voice, building off one another, creating an art in the presentation itself. At the end, we sometimes exchange poems, reading each other's verse as a sort of parting gift.

I have kept a personal journal since 1969. Some might consider it a peculiar sort of space, for it's not an entirely private diary nor is it written only for myself. I enter its world perhaps two or three times a week—sometimes more often, sometimes less. There I feel free to express myself quickly, easily, without trying to create a "perfect" product.

My journal is all process; it often contains half-formed observations, opinions I will later revise, an immediacy I like to share with a number of those closest to me. First drafts of poems. Ideas which may later become essays or stories. The work of others, mostly other women, also makes its way into these pages, when I want to explore or share it, move out from its stance or presence to a statement of my own. Again, this conscious use of others' work. I send my journal to a small group of friends. It has become a place where a group of us speak, question, share, even disagree. If asked to define with a single word these necessary pages, the word—again—would be process.

In my journal many ideas for more formal works are conceived or developed. And at least two recent books have come more directly from its practice: *Albuquerque: Coming Back to the USA* (a chronicle of my first year home, after twenty-three in Latin America)[4]; and *The Shape of Red: Insider/Outsider Reflections.*[5] The latter is a book of letters between my friend Ruth Hubbard and myself. The volume emerged from our correspondence, but I first addressed and tested many of our concerns in the pages of my journal. Ruth and I found that the more informal letter format invited readers into an open-ended conversation and allowed us to express ourselves without feeling we needed to draw tight circles around certain subjects, theorize excessively, or "have the last word." In other words, we concentrated on sharing the process rather than on producing an absolute.

The need for this kind of a process-oriented space is even more obvious in the world of art. And while we are taught that the art world is a place where innovation is encouraged, in fact it is just as rigidly controlled there as it is in academia, by male concepts of tradition, acceptability, market, and other considerations having nothing to do with creativity.

Artists steeped in the male tradition of "originality at all costs" will present anything new and different as a valid statement. Women, who know "originality" alone is of questionable worth, and that it is our feminist insight that best nurtures our creativity, often work with and through one another. Male criteria consider one of the most blasphemous ways in which we stray from the fold to be the use of one another's work which I mentioned at the beginning of this piece. But this practice produces some of the most profound and beautiful examples of our artistic expression.

From my own creative experience, I'd like to share moments that typify the many ways in which we women use one another's ideas, energy, words, images—pushing a sister's vision further (perhaps in another expressive form), watching that vision spread and affect a public hungry for it, then gathering from that same public the re-energizing response which in turn renews our capacity for expression.

One example I never tire of citing is related to the paragraph at the beginning of this essay. Miranda Bergman and Jane Norling are muralists living in Berkeley. Both of them, as well as Marilyn Lindstrom, have used faces from my photographs of Nicaraguan women and children as the models for the people in their murals.

In Managua, in 1983, Miranda and Marilyn worked on the front wall of that city's children's library. The Nicaraguans wanted to make sure the faces were those of Nicaraguan children; I provided dozens of pictures from which the women painted. Later, Miranda and Jane used my images of Nicaraguan women in their mural for the San Francisco Balmy Alley project (a series of community-based murals in solidarity with Central America).

In this way, the image of a child I had photographed in Bluefields became a youngster playing with letter-blocks on the Managua wall; my image of a market woman became a grandmother learning to read and write on the wall in San Francisco. In both places passersby see themselves and people they love reflected in the faces thus transformed: children feel at home with their images on the library; refugees north of the border feel a connection with the figures peopling Balmy Alley.

One woman's art has informed another woman's art, and its usefulness to the people for whom both are intended has been expanded. My click of a shutter has grown through another artist's brush; what has lodged itself in the eyes and hearts of the recipients will surely find its way into a continued expansion of that energy somewhere else. Some find it subversive that the notions of "originality" and ownership are being debunked. Some find it frightening. Women, for the most part, find it a relief.

Early in 1984, when I returned to the United States, one of the things I wanted to do was create a calendar with images of women. I wanted word images as well as pictures; and I wanted to include North American as well as Latin American women. From years of photographing in Cuba and Nicaragua, I had hundreds of negatives from those countries; I needed to make pictures of women here. So I traveled. In an immigrant market in Buffalo, a women's gym in Berkeley, New York's Central Park, among migrant fruit pickers in Washington's Yakima Valley, and on the vast mesas of the Southwest, I photographed women. I told prospective photographic subjects that they'd be part of "a calendar for us, for women to see ourselves strong and proud as we are." Without exception, the women I approached were enthusiastic about being included.[6]

Esther Parada is a computer artist, teacher, and critic of photography from Chicago. Some years back, she took two photos of the Nicaraguan revolutionary Nora Astorga: one published in 1978 in the *New York Times*, was a terrorist image; the other made by me when I interviewed Nora shortly after the war, showed the woman as she was. Parada worked them into a powerful collage, and added a text: those disinforming words used by the *Times* to describe Astorga, and Nora's own words taken from the interview I did. Viewers are left to their own ability to discern the truth about Astorga. The collage is art of the most compelling kind.

In 1979-80 I did the field work for my book *Sandino's Daughters*[7] (in which the interview with Nora Astorga appears). I recorded the stories of Nicaraguan women, and their voices weave a tapestry of collective memory, discovery, struggle. When the book had been out little more than a year, the women of At the Foot of the Mountain Theater, a feminist playhouse in Minneapolis, took six of the stories, added six U.S. women's lives, and created a play that went further than the original book in revealing the connections we can make. I was fortunate to be in the Twin Cities for a rehearsal as well as a production, and remember being thrilled, not only at the obvious intensity of the experience for the players, but at the audience reaction which—once again—took the connections and multiplied them by much more than the total input of those present.

In this experience, Nicaraguan women shared their stories— pieces of their lives—with me. The act of sharing undoubtedly made the women look at themselves in new ways. In my book, I in turn share their stories with the world. At the Foot of the Mountain further transformed the work in another medium. The possibilities don't, of course, end there.

Holly Near once talked about the energy for her own work which she gets from sister artists. She spoke of getting up in the morning, having a cup of coffee, maybe looking over at the bookshelf, and catching sight

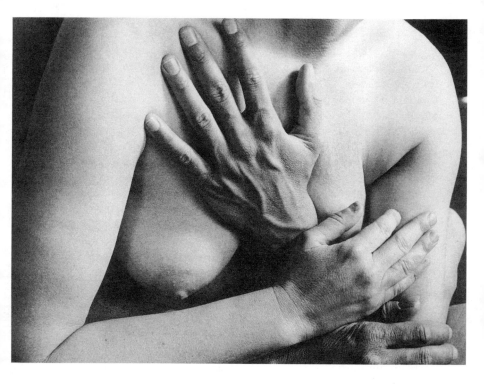

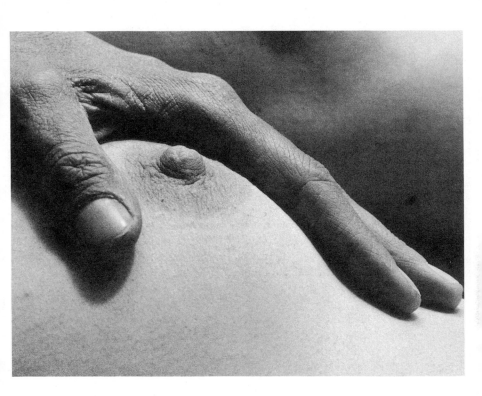

of certain books that have inspired her. She said she is conscious of the way she uses their power in whatever task she must face that day: writing, recording, performing. [8]

Sometimes simply mentioning what we do provides energy to a woman ripe to break through restraints on her own creativity. I remember during my first hearing before an immigration judge[9] being asked to describe myself to the court. The INS lawyer had just spent some time attempting to characterize me as a sexually immoral and dangerously subversive woman. I spoke of myself as a woman, writer, photographer, teacher, mother, activist, and oral historian, among other pieces of my identity. Later, in the courthouse lobby, a woman I didn't know grabbed my arm. She seemed excited. "I want to tell you how much it meant to me," she said, "to hear the words oral historian! I've been trying to explain to my advisor over at the college what it is I want to do, but I didn't know how. Now I do: oral history. That's exactly what I want to do!"

Sometimes the way one woman's work germinates in another woman's consciousness is neither so immediate nor so clear. It can be very powerful, nonetheless. I would like to end with a story about a story about a story.

In my New Mexican youth, I knew a woman named Alice Garver. She was a wonderful artist; I was a very young woman then, just beginning to feel the pull of my own creativity. Alice was married to an artist named Jack; they had three small children who seemed mostly her concern. I intuited issues of time to work, the fragmentation women who are artists and mothers feel. Alice and I never talked about these things, though; I was too young and she was ... well, she was seductive mystery.

Alice died young, leaving her children small, her by then ex-husband grieving, and a series of murals painted for each floor in the city's only skyscraper. Those murals had given Alice her first real recognition. But she didn't live to create more. Her art, her life, her mysterious death—they were all shrouded in questions. Words that could not be spoken. Or that I would not have understood. I never forgot Alice, and her struggle as partner, mother, artist, meant something special to my own.

Years later, returning to Albuquerque, another series of events involving a homeless man who lived in the streets around the university revived, in startling ways, images of my long-ago artist friend. Moved at the powerful energy unleashed by the connections, I wrote a story called

"Alice and Carlos: Three Stories." Read it next. It is another, more complex example of the ways in which one woman's art can affect another's.

—Saint Paul, Minnesota
Spring 1989

Notes

1. Meridel LeSueur, writer and radical activist born in Iowa in February 1900, lives in Hudson, Wisconsin and still gives generously of herself and her art to generations of younger artists and others.
2. See *The Women Troubadours*, Magda Bogin (Scarborough, UK: Paddington Press, 1976).
3. Quoted in *Every Woman Has a Story*, Gayla Wadnizak Ellis (Minneapolis, MN: Midwest Villages and Voices, 1982).
4. *Albuquerque: Coming Back to the USA*, Margaret Randall (Vancouver, BC: New Star Books, 1986).
5. *The Shape of Red: Insider/Outsider Reflections*, Ruth Hubbard and Margaret Randall (Pittsburgh, PA: Cleis Press, 1988).
6. This calendar idea eventually became a book of my photographs of Latin and North American women with texts from women of both continents. See *Women Brave in the Face of Danger* (Freedom, CA: Crossing Press, 1985).
7. *Sandino's Daughters*, Margaret Randall (Vancouver, BC: New Star Books, 1981).
8. Interview by Jack Levine and Lisa Knauer, on video as part of the research for a film.
9. El Paso, Texas, March 13-17, 1986.

Alice and Carlos
Three Stories

. . . we cannot develop and print a memory.
—Henri Cartier-Bresson

Can I call it Alice's story? All I knew were a few of the corners, tangled years sloughed off in memory.

Alice was a big woman. Stately, large-boned: those would have been the words used by people for whom it was all right to be big. A few might have said Amazonian. We were raised in an era of pinched waists. Petite as eager necessity. The chin and eyes tilted upwards in admiration and endless support for the men we were learning to adore no matter what. Definitely a preview to today's wistful anorexic disappearance act.

But Alice would not disappear. Her carriage was a statement. The clean openness of her face, eyes that took you in, straight on. Her eyes challenged me. The woman—Alice told me in her bearing—was big and beautiful. And she moved through her days with a particular grace.

Alice was grand. She looked down or straight across and took long easy strides, picking up one or another of her three small children with a strong yet gentle arm, gesturing endless amusement with the other. Endless possibility. She wore dirndl skirts, the New Mexican marriage of Indian and old Mexico, striped or solid chambray. Sandals and simple peasant blouses. Her breasts were heavy, full.

Alice was an artist. She painted and made prints, shaped clay pots in her large hands, demanded space for her work. And art was that work of hers. But she was also a wife. A housewife and a mother. Her husband, Jack, was a university professor, an artist too, and accepted as such in the community. Professional. Artist. Identities not in conflict.

Alice's three small children—and they *were* hers, in every daily battle—were towheads. Smelling of soggy crackers, they trailed loose wet diapers across a cluttered floor. Alice looked at her husband. Lifted and set down her children. Entering a room, she spoke, or her voice came from the next room over, the next project, something she was explaining or showing, her focus always for the work.

Perhaps I didn't really understand that then. Or, I didn't understand what must be sacrificed to that. It was part of the mystery, its staying power when she was gone. "Alice is strange," people would say. I couldn't, then, have articulated what they meant by that, nor exactly how I felt her presence and her strength. But I knew I wanted to be close to her.

I do not now remember the order:

Alice married to an artist, Jack. Alice herself an artist. Alice's work unnoticed. Sometimes not even getting done. Alice's work beginning to gain recognition. Was that the way it went? "Alice got a lucky break! She's been commissioned to paint a mural for the First National Bank Building!" Was that how it was?

Years later people spoke about *twenty* murals, one on every floor of that building which was then the city's only skyscraper. As if I should have known: there were twenty, not one. But I couldn't remember. Three decades later, when I returned to my city, I would make a pilgrimage to see those murals.

Alice was big. She was mysterious or crazy, take your pick. She had a husband, a professor, you know. And children. She painted those murals. Her work was just beginning to be noticed. Then Alice and Jack separated. They came apart. He came apart. Nothing much was said. His sadness and her anxiety were noted. A silence grew.

Alice was sick. She was very sick for a while, and when my mother visited her in the hospital she said, "I don't eat anymore." But later no one knew exactly what Alice's sickness should be called. They couldn't find anything *wrong*. "There's nothing wrong," they said. "It's all in her head ... psychological ... you know how women are...." And Alice went home, felt better, walked through her house with those long strides visibly slowed, picked up a child, pointed at a slash of color, the contour of a clay pot.

Then Alice was dead.

Alice died before the sun rose. Did someone find her? Someone must have. Was there surprise? Was there another story, crouched behind the first? No one said suicide, but the word hung in the air, displaced. No one mentioned the name of an illness. Her illness had no name. No one offered explanation, solution, there were no answered questions. The children disappeared. They must have gone with their father. Once, several years later in Mexico City, he appeared on our doorstep. I came from market to find him sitting there, head down, his sorrow like a blanket. Over two or three days: a half dozen words.

Alice began to visit me then. Over these years she has spoken to me of necessary space. When the angry demands of men close in, threatening to leave me without room for words or images, Alice appears, looking straight into my eyes. However I turn my head, she meets my gaze. Her large hand always palm-open, signaling. She makes me look at my work, at the space it occupies.

In 1984 when I came back to Albuquerque, I wanted to visit the murals. I had never seen them finished. After initial weeks during which I was reluctant even to leave the house, I began driving past the building. One day, almost a year after I'd returned, a friend and I talked as we drove. I looked up. There it was, now one of many such high-rise structures standing for progress, change. We had time, why not? And I turned the car into the parking lot, explaining as we ran: entering the space, pushing the glass doors, asking about the murals.

"What murals?"

All the foyer walls were office-gray. Nobody seemed to know. "Not in this building," one smiling secretary after another told us as we climbed from floor to floor. I was unwilling to give up, not ready to say this did not happen, it is a dream, imagined into memory. Then on the fifth floor, the suggestion we go to the seventh. "The receptionist there has been here longer than the rest of us. She might remember." Up we went. And she did. "Yes, they were beautiful," she agreed. "It was a real shame when they painted them over. They were peeling, you know, flaking...." By way of explanation. "They needed repair...."

This is how they repaired Alice's murals. They erased them completely.

I went, then, numb into the elevator, out the glass doors, slowly back across the parking lot, wondering if there was a way in which Alice's brush strokes might still inhabit that space, still visit the receptionists mix-and-matched on twenty floors. I wondered if the language of art can remain as a person does: presence and visitation.

Alice comes to me regularly now. Sometimes the folds of her white cotton blouse just graze the corners of my mouth when I rise before dawn to write or work in the darkroom. I smell her freshness beyond inks and chemicals. The odor of wet crackers Senlin, Gracie, or Carlos trailed as they laughed and ran.

*   *   *

Now I must tell a second story.

In the Albuquerque to which I returned in 1984, homeless people claim a space as they do across this country; a wandering, angry, growing group of men and women for whom a roof, a job, adjustment to society, are no longer givens but pieces of memory that have broken and fallen between the cracks.

On Central Avenue, along the few blocks that border the university, some of the homeless are familiar occupants: living from handout to handout, taking small shelter in doorways, foraging for scraps of food in the garbage bins behind El Patio or Pizza Hut.

One of these was The Rag Man. Some called him, simply, Rags. Ageless as so many who cannot harbor ambitions are, he possessed three qualities that set him apart. He was more than repulsively dirty. He was more than commonly angry. And he enjoyed being given some item or other which he would carefully pin to his tattered clothes. He liked bright colors especially, and often a student or someone in the neighborhood would present him with a cluster of ribbons, a strand of bright yarn, a bit of tinsel, a feather. Rags sometimes walked up close to people, threatening our composure with his sour breath, the sting of his eyes. His words pierced the carefully protected cleanliness of our determined forward motion. He would suddenly be there, close to a face, spewing a barrage of crude obscenities. Later, someone would remember: "Sometimes he could be the meanest bastard...."

Rags was angry. Righteously angry. Through the breakdown of conventional propriety, his anger seemed the one thing holding him together.

And so The Rag Man inspired fear in people. Some tended boundaries, tried to avoid allowing him too close. Some made a public point of dealing with his conduct. There was the winter he crawled beneath a second-hand shop called The Birdsong and lit a fire to keep warm. The place nearly went up in flames. A young woman student of mine once turned in a story she'd written about her relationship with Rags. She recounted a real or imagined afternoon on which she had invited him to her home, conversed with him at her table, offered him lunch.

I don't remember exactly when Rags began sleeping out in the small parking alley behind my brother's bookstore. It took getting used to the image to be able to distinguish the man's lean body wrapped in a dirty blanket or covered with scraps of cardboard. Then someone discarded a sofa, its stuffings running out through slits and sores in worn upholstery. Rags slept on the sofa, and he could be seen there dreaming through days as well as nights. The angry outbursts close up in the face of a passerby were less frequent. Maybe he was tired.

Then The Rag Man was murdered.

"It might have been for his money." Local lore had it his family kept him in small cash, perhaps paying him to stay away. He didn't beg, yet rarely lacked for coins.

"I'll bet it was a message from area merchants, trying to clear the neighborhood of homeless people." There was conjecture. Perhaps someone robbed him while he slept, beat or stabbed him, then soaked the body in gasoline and set it on fire.

"Or maybe someone set him on fire without looking for cash. Just for something to do."

The flames raged at three or four one morning. No one expects the police investigation to offer answers. But the people are speaking their own language of caring. Two or three, sometimes more, come to linger where the flames rose. Flowers, cigarettes, notes, poems appear on the spot where Rags was killed. Crosses and messages have been painted on the blackened wall. One poem signed by Kippa D. (age 15) says: "... I envy you raggedy man/your will to live another day ..." One night this altar too goes up in flames. The next day it reappears.

But it is the published obituary that quickens memory in my eyes, once again wets my lips in longing then throws me to my feet. For it tells me the Rag Man was Alice Garver's youngest son, Carlos. He was thirty-four. Survived, the papers say, by a brother in Alameda, California. A married sister in Albuquerque. "Carlos Garver was the son of Alice M. Garver, a painter specializing in Southwestern murals who died in 1966, and Jack Garver, a painter and sculptor who died last year."

Carlos's sister Grace McCoy speaks through the lines of the daily: "He was very imaginative, very creative, a very likable guy. He was very artistic. He loved to write. One of his hopes when I last spoke to him was to get a garage or a little room so he could draw. He still had it in him." The article goes on to say that Carlos was strung out on drugs from the age of fifteen, that he'd been on the streets since 1973. He had been treated at several mental institutions and his father tried to get him committed. But his sister Grace explains, "He would walk away, he would leave whenever it cramped his style."

* * *

The third story would have to be a question.

Would I find the answer if Alice appeared right now, if I could ask her about her own beginnings? How it was in her childhood, what passed as tenderness or rage between her own mother and father? How food was set out, or not, upon their early table? What flesh touched flesh, and how? Where the dark places on her way to school cried out, how they might have held her wrist or emptied her eyes of song?

How did Alice choose Jack, and Jack, Alice? Could she know her longings then? Were they forced to write the ritual of blood upon their sheets? Where did form and color stumble, fall, then pull themselves upright, growing against the tender side of skin? What happened to the art undone because of Senlin, because of Grace, because of Carlos? Or, put another way, which pictures belong to each of them? Was Senlin's canvas sold for money or for love? Did Alice offer the etchings made in Grace's name to a friend whose presence went unmentioned on her tongue? And what about Carlos?

I was fresh and muddled back then. I didn't really know if Alice and Jack belonged to my parents or to me. Sometimes I wondered, and my shoulders ached. My eyes learned to assume a serious knowing expression, I would nod my head thoughtfully, and avoid having to move through precise language when asked what I thought about a concept I didn't know or a name I'd never heard.

At twenty, knowing people like Alice and Jack, I had to begin halfway through a conversation among peers. They were eight or ten years older. It made a difference then. Today when Alice visits, we talk about these things. And I do not let the empty places bloat or gag in silence.

The third story would have to be a question containing within itself another question which in turn holds another and another, each new wondering smaller than the one in which it lives, like the Dutch Cleanser ad with the can of Dutch Cleanser upon which an ever diminishing little girl figure in folkloric cap and wooden shoes offers yet another can of cleanser and another and another. Like Sandra Cisneros's eleven-year-old birthday celebration, containing within it the ages of ten, nine, seven, six, five, four, three, two, and one.

If I ask why Jack's Mexican voice did not rise above a whisper, I also need to know what Alice's eyes were fixed on when she died. If I walk the journey backwards from the fire that ended Carlos's life, I must wade through the unforgiving temperature of a winter dawn, bits of colored yarn, a sister's right to her own map, the place of art in a woman's hands.

Alice, I am afraid. Will my own unknotted threads trap my eyes, mouth, tangle a detour before the finish line appears? These three stories no longer own beginnings, mid-points, ends. They are about process, how things happen because some other unnamed something happened first, wherever we come or go without insisting upon our space, the right to own our hands.

—Hartford, Connecticut
Winter 1988

About South End Press

At South End Press, a collectively managed, non-profit publisher, our goal is to provide books that encourage critical thinking and constructive action, thereby helping to create fundamental social change. Since 1977, we have released over 160 titles addressing the key issues of the day, focusing on political, economic, cultural, gender, race, and ecological dimensions of life in the United States and the world.

If you would like a free catalog of South End Press books, please write us at 116 Saint Botolph Street, Boston, MA 02115.

Other South End Press titles of interest

Yearning: Race, Gender, and Cultural Politics by bell hooks

Freedom Under Fire: US Civil Liberties in Times of War by Michael Linfield

The COINTELPRO Papers: Documents from the FBI's Secret Wars Against Dissent in the United States by Ward Churchill and Jim Vander Wall

A True Story of a Drunken Mother by Nancy Lee Hall

From Abortion to Reproductive Freedom: Transforming a Movement edited by Marlene Gerber Fried